Worthwhile Places

John D. Rockefeller, Jr., 1933

Horace M. Albright,
while Superintendent of Yellowstone National Park, 1923

Worthwhile Places:

Correspondence of
John D. Rockefeller, Jr.
and
Horace M. Albright

Edited by
Joseph W. Ernst

Published for
Rockefeller Archive Center
by
Fordham University Press
1991

LC 91–070235
ISBN 0–8232–1330–7

Printed in the United States of America

"Road engineers. . . seem sometimes to forget that
their services are only means to the larger end of
developing a well-located, beautiful, attractive road
that goes to worthwhile places."

John D. Rockefeller, Jr., to Horace M. Albright, June 6, 1939.

CONTENTS

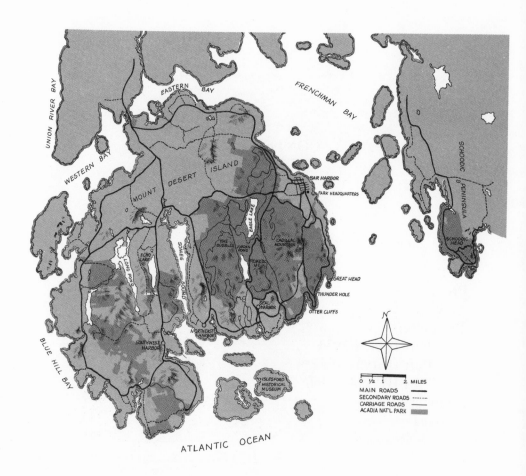

Acadia roads

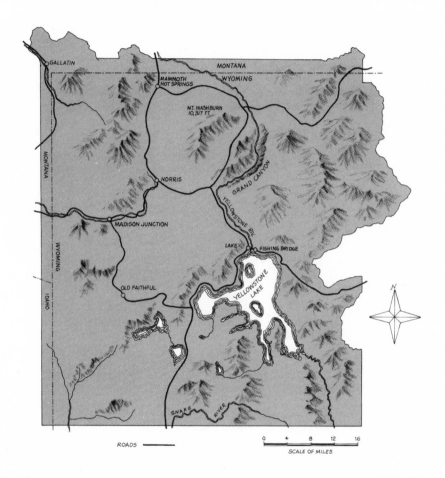

ROADS ━━━━━━

0   4   8   12   16
SCALE OF MILES

Yellowstone roads

PREFACE

John D. Rockefeller, Jr., a skilled and prolific letter writer, had wide and varied interests. With personal access to the nation's leaders, he corresponded with politicians, religious leaders, educators, landscape architects, and conservationists such as Horace M. Albright, Superintendent of Yellowstone National Park and later Director of the National Park Service.

His correspondence with Albright documents one of his most personal and long-standing interests - the national parks. The letters illustrate a remarkable public-private partnership that helped shape the growing park system. They portray a common concern and love of our natural heritage and the efforts which preserved countless scenic wonders for future generations.

The letters also reveal a highly personal relationship. While Rockefeller was always *Mr. Rockefeller* and Albright was always *Mr. Albright*, they both shared their feelings and ideas without reserve. The letters have three themes: the creation of more and better national parks, Rockefeller's concept of an ideal park, and the maturing of a warm and lasting friendship based on deeply shared mutual interests.

Between 1924 and 1960, Rockefeller and Albright exchanged over 1,300 letters. Rockefeller wrote from his offices in New York City, his homes in Maine and Williamsburg, Virginia, and occasionally while vacationing in Europe and Tucson, Arizona. Albright's letters came from Yellowstone

1

National Park, Washington, D. C., and, after he left the Park Service, his office in New York City.

Of these letters, 211, arranged in chronological order, are included in this collection. Rockefeller's copies of the correspondence are preserved in the Rockefeller Archive Center in Pocantico Hills, North Tarrytown, New York. The material is filed by subject matter at the Center. There are handwritten memos by Rockefeller, carbons of the letters he sent to Albright, and the originals of Albright's letters to Rockefeller with penciled comments and considered replies by Rockefeller. There are also related maps, clippings, and periodicals.

The letters appear exactly as they are in the archives. Nothing has been omitted and typing and spelling mistakes have not been corrected.

Rockefeller died in 1960, Albright lived until 1987. Until his death, Albright served as a conservation advisor to Laurance S. Rockefeller, John D. Rockefeller, Jr.'s son, and served on the boards of several Rockefeller conservation or restoration projects for much of that time. Correspondence flowed from Albright to Laurance S. Rockefeller as he continued and broadened his father's interests and activities in the nationwide conservation and park movement.

It is hoped that the publication of these letters will lead to a better understanding of how a unique and generous cooperative effort between the public and private sectors contributed to the development of the national park system.

AN OVERVIEW

John D. Rockefeller, Jr., first visited Yellowstone National Park between August 12 and 29, 1886. He was twelve years old. The park, created by Congress fourteen years earlier, was under the supervision of the General Land Office of the Department of the Interior. On August 17, 1886, at the request of the Secretary of the Interior, 50 men of Company M, First U. S. Cavalry, took control of the park. The Army replaced the unsuccessful and, for the most part, unpaid civilian organization that had administered the park since 1872. In time, the Army Corps of Engineers built and maintained roads and facilities while the Cavalry patrolled the region, fought fires, and provided guides for visitors. The Army stayed in Yellowstone until 1918, when it was replaced by the National Park Service created by Congress in 1916.

Young Rockefeller kept a diary of his trip to Yellowstone. The travel party consisted of his parents, his three sisters, an aunt, a minister, a doctor, and the doctor's wife. They visited all the major sights within the park, including the Norris Geyser Basin, Old Faithful, the canyon of Yellowstone, Fishing Bridge, and Mammoth Hot Springs. The diary describes the Morning Glory hot spring as "clear, deep. Terribly deep. Have measured 100 feet deep. All tasted the water very good and pure." At Canyon, he wrote, "After dinner walked about 3 miles up into the canyon and saw the upper Falls. 65 feet and then the lower

3

ones over 300 feet. Canyon beautifully colored. Saw eagle's nest." He rode a pony named "Peanuts" six miles to Cooke City and recorded that Old Faithful rose every 65 minutes. In 1989, the average time between eruptions had changed from 65 to 79 minutes. He did not mention the troops.

Thirty-eight years later, in 1924, when the National Park Service was eight years old, Rockefeller returned to Yellowstone with his three older sons, John 3rd, Nelson, and Laurance. Between these two trips to Yellowstone, there had been other trips to Mexico, California, Cuba, Panama, Europe, and the Orient. But his experiences on the 1924 trip accelerated his involvement in the care and use of park land.

Between 1924 and 1960, Rockefeller gave over $40 million to the nation for state and national parks and an additional $56 million toward the restoration of Colonial Williamsburg. During his life, he gave larger amounts to other sectors of society; $86 million to schools and colleges, $85 million toward religious causes, and $81 million to medical, charitable, and relief organizations. However, it was the parks and restorations that captured and retained his personal interest.

By 1924, he had given $420,000 for park purposes in Maine, where his association with the Park Service began a decade earlier. He entered into a partnership with the Service, building and caring for roads on public lands and giving land for park expansion in Lafayette National Park, renamed Acadia National Park in 1929. For over 40 years he was the principal private benefactor of Acadia, the first national park east of the Mississippi River.

Rockefeller discovered Mt. Desert Island in Maine, when he summered with his family in Bar Harbor in 1908. In 1910, he purchased the "Eyrie," a summer residence in Seal Harbor about seven miles from Bar Harbor. He purchased additional land around the homesite and built carriage roads for his own and his neighbors' use. He began contributing small amounts, from $5.00 to $500, to the Bar Harbor and Seal Harbor bridle path associations; he helped purchase small lots of land for local parks, and became an occasional contributor to the Hancock County Trustees for Public Reservations, the organization that fathered the national park. By 1924, he had contributed over $420,000 to the Trustees and to the park. By 1960, he had given Acadia National Park a total of $3.5 million in money, land, and roads.

With the assistance of experts such as Horace M. Albright, Frederick L. Olmsted, son of the famed landscape architect and a landscape planner in his own right with a growing reputation, and Grosvenor Atterbury, a noted architect, Rockefeller began a campaign to create his ideal national park on the island. He was guided by a clear vision of what he wanted for the park. Once, commenting on road engineers, he said, they "seem sometimes to forget that their services are only means to the larger end of developing a well-located, beautiful, attractive road that goes to worthwhile places."

Rockefeller had been building roads on public lands in the area since 1915. Carriage roads which passed over his lands and those of the park were built under an agreement he had made with the original owners of the park lands, the Hancock County Trustees. The agreement was continued when the lands became part of the national park system in 1919.

George B. Dorr, one of the original Hancock Trustees, was superintendent of the park when Rockefeller drafted a letter to himself which he proposed to have Dorr sign. The object of the letter was to get official permission to do work on carriage roads which crossed park lands. It states Rockefeller's vision of his role, his objectives, his methods, and his commitment to roads and forestry projects.

This is how Rockefeller saw himself in 1922:

Dear Mr. Rockefeller: July 15, 1922

    I want to express again on behalf of Lafayette National Park my genuine appreciation of the roadbuilding, forestry, planting, etc., which you have done under the authority of the Government in the Park lands. You have used excellent judgement in the way all of this work has been done and I not only cordially approve it in every detail but feel the park is most fortunate in having had so interested, genuine and intelligent a friend as yourself. While of course you are under no slightest obligation to the Park for the upkeep of the roads which you have constructed, may I say that in so far as you are willing to do this, in connection with the care of your own roads, it will be greatly appreciated by the Park authorities. I realize too, that you are constantly going over your own roads, having the trees cut which die from time to time, replacing or adding to the planting which had been done, bringing in or transferring top soil where further planting seems desirable, seeding bare banks, in order to more completely and rapidly restore natural conditions, pruning, etc. any such work you are willing to do along the Park roads adjoining your property, I shall not only appreciate your doing, but give you full authority as my representative to do; it being understood that no expense therefor will fall upon the Park.

I am writing this letter because of my appreciation of your great interest in the Park and because of my complete confidence in your familiarity with road building, forestry, planting, and the various matters above referred to, acquired through many years of experience in such work on your own places in various parts of the country.

While the letter was never sent, Dorr gave the necessary permission, and Rockefeller built carriage roads on park lands following these standards.

By 1924, John D. Rockefeller, Jr.'s contributions to the Maine national park were known throughout the Park Service. He was regarded as a potential benefactor for other parks and was treated as such. When his plans for the 1924 trip to Yellowstone and other western parks became known, Stephen T. Mather, Director of the National Park Service, instructed the park superintendents not to present any park problems, in fact, problems of any kind, to Rockefeller while he was visiting them. Mather did not wish to put any pressure on the philanthropist.

In preparation for the trip, Charles O. Heydt, a Rockefeller office associate, wrote to a concessionaire in Yellowstone Park asking for information. His letter was answered by Horace M. Albright, then Superintendent of Yellowstone National Park and Assistant Director of the National Park Service, who suggested an itinerary, a guide, and necessary clothing.

The party of four Rockefellers, John D. Jr., John D. 3rd, Nelson A., Laurance S., and a young doctor, left New York City on June 23, 1924. They returned to New York on August 10.

The family group visited the Grand Canyon, Mesa Verde, Sante Fe, Denver, Yellowstone, and Glacier National Parks. The visits to Mesa Verde, Yellowstone, and Glacier National Parks prompted Rockefeller to action. On July 10, while in Denver, he sent a check for $500 to Jesse Nusbaum, Superintendent of Mesa Verde, toward the cost of completing an interpretive museum. He pledged an additional $3,000 for the museum and for archeological work in the park.

Albright met the party on their arrival in Yellowstone. He did not accompany them on their visit through the park, which included a morning trip to the Amoretti Inn in Jackson Hole to view the Grand Teton Mountains. After two-and-one-half days, they went to Glacier National Park, where they spent three weeks.

Rockefeller returned to his home in Seal Harbor, Maine, where on August 15, he wrote similar letters to Charles J. Kraebel, Superintendent of Glacier National Park, and to Albright in Yellowstone. In a "spirit of helpful and constructive criticism," he commented to Kraebel on the unsightly conditions around the Many Glacier Hotel and along the roads in the park. Recognizing that the hotel company, a Northern Pacific Railroad enterprise, might have its own plans, he offered to contribute confidentially toward the cost of the work he was suggesting.

Kraebel thanked Rockefeller for his offer, but said he was unprepared to ask him for financial assistance. Rockefeller accepted the turndown, but kept the door open for a future request. The request never came.

While waiting for replies to his letters to the park superintendents, Rockefeller also wrote to the Secretary of Agriculture, Henry C. Wallace. Concerned about conditions he found in the Lewis and Clark National Forest while on a pack-train trip, he said some trails were in excellent condition, but others were impassable. Throughout the area, he saw wildflowers of great variety in marvelous abundance, but they were being damaged by large flocks of sheep.

Wallace replied two weeks later. He assured Rockefeller that the trails were being cleared as necessary. Furthermore, explaining the Forest Service philosophy of multiple-use, he wrote, the sheep had been on National Forest lands for years, and each year, the wildflowers bloomed anew. The sheep did not destroy them.

"That sheep grazing does not permanently destroy the wildflowers, I am glad to know," Rockefeller replied.

While in Glacier National Park, Rockefeller met Stephen T. Mather. Writing on September 24, Mather thanked Rockefeller for his interest in the parks and commented on the Rockefeller suggestions to the superintendents. Mather made no suggestions for support at this time.

A year later, Mather's restraint on approaching Rockefeller relaxed. In August 1925, he, and, at his suggestion, C. G. Thomson, Superintendent of Crater Lake National Park, wrote to Rockefeller asking for assistance in clearing the roadsides in the park. John D. Jr. declined the requests writing, "Perhaps sometime I shall be able to visit Crater Lake Park, and may then be inspired to cooperate in the clean-up work there." He did visit the park in 1926 and received extensive information on the work that needed to be done. While he gave Thomson a personal gift in recognition of his hospitality in the park, Rockefeller was not inspired to assist in road work in the park and gave no reason for his refusal.

But the results had been different in Yellowstone. Rockefeller's 1924 letter to Horace M. Albright fell on fertile ground. Describing the pleasure of his visit to the park, he wrote, "There was just one thing in the park which marred my enjoyment of that wonderful region, and I have wondered if I might be helpful to the park administration in improving that situation." He offered to help finance the clearing of down timber and stumps which lined the roadways.

Albright responded two weeks later. Road clearance was always one of his objectives for the park, he wrote, but he did not know what the work would cost since there were different conditions in different areas. Therefore, he proposed to clear short sections to determine costs and prepare budgets. Rockefeller agreed to this approach, and the work began.

Between August 1924 and March 1930, Rockefeller watched his ideas of what roadsides should look like systematically take shape in Yellowstone National Park. During this period, Rockefeller gave the Park Service $49,430 for the road work. The experience gained in Maine had now been extended to a large wilderness area in the West.

Albright wrote on May 26, 1927, "You started one of the most important movements ever undertaken in the national parks and the results obtained here attracted so much attention that there has been no difficulty in getting roadside cleanup recognized as an exceedingly important part of future road construction programs to be carried on by the Government."

The Yellowstone road project was soon overshadowed by an ambitious land purchase program in the West. In 1926, Rockefeller took his wife, Abby, and his three younger sons, Laurance S., Winthrop, and David on his third trip to Yellowstone. For Laurance, the middle son, this was his second in two years. Albright accompanied the Rockefeller party to Jackson Hole this time. The party visited the Bar B C ranch for an hour and, while the young men swam in the lake, Mr. and Mrs. Rockefeller enjoyed what has been called the best view of the Tetons. Albright took the opportunity to tell Rockefeller the history of the efforts to incorporate the valley into the national park system. These efforts extended back to 1898 and, since 1916, included personal drives by Albright and Stephen Mather.

Within a month after his return home, Rockefeller asked

9

WORTHWHILE PLACES

Albright for information on how the Jackson Hole country could be preserved for the nation. Albright provided an ambitious plan of action. Five months later, Rockefeller outlined his vision for the future of the Jackson Hole valley to Arthur Woods, an associate. He hoped to buy "all the land not held by friendly Dude Ranchers in the entire Jackson Hole Valley with a view to its being ultimately turned over to the Government...." There were two reasons, he said,

> 1st: The marvelous scenic beauty of the Teuton Mountains and the Lakes at their feet, which are seen at their best from the Jackson Hole Valley and
> 2nd: The fact that this Valley is the natural and necessary sanctuary and feeding place for the game which inhabits Yellowstone Park and the surrounding region.

Later, Mr. Rockefeller wrote, "I am confident that nothing short of the most comprehensive and complete program should be followed, fully believing that whether the program is carried out now or ten years later, it will ultimately be carried out, and for myself, quite willing to wait and let time do its work of adjusting and mollifying, rather than to seek an early settlement of the question through unwise compromise that would for all time mean a less ideal and worthwhile program."

To limit publicity about the plan and keep land prices from rising through speculation, the Snake River Land Company was created. Acting for Rockefeller, the company, by 1930, had bought over 30,000 acres for about $1 million. Little did he realize that twenty years would pass before the vision he shared with Albright would be realized. Although the 40-mile narrow range of Teton Mountains was made a national park in 1929, local and political opposition stalled the transfer of the valley lands to the nation until 1949.

AN OVERVIEW

Before 1933, Rockefeller made two other contributions toward parks in the West. Between 1927 and 1931, he gave $2 million to the Save-the-Redwoods League for the preservation of redwoods in California and $1.6 million in 1929 to the Federal government for one-half the cost of a sugar and yellow-pine forest fronting the sequoia giants of Yosemite Park.

He also made other large contributions in the East in addition to Acadia National Park. Colonial Williamsburg, not part of the National Park System, was the largest beneficiary.

John D. Rockefeller, Jr., first met the Reverend W. A. R. Goodwin in February 1924 and learned of his plans for the restoration of the historic Virginia village. Rockefeller visited Williamsburg again in 1926 and again met with Goodwin. Before the end of the year, he had authorized the purchase of the Paradise-Ludwell house, which was the beginning of the Colonial Williamsburg restoration. By 1960, he had invested over $56 million in the enterprise.

Horace Albright became a trustee of Colonial Williamsburg in 1934 and served until 1958. He and Rockefeller did not discuss Williamsburg at length in their correspondence, but their few letters provide sidelights on the project.

In 1929, Goodwin suggested to Kenneth Chorley, a Rockefeller associate who was involved in both the Williamsburg and Jackson Hole projects, that Williamsburg, Jamestown, and Yorktown should be connected by a parkway and made into a national park. Chorley presented the idea to Albright, then Director of the Park Service. On July 3, 1930, a park with plans for a parkway was authorized by Congress as part of the national park system.

In 1990, the Colonial National Historical Park consisted of most of Jamestown Island, the Revolutionary battlefield at Yorktown, 23 miles of parkway connecting these areas with Williamsburg, and the Cape Henry Memorial which marks the approximate site of the first landing of the Jamestown settlers.

Three other southeastern areas received Rockefeller's attention before 1933: Washington's birthplace at Wakefield, Virginia, Shenandoah National Park, and Great Smoky Mountains National Park.

11

WORTHWHILE PLACES

Shenandoah and the Great Smoky Mountains parks were authorized by Congress in 1926. They were the result of local campaigns for parks in the areas and Congressional desire for additional national parks in the East. To assist in the purchase of land for Shenandoah in Virginia, Rockefeller contributed the last $160,000 necessary to round out the area that the Park Service wanted. In 1929, he was instrumental in having the Laura Spelman Rockefeller Memorial, a Rockefeller philanthropy, contribute $5 million to the Great Smoky Mountains park, one-half of the total needed toward the purchase of land in North Carolina and Tennessee. Today, two plaques stand in Newfound Gap, at the state line, commemorating the gift.

The two plaques dramatize one of John D. Rockefeller, Jr.'s lifelong perplexities. He frequently told anyone who would listen that certain gifts were made by his father or by one of the philanthropic boards that his father had founded and not by him.

One bronze plaque which was approved by Rockefeller reads:

> For the Permanent Enjoyment of the People
> This park was given one half by the peoples and states of North Carolina and Tennessee and by the United States of America and one half in memory of Laura Spelman Rockefeller by the Laura Spelman Rockefeller Memorial. Founded by her husband John D. Rockefeller.

A second smaller but more accessible plastic-covered plaque reads:

> The Price of a National Park
> In the early 1920's the acreage that later became the park was productive farmland and timber country — over 6,000 separate tracts. Visions of a national park prompted many individuals and groups to donate money to the cause. North Carolina and Tennessee citizens donated $4.1

12

million. Their state commissions bought land, then turned it over to the federal government. Federal expenditures of $3.5 million and John D. Rockefeller, Jr.'s $5 million contribution in 1934 completed funding for the park.

Between 1924 and 1933, Rockefeller gave almost $6 million toward national and state park projects. His gifts included $500 to a proposed Appalachian park, $2 million for the national park in Maine, $1.6 million to Yosemite, and $2 million to the California state redwood forests. He had worked closely with his fellow conservationist, Horace M. Albright. By 1933, however, the financial and political events of 1929 and 1932 had changed the relationship of Rockefeller and Albright to the national park system.

The stock market collapse of 1929 and Albright's departure from government service created the new relationship. Rockefeller's net worth declined from a high of nearly $1 billion in 1929 to less than $500 million in 1934 and $291.1 million in 1939. Albright resigned as Park Director in 1933.

Between November 1932 and March 1933, they sought a commitment from the out-going Hoover administration that would permit the Acadia road-building projects to continue. After March 20, 1933, they courted the interest and support of the new administration and the new Secretary of the Interior, Harold L. Ickes.

As the Roosevelt administration's New Deal work programs expanded, federal funds were available for road work in Acadia, and Rockefeller's personal road building decreased. However, he and Albright kept a close watch on the problems and progress in Maine.

Albright resigned as Director in August 1933. He had served for seventeen years in the Park Service since its inception in 1916. From 1916 to 1929, he had been Assistant Director, and from 1919 to 1929, Superintendent of Yellowstone. When Stephen T. Mather retired as Director in 1929, Albright succeeded him.

He left the Park Service to become Vice President and General Manager of the United States Potash Company, with new operations in New Mexico and offices in Rockefeller Center in New York City.

In 1930, the company had asked Albright to join them as chief operating officer. He accepted the offer in 1933, after declining it in 1930 and 1931.

Albright's decision to join private industry was prompted by the promise of greater financial rewards than government service. However, he maintained his close, if now informal, relations with the National Park Service and with other appointed and elected officials of the Federal government as well as the organized conservation movement in America. His new employers encouraged his conservation work and promised him time off and extra help to care for special matters.

Albright has been described as a combination of P. T. Barnum and Florenz Ziegfield. He was effervescent, talkative and gregarious. In Yellowstone, and later in Washington and New York, he was always ready to entertain visitors and spread his gospel of the parks. He was an effective lobbyist for the conservation movement in the halls of Congress after he left Federal service in 1933.

Between 1933 and 1943, most of the Rockefeller-Albright correspondence dealt with Acadia National Park, its roads, bridges, land, structures, and a naval radio station that stood in the way of a shore road Rockefeller wanted to have built. The letters reflect the intense, personal interest Rockefeller took in the details of improving the park.

There had been one other major item pending on Rockefeller's agenda in 1933: the disposition of the 30,000 plus acres he had acquired in Jackson Hole. It was still pending in 1943. Opposition by the Wyoming delegation in Congress prevented adding the lands to Grand Teton National Park, which had been created in 1929.

Harold Ickes, Secretary of the Interior in the Roosevelt administration, became a frequent visitor to Acadia as well as an admirer of other Rockefeller projects. A friendship developed between Rockefeller and Ickes, who supported the plan to add Jackson Hole to the Grand Teton National Park.

In November 1942, Rockefeller told Ickes that because of the uncertainty of the times, he was anxious to dispose of the land which had cost him, including taxes and maintenance, more than $1.5 million. If the government was unwilling to accept the land as a gift, he would seek to dispose of it in some other way.

Ickes took the request to President Franklin D. Roosevelt and obtained his agreement to avoid a congressional confrontation over the National Park issue by creating a National Monument to accept the Rockefeller land. The Jackson Hole National Monument was created by Executive Order in March 1943.

But local opposition to the National Monument continued. Wyoming representatives in Congress again subverted the transfer of the land to the Monument by successfully introducing legislation that prevented Federal funds from being spent for the maintenance of the Monument. The opposition, which had found support in Congress, consisted of cattlemen who feared the loss of grazing rights on forest service lands, hunters who foresaw the loss of hunting areas, dude ranch operators who did not want the natural wilderness filled with tourists instead of dudes, politicians who drew upon the local fear of the eastern establishment, and local officials who feared the loss of tax revenues.

Unwilling to continue personal ownership of the land, Rockefeller transferred it to Jackson Hole Preserve, Inc., a private foundation. Laurance S. Rockefeller was president of the foundation which was incorporated in 1940. On December 16, 1949, after local opposition had diminished, Jackson Hole Preserve, Inc. gave 33,562 acres to the government. The Rockefeller lands, with other Federal- and State-owned lands in the valley, were incorporated into an enlarged Grand Teton National Park in September 1950.

The years 1933 to 1943 were a sharp contrast to the previous decade when Rockefeller's activities swept from Virginia to Wyoming and California to Maine. It was a period of retrenchment and caretaking. World War II slowed road and bridge building in Acadia; Jackson Hole had been on hold since 1933; the Colonial Parkway, connecting Jamestown and Williamsburg, would be built with Federal funds. Rockefeller's direct participation in park affairs was steadily decreasing.

15

There were other areas, however, in which his interests were aroused. In 1943, Mr. and Mrs. Rockefeller heard of a possible threat to Indian pueblos in New Mexico because of plans for dams on the upper Rio Grande. He turned to Albright for information and advice on how the pueblos might be protected.

In a similar vein, but with a more personal sense of urgency, Rockefeller turned to Albright over the explosion of the deer population in Acadia. The deer, he reported, were disfiguring and destroying the forest undergrowth. He was tired of official surveys of the deer population — he wanted action. But, as Albright pointed out, the deer were under the protection of the laws of the state of Maine.

Rockefeller's giving for all park purposes exceeded $30 million by 1944. In addition to the gifts to the Federal Government, there were gifts to the Palisades Interstate Park in New York and New Jersey; city parks in New York City and in Cleveland, where his father's business career had started; and county parks in New York and New Jersey.

Between 1944 and 1960, he gave Jackson Hole Preserve, Inc. over $19 million in land and funds which enabled the foundation to buy additional private lands within the Jackson Hole National Monument, and later Grand Teton National Park; a grove of giant sequoias in California; a cypress swamp in Florida; and land on St. John's Island in the Virgin Islands. The funds were also used to build tourist facilities in the Jackson Hole region and in the Virgin Islands. He continued to support the national park system, but now he used an intermediary. As large as his contributions were to the various kinds of parks, they did not match his support of Colonial Williamsburg. "We made no mistake in the investment we have made in Williamsburg. No one has gotten more pleasure from what has been done there than I have," he wrote in 1952.

After 1944, Rockefeller made only two personal gifts for park purposes, other than land in Maine. In 1947, he gave $100,000 toward the purchase of a scenic gorge and falls, Linville Falls, fronting on the Blue Ridge Parkway north of Asheville, North Carolina. In 1956, he gave $19,000 to purchase a small section of natural prairie in Kansas. A $1 million gift toward the purchase of land in the South Calaveras Grove in California was made through Jackson Hole Preserve, Inc.

While his direct giving for park purposes all but ceased, Rockefeller continued his personal interest in Acadia.

With the end of World War II, Rockefeller turned to Albright to start things moving again in Maine. There were roads and bridges to be built and Federal funds to be found to do the work. As Federal funds were slow in coming and as post-war inflation multiplied the cost of construction, Rockefeller considered building some of the bridges himself, or at least contributing toward the cost of the work with grants to the government. He was not called on to make these contributions and, slowly, the work wound itself to a satisfactory conclusion.

In October 1947, Acadia was ravaged by a devastating fire. Holding to his belief in a better future, Rockefeller stoically accepted the blow and began reworking the roadsides using his own employees to do the work. Now there was a change. Criticism was leveled against the manner in which the Rockefeller crews were working the roadsides, and Rockefeller had to defend his superintendent's methods through Albright. And defend them he did.

While changing conditions in Acadia held Rockefeller's interest, a dark cloud spread over the entire park system. Articles in *Harper's*, *Reader's Digest*, *The Saturday Evening Post*, and other publications decried the poor conditions in the parks resulting from neglect during the war years and the increasing pressure on the parks by the growing number of visitors. Looking for reasonable answers, Rockefeller turned to Albright while lamenting the apparent decline of the parks since the days when Albright had been in charge.

Albright, President Dwight D. Eisenhower, and Secretary of the Interior Douglas McKay, all assured Rockefeller that while there were problems, conditions were not as bad as they were painted in the articles. Accepting these assurances, Rockefeller was suddenly surprised by what seemed to be an attack on the National Park Service itself.

In 1953, the Civil Service Commission removed the protection of the Civil Service rules from the top six officers of the Park Service. These positions had had this protection since the Service was established in 1916.

Between 1916 and 1961, there had been three Democratic administrations: Wilson, Roosevelt, and Truman; four Republican administrations: Harding, Coolidge, Hoover, and Eisenhower. During those 45 years, there were six directors of the National Park Service: Stephen T. Mather (1916-1928), Horace M. Albright (1929-1933), Arno B. Cammerer (1933-1940), Newton B. Drury (1940-1951), Arthur E. Demaray (1951), and Conrad L. Wirth (1951-1964).

Only one, Newton B. Drury, was appointed from outside the Service and had no previous national park experience. The others, from Albright to Wirth, had risen through the ranks to the top position. Mather and Albright shared in the creation of the Park Service. Drury was a highly regarded conservationist. For many years he had been Executive Secretary of the Save-the-Redwoods League and had been active in the California state park system.

President Wilson had put the top positions of the Park Service under the purview of Civil Service laws and regulations and, with the practice of promotion from within the organization, national politics were not an important factor in the life of the Park Service.

Until the 1950's, each change in directors brought a response from Rockefeller, usually a letter commenting on the man's activities and including a small gift. Albright's departure from government service in 1933 led to public recognition of Rockefeller's contributions to the parks by Harold Ickes, Secretary of the Interior. He gave a speech based on information supplied by Albright, which emphasized the Rockefeller park contributions. Albright expressed concern about Rockefeller's possible negative reaction to the publicity, but to Albright's surprise, Rockefeller appreciated the remarks.

Twenty years later, the removal of the six top Service positions from the protection of Civil Service sent shock waves throughout the organization. Albright wrote Rockefeller about the change. Rockefeller contacted his son, Nelson, then Undersecretary of Health, Education and Welfare, and Nelson went to the Secretary of the Interior, Douglas McKay. McKay quickly assured John D. Rockefeller, Jr., that the change was an overall change throughout the government and that it would not impact adversely on the Park Service. McKay's prediction held for twenty years, when, during the Nixon administration, a purely political appointment was made. Later appointments to the top post were generally from the professional ranks of the Park Service.

Rockefeller's concern about the welfare of the National Park Service did not start with the Eisenhower administration. The long delay in transferring the Jackson Hole lands to the national government had been a burden. In 1949, he told Albright that his enthusiasm for the Park Service was considerably dampened. In 1953, he wrote Park Service Director Conrad L. Wirth that he thought the parks should have an interpretive program, but should not try to educate the visitor.

Albright assured Rockefeller that his intervention during the Civil Service crisis had served the Park Service well. His vigilance in protecting both the parks and those who managed the parks was one more contribution Rockefeller made to the heritage of every American.

During the last years of the Rockefeller/Albright correspondence, the content of the letters changed from concern with the present and future to memories of the past. Rockefeller and Albright warmly embraced their remembered association and successes. Occasionally, Albright would offer opportunities for Rockefeller giving, but they were usually declined. Among such declinations were support for an oral history program for surviving western pioneers, the American Trail Association, the purchase of Alston House in North Carolina, and Castillo de San Marco in St. Augustine, Florida.

Albright's association with the Rockefellers included his service on the boards and commissions of the American Youth Hostel, Colonial Williamsburg, American Conservation Association, Jackson Hole Preserve, Inc., and the Palisades Interstate Park Commission.

This professional association was paralleled by his deep personal interest in the Rockefeller family. For over 60 years, he watched their activities. His letters provide a contemporary commentary on the joys, sorrows, and political victories and defeats of the family.

He did not expect, nor did he always get, replies to his sometimes rambling letters. In retirement, in California, he continued in the national conservation scene. Corresponding with Laurance S. Rockefeller and his associates, Albright commented on Lyndon Johnson's "Make America Beautiful" campaign. He hoped to tutor Ronald Reagan on conservation matters, and he relived, again and again, the Rockefeller visits to Yellowstone and Jackson Hole. Horace M. Albright was one of John D. Rockefeller, Jr.'s long and lasting associates.

Joseph W. Ernst

PART I
1924 – 1933

Acadia National Park, Colonial Historical National Park, Colonial Williamsburg, George Washington Birthplace National Monument, Grand Teton National Park, Great Smoky Mountains National Park, Jackson Hole, Lafayette National Park, Mesa Verde National Park, Palisades Interstate Park, Public Highways Beautification, Shenandoah National Park, Yellowstone National Park, Yosemite National Park.

WORTHWHILE PLACES

May 14, 1924

Mr. Chas. O. Heydt,
26 Broadway,
New York, N.Y.

My dear Mr. Heydt:

I have been absent from Yellowstone National Park for several months, and have just returned. Mr. E. H. Moorman, of the Yellowstone Park Camps Company, forwarded to me your letter to Mr. Hays, dated April 11th, in regard to the trip in this park proposed by Mr. Rockefeller, but it did not reach me immediately.

I very much hope Mr. Rockefeller will make the trip he is contemplating. It can be handled according to his desires as to every detail. It happens that I will have available for detail, as a guide for the party, one of my oldest and ablest rangers. He has guided many parties through the wildest sections of the Park, and knows exactly what a party such as Mr. Rockefeller's will require. He is one of the best fisherman in the Yellowstone region.

As to an outfit, a thoroughly satisfactory outfit for an independent trip would cost about $20 per day per person including saddle horses, pack horses, guides, food, slickers, etc. Clothing for the party itself, and fishing tackle would be extra. Fishing tackle can be procured here. I cannot conscientiously recommend Mr. Walter Shaw.

If Mr. Rockefeller and his boys have not seen the Yellowstone, I would suggest that they enter the Park via Cody, Wyoming, Buffalo Bill's former home, and then make a four days automobile trip over the road system of the Park, visiting the geysers, Lake Yellowstone, the Grand Canyon, and the Great Terraces at Mammoth Hot Springs. From Mammoth, which is the headquarters of the Park, they should go to Camp Roosevelt, 18 miles East, and there take the saddle horse outfit. A week or ten days on the trails of the Yellowstone is not very long, because this is a big country - as big as Delaware and Rhode Island combined, but such a period would be sufficient to take the party through the country where the wild buffalo roam, high into the Absarokas, and along the shore of Lake Yellowstone into the country of the moose — all a great wilderness, and full of game and fish.

I would suggest that the party plan to spend from two to three weeks if possible, and to come about July 20th.

If you will give me the exact dates of the trip, the number in the party, and all suggestions you have as to its organization and equipment, I will have all arrangements made, and there will be no publicity. I will send you a complete itinerary, and all necessary information. Mr. Rockefeller knows my chief, Hon. S. T. Mather, the chief of all the national parks, and also Mr. Geo. B. Dorr, the Superintendent of Lafayette Park in Maine.

Yellowstone is a great boys' park, and Mr. Rockefeller's sons are just the right age to thoroughly enjoy the place.

If you write me again, mark your letter "confidential", and if you want to use an assumed name for the party, please give that to me.

Sincerely yours,
HORACE M. ALBRIGHT

Charles O. Heydt. Rockefeller office associate.

Stephen T. Mather. Director of the National Park Service, 1917-1929. Independently wealthy from a fortune made in the borax business, he was appointed first director. Mather became ill in 1917, and Horace M. Albright was made acting director. In 1929, when Mather retired from the service, Albright succeeded him as director.

George B. Dorr. Scion of a wealthy Boston family. Dorr made his summer home on Mount Desert Island in Maine. A bachelor, he was one of the first members of the Hancock County Trustees for Public Reservations, an organization formed by President Charles Eliot of Harvard, and others, to assemble land on Mount Desert for preservation and public use. The Trustees' lands were donated to the Federal Government in 1916 as the Sieur de Monts National Monument. The Monument became Lafayette National Park in 1919 and then Acadia National Park in 1929. Dorr made large contributions of land and money to the growing

WORTHWHILE PLACES

park. He became superintendent of Lafayette National Park in 1919. He died in 1944.

August 15th, 1924.

Dear Mr. Albright:-

Our Western trip ended on Sunday last, at which time we reached New York, coming on Monday night up here to Maine, where we have a summer home.

I want to tell you how much we enjoyed our tour through the Yellowstone, how interested we were in all that we saw in the Park and how greatly we appreciated the courtesy of the rangers wherever we went, who were acting, we realized, under your kindly directtion. The chauffeur, who conducted us through the Park, lived up fully to your recommendation. He proved himself to be an expert driver, a competent guide and a thorough gentleman.

There was just one thing in the Park which marred my enjoyment of that wonderful region, and I have wondered if I might be helpful to the Park administration in improving that situation. I refer to the vast quantities of down timber and stumps which line the roadsides so frequently throughout the Park. Of course I realize that this dead material comes in part from the roadway itself, having been thrown out when the road was cut through, and also that it is due to some extent to the character of the forests which is such as to cause many trees constantly to die and fall. I know also from personal experience that it is costly to cut up and burn dead timber, down as well as standing.

It seems to me, however, that if the accumulation of dead trees and stumps alongside of the roads to a width of from fifty to a hundred feet from the roadside could be done away with, much of the beauty of the woods and the scenery generally would be enormously improved. I wonder, therefore, if you would agree to the desirability of such work if it could be financed, and if so, what you think it would cost, the work to be done in the off season, probably largely when there is

24

snow on the ground and in the most economical manner possible, even if it extended over several years. Probably it would be difficult to make any worth while estimate of the cost of such an enterprise. If the idea appeals to you, it might be better for me to state some amount that I would be willing to contribute at least as a starter, and let that be used in whole or in part this coming winter, as a result of which it would be possible to determine better what further sums would be necessary.

Without, therefore, making a committal as to any contribution, I am simply throwing out the suggestion that I may have the benefit of your frank opinion as to its desirability, together with some rough indication of your thought of the possible cost of such an undertaking.

With renewed expressions of thanks for your courtesy to us and with hearty congratulations upon what you have done and are doing in Yellowstone, I am

Very sincerely,
JOHN D. ROCKEFELLER, JR.

September 2, 1924

My dear Mr. Rockefeller:

The work of completing our next year's budget and preparing the annual report on operations in Yellowstone Park have been responsible for some delay in answering your letter of August 15th, which I want to tell you in the beginning of this reply, is one of the most inspiring communications that I have received since I entered the National Park Service over 11 years ago. Interest such as you have shown in Yellowstone Park spurs one on to greater effort and makes one feel more than ever that we are in a public work that is worth while.

I doubt if any other one thing associated with Yellowstone Park has troubled me more in planning for the future than the dead and down timber along our roads. This condition of the roadside is unsightly and there can be no question but what it detracts a great deal from the pleasure of the Yellowstone trip in the case of many, many visitors. In the course of a year dozens of people comment on this dead and down timber and since your letter reached me I have had two communications regarding the unsightly roadside conditions. I attach copies of these letters, which are typical of dozens that I receive in the course of a year.

Back in 1915, the first time Mr. Mather and I came to Yellowstone, we took up the question of clearing the roadsides. The Army was in charge of Yellowstone at this time and we asked for estimates on the cost of cleaning up the dead and down timber and improving roadside conditions. The estimates as to cost almost paralyzed us but we took them at their face value. We know now, however, that the work could be done for a fraction of what the Army estimated the work would cost. However, we took hold of the park at the time of the war and we have been on a rock bottom financial basis ever since, so that we have had no opportunity to actually undertake any of this work of cleaning up the timber left along the roads, except in connection with getting out our winter supply of wood, and, of course, we require so little wood and the wood cutting operation is so different from a clean up program that I have little to go on now in the way of making an estimate.

I wonder if the following idea would appeal to you as practicable and sensible.

Let us take a half mile of the roadside, say between Mammoth Hot Springs and Norris, where there is so much dead and down timber, and clean up this under the direction of a good foreman and with constant personal supervision by myself. The results of this operation would give us a very accurate idea of what the heavy clean up work would cost and we could survey the entire road system to classify the heavy work and the light work as well. Also, in order to get an idea of what the cost of the light clean up would be we could take another half mile and clean it thoroughly, keeping accurate record of costs. I could then submit these two cost records to you.

26

The latter part of this month is the ideal time to undertake clean up work of this character. There is not much travel on the roads and we can pull the debris into the road and burn most of it, afterwards hauling away the ashes. The winter snows will restore the natural conditions so that in the spring all evidence of disturbance of natural conditions involved in the clean up will be gone.

As stated above, the most unsightly section of road is the 20 miles between Mammoth Hot Springs and Norris, but after all there is only about 10 miles of road that runs through the timber and much of this requires only light clean up work. Leaving aside the 11 miles of road between Canyon Junction and Norris Junction, a section that you did not cover when you were in the park, I doubt if there is over 35 miles of road in the entire park that requires cleaning up. All of the roads in the northeastern section of the park, particularly between Canyon and Mammoth Hot Springs, via Tower Falls, were very well cleaned up when built and as the timber is mostly spruce and fir there is not so much fallen timber in the forests. It is characteristic of lodgepole pine, which predominates in the park, to go on the theory of "the survival of the fittest" and hence weak trees are constantly dying and falling. It is also characteristic of the trees in lodgepole pine forests to grow very thickly when young and then as they grow bigger to force out the weaker trees.

You have taken interest in a Yellowstone problem that is as important from the purely landscape standpoint as any this park has ever faced, but it should also be said that it is the problem that we have the least chance of having Congressmen consider. I have called it to the attention of several Congressional committees, two of which were sub-committees of the Appropriation Committee of the House of Representatives. I suppose I have talked over the problem with fully forty individual members of Congress. I have discussed it with three Congressmen within the past month and there are two more here this week that I shall talk with about the dead and down timber, but I do not expect much interest to be taken because these men feel that there are many other things which ought to be done before we begin cleaning up the forests. They do not see the strictly park point of view.

If the plan suggested above appeals to you and you would like to assist in making the experimental clean up I would appreciate it if you would let me know your views at an early date as I would like to get the work done during the last two weeks of this month. At any event, however, I am going to undertake the clean up of a few hundred yards of roadside with some road or telephone crew in order to get some idea of costs, but, of course, this will be an unauthorized project and I will not be able to let these men work more than a day or two on a project of this character. I am inclined to think that our record of cost will show that the work can be done very cheaply.

I had a very pleasant visit with Colonel Stewart, of the Standard Oil of Indiana, who was in the park for about ten days with his two boys, and only yesterday Mr. T. A. Dines of the Midwest Refining Company left the park after a visit of several days with his family. Colonel Stewart, I thought, has one of the most pleasant personalities that it has been my fortune to meet.

With sentiments of highest esteem and thanking you heartily for your interest in the Yellowstone, I am

Very sincerely yours,
HORACE M. ALBRIGHT

Colonel Robert W. Stewart. President of the Standard Oil Company of Indiana. In 1929, John D. Rockefeller, Jr., forced Stewart out of that position in a highly publicized proxy fight. Rockefeller was incensed with Stewart's responses before a Senate investigating committee in 1928. He was charged with perjury and contempt of the committee. The committee was investigating the implications of the Teapot Dome scandal.

Thomas A. Dines. President of the Midwest Refining Company, a subsidiary of Standard Oil of Indiana.

September 8th, 1924.

Dear Mr. Albright:-

Your letter of September 2nd is received. I have just telegraphed you as follows:

> "Letter second received. Fully approve your recommendation and authorize work at my expense on two half mile sections. Assume cost will not exceed a couple of thousand dollars."

In saying "assume cost will not exceed a couple of thousand dollars" I simply wanted to make some record of financial commitment. The cost of this experiment will probably be less; it may be more. To the extent of $2,000 you are at liberty to draw on me as required for this purpose, and as the work proceeds, if you find it is going to cost more in order to complete the experimental sections, please advise me.

I am glad you feel as I do about the desirability of clearing up the roadsides in Yellowstone Park, and hope as a result of the experiment, a program can be worked out which will make possible the accomplishment of this much needed improvement.

Very sincerely,
JOHN D. ROCKEFELLER, JR.

September 15, 1924

My dear Mr. Rockefeller:

I have received your telegram and letter of September 8th and it is hardly necessary, I think, for me to tell you that both of them gave me great happiness and inspiration.

WORTHWHILE PLACES

On Saturday, the 13th, I organized a small crew of men under a competent foreman and started the experimental clean-up work on a half mile of road some eight miles south of park headquarters on the main road to Norris Geyser Basin. This half mile of road will require heavy work, and just beyond I have selected another half mile that will require light work. I spent half a day with the crew outlining the work and watching its progress. I went back again after twenty-four hours and was much gratified by the results already obtained. I could scarcely recognize the small section of road that had been cleaned. It looked wholly different and although not yet raked up was most pleasing in appearance.

With the small crew that I have it will require a week or ten days to clean this half mile of dead and down timber, but I do not anticipate that it will cost more than $500 or $600 for the half mile. When the heavy work is completed the crew will clean up the half mile requiring light work and I think this can be done for about $200.

I have made up a report which I attach hereto, giving you a statement of the exact condition of each foot of road between my office at park headquarters and Norris Junction, which is very near the Norris Geyser Basin, a section approximately 20.5 miles long. I am also attaching a series of blue prints on which I have had the engineers plot the conditions of the roadsides so that at a glance you may see just what work is required in order to obtain the end you desire. As soon as the experimental work is completed I will send you a telegram giving you the exact costs, which in conjunction with the report attached hereto will, I think, provide you with sufficient data upon which to make a decision as to whether or not you will want me to proceed with further clean-up work this year. I shall also submit pictures showing the condition of the roadsides before experimental clean-up work was made and other views of the same roadsides after the work is completed.

I hope our costs will be such as to impress you with the practicability of cleaning up Yellowstone's roads and that you will feel inclined to authorize me to clean up this autumn the section between park headquarters and Norris Junction. This road is probably traveled as much as any other road in the park and no other section of road has more unsightly sides and adjacent slopes than this stretch between Mammoth Hot Springs and Norris. This is work that can be done more advantageously in the autumn; debris can be burned safely at this time of the year and men and teams can work along the road without interruption by heavy automobile traffic. Also, at this time of the year, we can organize crews of unusually competent and loyal men. Most of the transient laborers have already left the park region and only the substantial, hardworking fellows who want to save a little money remain.

My thought is that if the continuation of work appears to you to be practicable the clean-up should proceed over a period of about three years, perhaps four. This year we would clean the road sides to Norris Junction, approximately 20 miles. Next year we would clean up the road sides all the way to Old Faithful and down to the Western Entrance at West Yellowstone. The third year the road over the Continental Divide and the South approach road from the West Thumb to the South Entrance could be taken care of and also most or all of the road from Sylvan Pass to Lake Junction. This would leave to be accomplished later only the small sections that will require cleaning between the outlet of Lake Yellowstone and Mammoth Hot Springs by way of Grand Canyon, Dunraven Pass and Tower Falls. There is very little work to do along sides of these sections of the highway system. Of course, there would still remain a section 11 miles in length between Norris Junction and the Grand Canyon but we ought to plan to clean up this section of the road system in connection with the location of a new telephone line.

Speaking of telephone lines, you will recall that many of the most beautiful sections of the Yellowstone road system were made unsightly by two pole lines, one on each side of the road. One of these lines belongs to the Government, the other to the Yellowstone Park Hotel Company. This year the Hotel Company and the National Park Service have arranged through me to rebuild in a period of three years all of the telephone lines, putting both systems on one pole line and placing this pole line in a swath cut through the timber a short distance from the roads. The first section of this new telephone system is nearing completion. This is the section between Mammoth Hot Springs and Norris Junction, the same section that I am proposing we shall first clean up if the plan appears to you to be practicable. Already, most of the old poles on this section are down. Therefore, if you authorize the cleaning up of the road sides between headquarters and Norris Junction next year we will have an exquisitely beautiful highway for the first 20 miles toward the geysers, clear of debris and dead and down timber and likewise, clear of unsightly telephone poles and wires.

" 'Tis a consummation devoutly to be wished."

Awaiting your further instructions which, of course, I shall not expect until you have received our telegram regarding costs of experimental work you authorized, and with sentiments of highest esteem, I am

Very sincerely yours,
HORACE M. ALBRIGHT

September 15, 1924

Abstract

Report
on the
*Condition of the Roadsides Between the superintendent's Office
at Mammoth Hot Springs and Norris Junction*

The distance between the Superintendent's office at Mammoth Hot Springs and Norris Junction by the speedometer of Engineer A. W. Burney's Dodge car is 20.5 miles. The following description of the condition of the roadsides between headquarters and Norris Junction is based on inspection made on September 13th by Superintendent H. M. Albright and

Engineer Burney. Mileage figures used below are from the speedometer of Engineer Burney's official car.

1.5   At this point the road enters the region of an old forest fire. Old timers in the park assert that in 1883 forest fire burned a Douglas fir forest stretching from Terrace Mountain on the West to Bunsen Peak on the East. Many sections of this fire scar immediately re-forested. However, much of the region through which the road runs was not covered with a new growth of timber. The burned trees were afterwards cut down for wood for Fort Yellowstone and the Mammoth Hotel but for more than thirty years hundreds of stumps have stood near the main highway, giving visitors the impression that at one time or another it was the policy of the government to permit the operation of sawmills in the park and that a very fine forest had been cut down to furnish lumber for buildings in the park and perhaps for shipment away from Yellowstone. Tests reveal the fact that these stumps are now very rotten and the smaller ones can be kicked over by the strength of a man's foot. The bigger stumps can easily be pulled by a team of horses. ...

3.0   At this point the road turns sharply into the Hoodoos proper. The Hoodoo region is covered with great blocks of travertine rock thrown down from Terrace Mountain by an earthquake or other cataclysm. A forest grew on the white rocks and was burned in the 1883 fire. However, the ghostly tree trunks seem to be very appropriate to the Hoodoos and it is believed that removal of the trees from this area would rob the Hoodoos of some of their interest for the visitor.

8.45   From this point for a half mile the roadsides are littered with timber cut from the original right of way with other timber that has fallen since the road was built, with logs brush and debris.

15.5   Semi-Centennial Geyser. To 15.9, Roaring Mountain, heavy clean up is required, including the removal of a large amount of dead and down timber along the roadsides. There is much dead timber between the road and Roaring Mountain but as this timber was killed by hot water from Roaring Mountain and it appears to be the natural result of the activity of Roaring Mountain, this timber should not be cut.

20.3   From this point to Norris Junction at 20.5 the road crosses a timbered area which was struck some years ago by a cyclonic wind, most of the trees being uprooted and the whole area made desolate and unsightly.

It will be noted from the above that the roadside conditions of the section between headquarters and Norris Junction require the following clean-up work:

6.4 miles no work required

7.2 miles light clean-up

6.9 miles heavy clean-up
‾‾‾‾
20.5 Total

October 8, 1924

Report on Roadside Clean-up

This is a report on the experimental work of cleaning up roadsides in Yellowstone National Park, authorized to be done by an eastern friend of the park.

On August 15, 1924, this friend of the park wrote me a letter, stating his belief that the roadsides in Yellowstone Park should be cleaned up, and asking me what this work would cost....I suggested cleaning up a half mile of road that required heavy work and another half mile requiring only light work.

On September 7, 1924, the friend of the park wired me as follows:

Letter second received wholly approve your recommendation and authorize work at my expense on two mile sections. Assume cost will not exceed a couple of thousand dollars.

Brief Description of the Work

Briefly the work accomplished is a complete clean-up of the roadsides from 15 to 100 feet back from the ditch line of the road on both sides, depending upon the visibility of the roadsides from an automobile driven along the road. The average clean-up would not exceed 50 or 60 feet on each side of the road. All dead and down timber, dead brush, debris, etc., have been pulled away with teams or loaded on truck or wagons and hauled away. Rotten logs, too far decayed to pull out and too difficult to take up in a shovel have been spread over the ground like fertilizer (which these rotten logs really are when decayed to a point where they fall to pieces. Where such logs are within 15 feet of the road, they are raked up and hauled away.

All standing dead trees within ten or fifteen feet of the road are cut down and hauled away. Other dead trees are left standing unless ready to fall down or unless they seriously impair the landscape.

All young trees, especially near the road are scrupulously protected. Likewise all native shrubs are protected. It has been our aim to restore the roadsides to a natural condition minus the down timber that is usually found in a lodgepole pine forest.

Landscape Betterment

The clean-up work above described and the removal of the telephone lines between Mammoth Hot Springs and Norris Junction, if completed before the opening if next season, will give us a 20.5 miles section of highway of great beauty. It is beyond my power to describe the transformation in the appearance of the roadsides wrought by the clean-up work. I am sure that if the public-spirited gentleman who has made this work possible could see the results of his generosity he would experience a thrill of intense pride. I trust he can see it next summer. As for those of us who are living and working in the park, the spirit of the donor of funds for the work and the clean-up project itself have immensely encouraged and inspired us, and all who know and love the Yellowstone feel that in improving the roadsides, not only is a great landscape work being accomplished, but the wilderness beauty of the great park is being restored.

October 9, 1924

Dear Mr. Albright:

Your letter of September 15th and your several telegrams have been received. On the strength of the experiments which you have made, I wired you the other day as follows:

"Telegram third received. On basis of cost to date authorize you to do as much work as can be done to the best advantage and to the greatest economy this fall."

In line with your telegraphic request of the 8th, I have instructed my office to send you check for $1,000 on account of the work done to date. Further payments will be made when and as requested by you.

Without any committal as to the future, it would seem to me that it was wise to go ahead with such work as can be economically and well done this fall, and let the decision about further work be based upon the results obtained this season. You will note that my committal was not made in dollars, but in the amount of work that could be well and economically done this season. The latter seemed a better measuring stick than the former, and in view of costs to date, the total amount that could be wisely spent this fall would not be very large.

I am glad that you feel so enthusiastic about what has been accomplished, and am sure that you have greatly improved the appearance of the roadside where you have worked.

Very sincerely,
JOHN D. ROCKEFELLER, JR.

October 16th, 1924

COPY OF WESTERN UNION TELEGRAM
MR H M ALBRIGHT
YELLOWSTONE NATIONAL PARK
WYOMING

YOUR LETTER OF OCTOBER NINTH AND INTEREST-
ING REPORT RECEIVED STOP AM WONDERING
WHETHER DEAD TREES STUMPS ETC CANNOT BE
BURNED IN PILES WHERE THEY LIE OR IN THE ROAD
THUS AVOIDING LOADING ON TRUCKS AND HAUL-
ING THEM AWAY STOP DAMAGE TO GREEN COVER
IN OPEN SPACES ALONG ROAD SIDE WOULD BE ONLY
TEMPORARY QUICKLY GROWING OVER STOP
SHOULD NOT IMPORTANT DEDUCTION IN COST BE
MADE IN THIS WAY STOP OUGHT NOT STANDING
DEAD TREES BE CUT TO A GREATER DISTANCE
FROM THE ROAD SIDE THAN TEN OR FIFTEEN FEET
STOP AM WRITING

> JOHN D ROCKEFELLER JUNIOR
> CHARGE JOHN D ROCKEFELLER
> 26 BROADWAY

October 17, 1924

My dear Mr. Rockefeller:

Your telegram of October 16th reached me this morning.
The suggestions you have made in regard to burning of dead
trees, stumps, etc., I agree to entirely, and in fact, I am working
along these lines at the present time. We are not moving a
stick of timber or particle of brush that can be burned where
it lies or in an immediately adjacent open space.

However, in the case of the heavy clean-up work that was
done under the authority for the experiment and other heavy
clean-up work that must be done later, and which must be
accomplished in extremely heavy timber where even a very small
fire would damage trees and undergrowth, it is necessary to
haul away debris in trucks or wagons. Since we have had a
light snowfall we have been burning in the road with very
satisfactory results. The report I submitted with my letter of

October 9th contained a statement that I felt we would be able to do future work cheaper than the figures produced by the experimental work. This statement was based on my belief that we could materially cut costs on many sections of the road by burning on the roadsides and in the road itself.

As to standing dead timber, I think that you again have the correct viewpoint and I am having some further experimental work done with a wood cutting crew to get the effect of an entire roadside free of dead timber back to fifty and one hundred feet where this much clearing of dead trees is necessary in order to get this useless timber out of the landscape. This experimental work is being done this week and the wood is being cut for administrative purposes. Hence, the cost will not enter into the existing project except as a matter for reference and use in computing costs of future clean-up work.

I am anxiously awaiting your more detailed statement regarding my report and also I will be exceedingly glad to have any suggestions that you have included in your letter. I hope you will be exceedingly frank in stating your feeling about our methods and our results. This is work that is more or less new to us and we are very desirous of getting all of the suggestions and ideas that may be useful to us in carrying out this project. I am glad to report that the crews are making very satisfactory progress this week. While in my report I stated that I was going to add two more crews I finally decided to add but one.

Thanking you for your wire, I am

Very sincerely yours,
HORACE M. ALBRIGHT

November 4, 1924.

Dear Mr. Rockefeller:

I have received another check for $1,000 from Mr. Robert W. Gumbel. This makes a total of $2,000 that we have received from you to-date. I have done some very careful figuring on the cost of our clean up work that we have done this fall and expect to do before taking the crews off and I find that the total cost of the work will amount to approximately $4,500. Up to and including October 31st we had actually expended $3,051.12, so that in order to meet all of the October expenses we will need about $1,100 more. November activities will not require more than $1,500. Very gratifying progress is being made with the work and when we take off the crews about November 15th we will have cleaned all of the roadsides requiring cleaning from headquarters to Apollinaris Spring, almost eleven miles of the road to Norris.

The second crew that I assigned to clean up work between Mammoth Hot Springs and Golden Gate went to work on October 11th in the area of the big fire of 1883. This crew has been engaged in pulling thousands of stumps, clearing away old dead and fallen timber, and burning both stumps and rotten timber and debris where found. In many respects the improvement of the landscape in this enormous open stump field, through the heart of which the road ran, is a more effective piece of clean up work than the improvement of the roadsides in the timber. In connection with this work the shores of a small lake lying near the road were entirely cleaned. This lake was very unsightly and improvement of the landscape at this point is most pleasing. We found, however, that in clearing away these stumps we had to go back a little farther than we had anticipated because with the stumps gone from the immediate vicinity of the road those in sight on adjacent hillsides became more conspicuous than they were when they were simply a part of the immense stump field.

Taking everything into consideration, however, we find that our costs are running very close to the estimates; perhaps a little closer than I anticipated when I wrote my report of October 9th, wherein I stated that I thought the roadsides could be cleared all the way to Norris Junction for about $10,000. I have no reason to believe that the statement in my report of October 9th will not be demonstratd to be correct when this section is finished, but the baffling effect of the stumps, the removal of a very considerable amount of dead timber just beyond the Obsidian Creek Bridge at the entrance to Willow Park, and one or two other unexpected situations ran the cost of some of the work higher than I had already estimated. However, as each day passes we realize that we are becoming more experienced in this very interesting landscape work and that we are getting better and better results. We now have a sufficiently large enough section of the roadside cleaned up to give us a very good idea of what the general effect of this work is going to be and to observe the impression that it makes upon everyone who travels along the roads. The work has aroused the interest of all of the local inhabitants and I can see that one of the results of the work is going to be a vastly greater interest in landscape work in general throughout the park.

We have always had great difficulty in keeping our foremen and laborers, in their work along the roads and trails, from cutting trees for repair of bridges, culverts or buildings, and I have never had to face a harder task than to stop the borrowing of gravel from along the roadsides. The clean up work that is being undertaken at the present time has created such an impression upon our foremen and upon other employees of the park that I do not believe that we will ever again have much trouble in the preservation of the roadsides from mutilation through the cutting of trees or the digging of gravel pits. On the other hand, I believe that in the normal work of keeping the roads in repair there will be a disposition on the part of road crews to go away from the roads themselves and do clean up work that will maintain them in the sightly and attractive condition that they will be in when the work we are now doing is completed. On the other hand, of course, we expect to make it the duty of every road section crew not only to keep the road in good condition but also to remove dead trees from the roadside and clean up all debris that may accumulate along the highways. We are also going to improve the slopes of the roads to remove the old gravel pits and do other work of this character that can be classed as road maintenance operations.

I am under orders from Director Mather to meet him in Yosemite Park about November 16th and it shall be my purpose to bring the roadside cleaning work to a close as soon as the crew reaches Apollinaris Spring. The crew ought to reach this point very shortly after the middle of November. We will then be able to say to you, when you come out next summer, if you find a trip to the Yellowstone practicable in 1925, that you will find the roadsides all the way from headquarters to Apollinaris Spring, a stretch almost eleven miles in extent, as clean and beautiful as any similar stretch of road in the western part of the United States, except perhaps where millions have been spent on landscape improvement, such as along the Columbia River Highway. I can truthfully say that the results we are obtaining in this clean up work are beyond my expectations. Truly, no more important work has ever been undertaken in this park than the landscape improvement that you have authorized and I find that I personally am getting more pleasure out of supervising this work than almost anything else I have undertaken.

If you can send us $2,500 more, I am certain that this will cover all the costs of this year's work. When we take off the crews I will have a final accounting made to you showing just what portion of the money went to labor, to horse hire, to provisions, etc. There can be no question about our ability to do this work very much cheaper next year because, first, we will have experience of this year to guide us, second, we will be able to start the work when we can make a better selection of men and teams, and third, we will not be interrupted by bad weather. We have had two or three storms recently that have somewhat impaired our efficiency, although they were not accompanied by sufficient precipitation to justify stopping the work. If you feel that our work this fall justifies your continuing next year, I would like to begin not later than August 15th, with several more crews than I have been able to assemble this fall. I have been very careful to keep the crews small in order that I might personally work with them in order to develop the best and most economical methods of operation.

This is a rather long and rambling report and not up to the standard that I usually maintain, but I am working under very heavy pressure in an effort to meet Mr. Mather's wishes in regard to joining him in California.

I will be in Washington during the month of December and if you feel that you would like to talk with me about this work personally I would be glad to go to New York to see you. At that time I might perhaps be able to express to you in conversation, better than by letter, what an inspiration your work has been to me, and perhaps also I can tell you better than in writing just what we have been able to accomplish.

Sincerely yours,
HORACE M. ALBRIGHT

Robert W. Gumbel. Secretary and office manager for John D. Rockefeller, Jr.

November 11, 1924

Dear Mr. Albright:

Your letter of November 4th is received, I am much gratified at what you have accomplished this fall in cleaning up the roadsides. That your original estimate should also have been so nearly correct is also highly satisfactory.

I am asking my office to send you a further check for $2,500, making a total payment of $4,500 to date, which I understand you to say you expect will complete the eleven miles of road from Mammoth Hot Springs to Apollinaris Spring.

The interest which your office and your employes are taking in this road-cleaning work only goes to show that even the untrained eye likes the beautiful and the orderly better than the ugly and the untidy, when an opportunity to compare the two is given. If this work shall prove to be educational to your own force and helpful in making them more careful and considerate in their road work in future, that will give both you and me added satisfaction.

While I should be happy to see you should you be in New York during the winter, you have written me so fully of what you have done that I have all the information I need, and would not feel justified in permitting you to come here just for the pleasure which it would give me to see you.

With the expression of my satisfaction in having been permitted to cooperate with you in beautifying Yellowstone Park, and with much appreciation of the able manner in which you have handled the matter, I am,

Very sincerely,
JOHN D. ROCKEFELLER, JR.

May 16, 1925

My dear Mr. Rockefeller:

I have just had an opportunity to inspect the section of the park highway system on which we conducted clean-up work last fall. I find that conditions are such that about June 1st, or perhaps a week earlier, we can put on a crew to work with the assurance that excellent results can be obtained in clean-up work before the opening of the tourist season on June 17th. It will be particularly advantageous to finish the section that we worked on last fall. This is in the neighborhood of Apollinaris Spring where all the tourists who visit the park stop enroute to the geyser basins.

We will be working at Apollinaris Spring with a crew of masons, making this spring more accessible and sanitary. This crew will be under the direction of our Chief Landscape Engineer who could also assist me in superintending the roadside cleaning work which would extend one quarter of a mile south of Apollinaris Spring and nearly three-quarters of a mile north. If you think well of going ahead with the work for say, three weeks, and at a cost of approximately $1,000, I would appreciate it if you would send me the requisite authority.

You will be interested to know that the work done last autumn is particularly pleasing to the eye this spring. A heavy winter snow has done much to restore the natural condition of the forest floor. Here and there one can observe a pile of ashes but they are hard to see. It is remarkable how few living trees were killed by the burning operations in the timber after we changed our method of disposing of dead and down timber and debris. I do not think that over twenty-five or thirty trees were killed. These, of course, will constitute no loss to the forests but we will have to go back over the work and cut them out. It was impossible to tell that these trees were being killed while the fires were burning because the flames did not ignite either the bark or the needles. They were killed through excessive heat and I do not see how this could have been avoided as these harmful fires were built in very dense thickets or lodgepole. However, as I have stated, the forest has been in no manner harmed by the loss of these few puny trees.

I sincerely hope that your summer plans contemplate a visit to the park so that you can personally observe what we have been doing with your aid. I would like particularly to have you come out late in August when we have planned a Buffalo-Plains Week in the Upper Lamar Valley where our big buffalo herd can be seen to advantage.

Very sincerely yours,
HORACE M. ALBRIGHT

July 18, 1925.

My dear Mr. Rockefeller:

I should have reported earlier on the roadside clean-up work undertaken in June, but have been unable to do this for two reasons: (1) because of pressure of business incident to the beginning of the fiscal year, and (2) because of delay in getting in some items of information in regard to costs of the clean-up work.

I find that with all costs in, excluding costs of equipment repair which of course have not and never will be charged against the clean-up work, we expended a few dollars over the fund of $1,000 which you placed at my disposal this spring. The excess costs of the work done this spring seem to me to be properly chargeable against the maintenance of the road in view of the fact that we have worked out a policy which contemplates perpetual maintenance of the cleaned up area as a charge against road maintenance. We went back over the roadsides cleared last fall and took out several trees that blew over this spring during a violent wind storm, and did other items of work that are responsible for going over the allotment slightly.

The roadsides are now splendidly cleared to a point from one-eighth to one-quarter of a mile south of Apollinaris Spring, or for a distance of approximately eleven miles south of headquarters at Mammoth Hot Springs. The work done this year covered just about one mile of road and half of this section was very heavily littered with dead and down timber and stumps.

You will note that the work this spring was done a little cheaper than last fall. This is partly due to two reasons: (1) we had our experience of last fall to guide us toward better and more efficient work, and (2) we have a new foreman by the name of Emil Furrer, a Swiss, who caught the idea of roadside improvement far better than any man we had last year. In addition to this, he proved to be an indefatigable worker, and his intelligence and energy brought surprising results. Should you conclude to go on with this work toward the end of the month, I plan to put Furrer in full charge and expect to see exceedingly fine work done during the fall when he will not be under any handicap of traffic along the roads.

I enclose some pictures showing the piles of dead timber and also enclose one view showing the results of last fall's work. When I wrote you on May 16th the snow was just leaving the roadsides and the grass and flowers had not yet come out in profusion. Before the tourist season opened, the woods and roadsides which had been cleared were marvellously beautiful, due to the rank growth of grass and wild flowers. It was certainly a joy to ride along the cleaned up area and note the changes wrought in one year.

I enclose also some pictures showing some landscape work done at Apollinaris Spring. This was in our National Park Service construction program and was carried out by the Landscape Engineer personally. He gave more than usual attention to this project because it was situated within the area of your roadside clean-up activities. However, all of the work around Apollinaris Spring, including the cleaning up of the dead and down timber at that immediate point as well as the debris left there by the construction crew, was accomplished with National Park Service funds available for sanitation of the park.

I cannot tell you how earnestly I hope that you will let me go on with this work when the travel begins to decline toward the end of next month. This Swiss and his crew can complete the work to Norris Geyser Basin this year despite the fact that there is about four miles of very heavy clean-up work to be done. I feel more confident than ever that our estimates of last fall were too high and that, as we go forward with this work and gain experience, costs can be lowered more and more. With Furrer available, I know we can make a tremendous showing this autumn.

At your convenience I would be grateful to you if you would let me have your views as to proceeding with the work, say, on August 20th or 25th, with a program contemplating a complete clean-up of the roadsides to Norris Junction, a little over nine miles. We have now spent $4,491.72 of your funds in this work. The estimate for the Mammoth-Norris section was $10,000. I firmly believe we can finish this project for $5,000.

With sentiments of highest esteem, I am

Sincerely yours,
HORACE M. ALBRIGHT

July 22nd, 1925.

Mr. Stephen D. Mather
Crater Lake National Park
Medford, Oregon.

Dear Mr. Mather:-

Your letter of July 10th is received.

I am much interested to know that you find the cleaning up work along the roadsides, which Mr. Albright has been doing in Yellowstone Park so satisfactory.

I doubt not there are many other places throughout the national parks where such treatment would yield similarly worthwhile results. Some day I may visit Crater Lake Park, and if so, may be interested to cooperate with your superintendent there, as I have been with Mr. Albright.

My boys and I are spending this summer at our home here in Maine, and do not expect to be in the West. Within the next year or two, however, we shall some of us be visiting the West again, I hope, for our trip last year was most successful and enjoyable.

The rapid strides which you have made during the last few years in the development of the national parks is truly astonishing and reflects the greatest credit upon you as the head of the national park service.

With thanks for your letter, and cordial regards, I am

Very sincerely,
JOHN D. ROCKEFELLER, JR.

January 11, 1926.

Dear Mr. Albright:

I returned from Europe just before Christmas, and only recently have had time to catch up with the mail that was awaiting me. Among the letters which I have just read is yours of November 28th, with the interesting report in regard to the clean-up work along the roads in Yellowstone Park. You certainly have been confronted with difficulties this fall, but nevertheless have made some progress. I have wondered whether it would be easier to work in these swampy places when the ground was frozen, but perhaps there is too much snow then. I feel confident that you have done the best that could be done under the circumstances, and shall be glad to enlarge the credit as you request to whatever sum may be needed up to a total from me of $14,430, the amount contemplated in your original estimate. You have spent to date $8,225.97, thus leaving a credit of $6,204.03.

I am glad if it is true that as the result of the emphasis which you are putting on the road clean-up work, this work is being done in connection with the construction of any new roads in the park. That in itself is a step of progress.

You speak of some clean-up work along the lake share in which you are hoping I may be interested. Would it not be well to finish the road from the Mammoth Hot Springs to Norris Geyser Basin first, so far as the use of any moneys contributed by me is concerned? Then too, if I recall rightly there is more clean-up work required on other roads in the park. My present feeling is that my interest would be to consider roadside cleaning first before turning to the lakeside. But I am open to conviction.

I hope you are getting some rest and that you will give yourself time to recover from the overwork of the past year.

Mrs. Rockefeller, our three younger boys and I are planning a trip West this summer, which will include a few days in the Yellowstone. Of the details I will write you a little later. You spoke once of the beauty of a pack train camping trip in the Yellowstone and expressed the hope that we might some time let you arrange such trip. I shall be interested to learn from you at your convenience where such a trip could be made and how long it would take. Mrs. Rockefeller of course could not join us on such a trip but would have to stay at one of the hotels. The youngest of the three boys who are going is ten, the next twelve and the next fifteen, the latter being one of the three who came with me two years ago. They all ride and are at home in the saddle, but the younger boys not having previously been on such a trip, I had thought for the first experience a trip of not to exceed a week in length, less rather than more, would perhaps be better for them, and that we would see the objects of interest in the park from an automobile as we did before, rather than from horseback, the horseback trip being in the back country. Any suggestions you have to make in regard to such a trip will be much appreciated.

I am writing thus early that we may have plenty of time to plan it, since we are also going to the Yosemite, Mesa Verde and the Glacier National Park, and you will see that we ought not to spend more than ten days in the Yellowstone, including the camping and motor trips.

Very cordially,
JOHN D. ROCKEFELLER, JR.

January 18, 1926

My dear Mr. Rockefeller:

I am more delighted than I can well express with the news contained in your letter of January 11th, telling me about your tentative plans for the summer. Of course, a camping trip in Yellowstone is just a little difficult to plan without definite knowledge of the time of your visit.

I am assuming that you would naturally go to Mesa Verde Park first, because it is farther south and opens earlier, also because you would want to avoid the crowds in that park. I also assume that Yellowstone would be likely to be the next park in your itinerary and I suppose you would plan to arrive here around the 20th of July. This would be about the right date to start your Yellowstone trip. It would be all right to come any time between July 20th and September 1st, but early in July we have the mosquito nuisance to contend with. Owing to the open winter I anticipate that the mosquitoes will all be gone by July 1st this year, but a cold spring would make up for the deficiency in moisture this winter and prolong the mosquito evil. Under the worst weather conditions the mosquitoes are gone by July 15th, so assuming that you would come about that time, on, say, the 20th, I have the following tentative itinerary to offer to you:

First Day, July 20th. Arrive Gardiner, 11:30 A. M. Spend the remainder of this day at Mammoth Hot Springs and the night at the Hotel. This would give you ample time to see the wonderful hot spring terraces here, and hear the ranger-naturalist talks in the evening on the natural history of the park. There would also be time for an automobile ride around Bunsen Peak, where there would be an opportunity to see the third finest canyon in the park and the second highest waterfall - Osprey Fall. Also, you and I would be able to discuss the details of your tour by automobile and the subsequent camping trip.

Second Day, July 21st. Get an early start to the Geyser Basins, leaving at 7:30 or 8:00 o'clock. You could easily reach Old Faithful by noon and take plenty of time to stop along the way. You would be ahead of the busses and would get the advantage of the clearer, fresher air of the morning and freedom from dust.

Third Day, July 22nd. Leaving Old Faithful about 8:00 o'clock, go down to the Teton Mountains. I would recommend spending the night at the Jackson Lake Lodge where you took luncheon in 1924. This would give you ample time to go farther down into the Tetons in the afternoon. We hope by that time that Congress will have made the Teton Mountains a part of the park.

Fourth Day, July 23rd. Leave Jackson Lake Lodge early and come up to the Thumb of Lake Yellowstone. There, we can have a speedy motor boat waiting for you and take you across to the Lake Hotel, or, you can go on via automobile along our new Lake Shore road to the Lake Hotel for lunch. After lunch, drive down to the Grand Canyon of the Yellowstone and spend the afternoon driving along both rims of the Canyon. Or, if you prefer, you could use the trails, at least on one side. In fact, a trail will have to be used from Grand View to Inspiration Point on the west side, a distance of little over a mile, because of the fact that we will be reconstructing the road. The night would be spent at the Canyon Hotel.

Fifth Day, July 24th. Via automobile, over Mt. Washburn, and down to Camp Roosevelt for lunch. Here, the use of horses would begin. For the afternoon of this day I would recommend a short horseback trip to the Beaver Dams and Petrified Trees, and possibly up to Lost Lake to see a moose. The night would be spent at Camp Roosevelt.

Mrs. Rockefeller might like to stay at Camp Roosevelt while you are on the little camping trip. We could have one of the log cabins made available for her and unless she is timid she would enjoy being there more than at one of the hotels. However, if she would prefer to come on in to Mammoth Hot Springs, Mrs. Albright and I would like you to let us have her as our guest in our home, which is very spacious. It is only 18 miles from Camp Roosevelt to Mammoth Hot Springs.
Sixth Day, July 25th. The horses would be sent ahead early in the morning to the Mail Box, on the Cooke City road, about ten miles northeast of Camp Roosevelt. You and the boys would go there by automobile. The trip would be made up Slough Creek that day, probably to the park line, where the Silvertip Lodge is located. This is Mr. Thomas Cochran's lodge which he has doubtless told you about. Fishing should be excellent in Slough Creek. This will be a delightful day and the scenery will be good.
Seventh Day, July 26th. Ride up Slough Creek to its headwaters in Lake Abundance. Here, there will be some more fishing, and the camp will be beautiful.
Eighth Day, July 27th. To the Grasshopper Glacier, with camp on Goose Lake. You have heard of the Grasshopper Glacier with its millions of grasshoppers imbedded in the ice, lying at the head of the Rosebud River, well toward the highest section of the Beartooth Mountains.
Ninth Day, July 28th. Goose Lake to Cooke City. Make camp on Soda Butte Creek just inside the park. Cooke City is a picturesque mining town, often spoken of in the West as a "Ghost City". It once housed many people, but it is now in the last stages of decay. All of the buildings are of log.
Tenth Day, July 29th. Ride down Soda Butte Creek to its junction with the Lamar River, thence, up the Lamar River to the summer range of the big buffalo herd, now numbering nearly eight hundred animals. This trip would be under the chief guidance of the Chief Buffalo Keeper and will be about

51

as interesting a day as the three boys will have in all their lives.

At the end of this day, which would be the longest, involving a horseback trip of close to twenty miles, the automobile would take the party back to Camp Roosevelt for the night.

Eleventh Day, July 30th. Leave Camp Roosevelt early and catch the night train at Cody. This train carries a Glacier Park sleeper, which will be set off at Glacier Park Station the following night, and on the morning of August 1st you would be ready for your Glacier Park tour.

This trip can be varied in several different ways. For instance, from Upper Slough Creek the trip can be made back through the mountains on a very spectacular trail built by Mr. Cochran, to the Buffalo Ranch, thence up on the summer range of the buffalo, thence over Speciman Ridge, with its wonderful petrified forests and other fossils, to Camp Roosevelt. One day could be cut from the itinerary by such a readjustment. Or, the party could go right from Camp Roosevelt to Hellroaring, thence over the high divides to the eastward, to Slough Creek, thence to the Buffalo Ranch, and the summer range of the buffalo. Any one of these combinations will make an exceedingly interesting trip for you and the boys. This is our finest big game country, and while on the trip you would see antelope, elk, deer, buffalo and probably mountain sheep and moose. The forests of this section are varied, containing lodgepole, limber, and Whitebark pine, Douglas fir, Alpine fir and Engelmann spruce. The whole region is a wild flower garden.

As I recall it, the trip I spoke to you about would have been about a three weeks' trip, but the first five days would have been in the northeast corner, where I now propose to take you for the short trip. The other two weeks of the trip which I discussed with you would have involved a ride over the trails all along the mountains in the eastern part of the park, to the head of Lake Yellowstone, thence across the south line to the Bechler River region and up the Bechler River to Old Faithful.

I hope the above will give you sufficient information on which to base your preliminary plans, but if I can give you any more information please command me. I am enclosing a map which will show you at a glance just what I have proposed.

Referring to the clean-up program, I am very grateful to you for what you said about the work of the past summer and for your commitment as to completing the work between Mammoth Hot Springs and Norris. I certainly agree that it is desirable to complete this project as soon as possible. What I had in mind in regard to the work at Lake Yellowstone I feel I did not make very clear to you.

We are building from the Thumb of Lake Yellowstone to the Lake Hotel a new road, or, rather, we have entirely rebuilt and realigned an old road, a large part of which has been abandoned for twenty-five years. All of the new road, which is really the section approximately twelve miles long, which has not been used all of these years and on which the bulk of our funds are being expended, is being cleaned up under our appropriations. Between Lake Junction, where the Cody road comes in to the Grand Loop, and the beginning of this new work at Bridge Bay, approximately four miles, there is some badly needed clean-up work to be done. I imagine that altogether there is about a mile and a half of this section that requires intensive work, the litter being on both sides of the road, but principally on the lake side of the road, thus obstructing or ruining many beautiful views. What I had in mind was that in view of our own government work on this West Thumb-Lake outlet road, you might feel that it would be a desirable thing to do roadside clean-up work on that part of this section which is not under government construction, on the ground that as an automobile drive the Lakeshore road will be one of the most beautiful in the park and should be freed of roadside litter ahead of some of the timbered sections of the Mammoth-Norris road, which remain to be cleaned.

I have sketched on one of the attached maps the Lakeshore road project. The section in blue is the government construction project - the sections in red, the old pieces of road, parts of which remain to be cleaned up, the northerly section being the more important one.

There is no question but what your initiation of roadside clean-up in Yellowstone National Park has had a profound influence on all National Park road projects. Extraordinary attention is being given to cleaning up the roadsides in connection with the building of all new roads, not only in the Yellowstone but in all of the other parks. I am sure you will be greatly pleased with what you will see in the parks next summer.

At the risk of making this letter too long I am going to add one paragraph regarding our game protection program. A letter from Mr. Cochran today tells me that you have made a very liberal contribution to the fund he is raising to acquire lands for the winter feeding and protection of animals north of the park. This, I appreciate more than I can well express. Another reason why I am anxious that you should spend your first day of your next trip to the Yellowstone at Mammoth Hot Springs is that it will afford me an opportunity to give you a view of the lands that are being acquired under this game protection project. Your train will arrive at 11:30 and we will have time to run down to the winter range before coming to headquarters for lunch.

One thing more, the enclosed clipping with reference to the establishment of the Aileen Nusbaum Memorial Hospital in Mesa Verde National Park, I know, will be interesting to you, as it is to everyone in the National Park Service. This extraordinary tribute to Mrs. Nusbaum is most richly deserved, but it is particularly inspiring when one realizes that her work has been recognized by Congress.

I have taken the liberty of sending a copy of your letter of January 11th, together with a copy of this reply, to Mr. Mather.

With all good wishes, I am

Sincerely yours,
HORACE M. ALBRIGHT

Mr. Thomas Cochran. New York financier. John D. Rockefeller, Jr., purchased $10,000 worth of stock in his company, Camp Preservation Company, organized to buy land adjacent to Yellowstone Park for an antelope refuge.

February 1, 1926.

Dear Mr. Albright:

Your good letter of January 18th is received. Many thanks for all the trouble you have taken in regard to the trip for my boys and me next summer. I will write you about that shortly.

As to the clean-up work which you had in mind along the lake, I has not fully understood just what was intended in your previous letter. I now see that to complete this entire lake road work requires work on only a portion of four miles; namely, the stretch between Lake Junction where the Cody Road comes into the Grand Loop and the beginning of the new work at Bridge Bay. You further estimate that probably not over a mile and a half of this section requires intensive work. You do not tell me what you estimate it will cost to do this clean-up work; that I shall be interested to know. My disposition, however, would be to finance it, and I will write you definitely upon hearing from you as to your rough estimate of the cost.

The tribute to Mrs. Nussbaum, as set forth in the clippings which you enclosed, is most interesting and gratifying, and well deserved. I rejoice for her and her husband at this fine recognition.

Very cordially,
JOHN D. ROCKEFELLER, JR.

WORTHWHILE PLACES

*Jesse and Aileen Nusbaum. Jesse was superintendent of Mesa
Verde National Park when Rockefeller visited the Park in 1924.
Rockefeller later made several contributions toward the cost
of medical treatment for Mrs. Nusbaum.*

February
Fifteenth
1 9 2 6

My dear Mr. Rockefeller:

I have received your letter of February 1st and I am glad
to know that the material I sent you for use in planning your
trip is about what you wanted.

As to the Lake Shore clean-up; the Engineer of the park
and I have gone very carefully over our data on this job and in
the light of the cost of our own work out there we feel that $1200
ought to make an excellent job of this section between the Lake
Junction, where the Cody road comes into the Grand Loop, and
Bridge Bay, where our new work ends. The heavy clean-up work,
involving a little over a half mile of the road, will cost very close
to $800, the remaining 2.8 miles to be taken care of for $400.

This is a job that we can do in the spring because we
should be able to use not only the road for burning debris
but also the Lake Shore before the water rises too much.

I have just been going over some old historical material
and I ran across a report made in 1889 by Hon. Francis E.
Warren, for nearly forty years United States Senator from the
State of Wyoming. The report to which I refer was written
by him when he was Territorial Governor. He visited the park
in August, 1889, and became very enthusiastic over its beauties
and wonders. While returning to Cheyenne he wrote this report,
and among other recommendations offered the following for
the consideration of the Federal Government: "That $100,000
be appropriated to clear away the fallen timber in the park".

I recently recalled this recommendation of Senator Warren's to Mr. Mather's attention, and suggested that he see the Senator and tell him that his recommendation is now being carried out, not by the use of Federal funds as he suggested, but through the public spirited contributions of a private citizen.

I thought you would be interested in this little historical incident.

With all good wishes, I am

Sincerely yours,
HORACE M. ALBRIGHT

September 16, 1926

Dear Mr. Rockefeller:

I feel very badly that I have not had an opportunity to make an earlier acknowledgment of your telegram in regard to your Yellowstone trip and also of your letter of September 6th which reached me several days ago. Both Mrs. Albright and I appreciate your very kind words more than we can well express. We feel that Mrs. Rockefeller and you have been too kind to us, both in what you have said about your trip and in the gifts that you have sent to us.

I do not know when Mrs. Albright has received anything that has made her happier than the beautiful bag which Mrs. Rockefeller sent to her and the three books of biography which she sent to me, I am just now enjoying as I am getting time to read. I remember now that Mrs. Rockefeller and I discussed biographies several times while on our trip and I was particularly interested in what she told me about the compilation of her father's life story. Therefore, in sending me some books of biography, she picked out what pleases me most.

I presume that Mr. Cammerer told you that immediately after you left the Yellowstone, I was ordered to Glacier National Park to assume charge of the forest fire fighting work there.

WORTHWHILE PLACES

I was in Glacier Park on the fires for three weeks. From many standpoints it was very disagreeable work but from others, it was interesting. We do not have complete statistics available but upwards of 40,000 acres of forest land were burned and we had to build over one hundred miles of fire trench. The total cost was more than $175,000. The fires had been burning two weeks when I arrived with my two best Yellowstone fire-fighters. After the fires were controlled I motored through four of the Canadian national parks, including the parks along the line of the Canadian Pacific Railroad.

I was particularly shocked in the Canadian national parks to note what little attention had been given to the preservation of the landscape. Some of the buildings in the parks, especially the Chateau Lake Louise, the great Canadian Pacific Hotel, were atrocious structures to be erected in a national park. The entire Lake Louise Valley was spoiled for me on account of the hotel and the formal gardens and lawns.

The Yellowstone season is now drawing to a close. Nearly 185,000 people have been entertained here during the summer and we have begun roadside cleanup between Yellowstone Lake and the Canyon in accordance with our discussion while you were here. I will present in another letter, our plans for the autumn work. Of course, we also expect to finish the Mammoth-Norris section and we have a crew on that project at the present time. I believe we will be able to economically and satisfactorily expend approximately $5,000.00 this autumn provided, of course, weather conditions are good.

With all good wishes to Mrs. Rockefeller, the boys and yourself in which Mrs. Albright cordially joins me, and with more thanks for your kindnesses to us, I am

Sincerely yours,
HORACE M. ALBRIGHT

Arno B. Cammerer. Joined the staff of the National Park Service in Washington in 1917. Became Director of the Park Service in 1933 and served until 1940.

In 1988, over 2,100,000 people visited Yellowstone.

September 16, 1926.

Dear Mr. Rockefeller:

The 1926 tourist season of Yellowstone National Park is drawing to a close. Our maintenance work and other activities of the summer are completed and we are ready to engage in continuance of the roadside cleanup work which you have authorized us to undertake here.

Recalling our discussion of the cleanup projects when you were in the park this summer, we have planned during the months of September, October, and as much of November as the weather will permit us economically to work, to engage in the cleanup of the roads between Yellowstone Lake and the Grand Canyon, the road to Artist Point on the east side of the Grand Canyon, the small section of five miles between West Thumb and the southern end of the new Lake Shore road and the remaining mile and three-quarters between Mammoth Hot Springs and Norris Junction. I have not had the time, owing to my absence in Glacier National Park fighting fires, to carefully estimate the cost of this work and I am unable at this time to present all of the figures that should go with this program of cleanup activity.

I feel, however, that should we enjoy good weather we can economically expend approximately $5,000.00 and I would appreciate it if you could send us $3,000.00 at this time in order to meet the September payroll and procure the necessary provisions and supplies for October work. We now have four crews engaged in cleanup work and several of them have been at work since shortly after the first of September, the principle one being engaged on the completion of the work between Norris and Mammoth Hot Springs under the first project that you approved. Within two weeks I shall forward you a complete program together with a map showing just what we expect to accomplish.

WORTHWHILE PLACES

In regard to the Mammoth - Norris project, in my report of October 8, 1924, I stated that I thought that this work would cost approximately $14,430.00. Last year you will recall we met some unexpected obstacles in cleaning up the swamps in the vicinity of Obsidian Cliff and Beaver Lake. Otherwise, this estimate would have proved to have been too high.

Up to the present time we have expended on this project the following sums:

1924 Fall	$3,491.72
1925 Spring	855.14
1926 Fall	3,879.11
1926 Spring	4,033.58
Total	$12,259.55

This leaves a balance for the 1926 fall work between Mammoth and Norris of approximately $2,170.45 which I think is just about what will be required to complete the project.

The Lake Shore project covering the road between Bridge Bay and Lake Junction, undertaken last spring, cost $1,155.53. The advances that you have made for both projects total $14,368.37. Credits for work done by cleanup crews in piling and burning brush on telephone rights of way, meals served to other departments, etc., amount to $953.29, which amount my accountant has just advised me is held here in cash to the credit of the cleanup projects. I am sorry I did not know about this earlier as I would have returned this fund to your New York office in accordance with your policy of handling these funds.

The net expenditures to date are $13,415.08, which is the sum of $12,259.55 on the Mammoth - Norris section and $1,155.53 on the Bridge Bay - Lake Junction project.

You will be interested to know that we also have two cleanup crews at work on our own new roads, this work being done as part of our construction costs. As I explained to you when we were driving over the new Lake Shore road, the balance of our construction funds for that project is inadequate to complete the cleanup work, this deficiency being due to the fact that the job was estimated early in 1924 before the cleanup program was adopted. As I recall it, you offered to assist in this cleanup project should we need help, up to about $3,000.00. If my recollection of this conversation is incorrect, I hope you will set me right.

I trust that in submitting this general idea of what we hope to accomplish during the present autumn, I have correctly interpreted your own idea as to how this work should be continued. I would appreciate your early comment on this letter and I will greatly value any suggestions that you have to make regarding our fall work. As soon as possible I will submit our plans more concretely and a map will accompany that report, showing the status of all cleanup that already completed, as well as what we hope to accomplish this fall.

Sincerely yours,
HORACE M. ALBRIGHT

The $12,259.55 spent by Rockefeller on roadside clean-up between 1924 and 1925 would be over $82,000 in 1990 dollars.

September 29, 1926

Dear Mr. Rockefeller:

Referring to our day in the Jackson Hole and to our discussion of the desirability of protecting the approach to the Tetons from dance halls, lunch stands and other objectionable structures, I have at last secured the information you asked me to obtain. I have been amazed to find that there was vastly more settlement in the area between the Teton Mountains and the Snake River than I had supposed there was. I have had two Jackson Hole business men, who are close friends of mine and who have been working hand in hand with us in the park for years, make a study of the settlement in this area and land values.

I quote the following from a letter just received from Mr. Winger, one of these Jackson Hole men:

WORTHWHILE PLACES

"Beginning at the section line running east and west one mile north of the town of Wilson, and taking everything on the west side of Snake River above this line to Jackson's Lake, there are approximately 14170 acres of privately controlled lands, not including the Geraldine Lucas and Bar B C Ranches and only parts of the J Y Ranch. We have included approximately 1000 acres recently purchased by the J Y as a matter of protection to themselves against the probable incursion of such calamities as the Elbo Land and Cattle Company. It is doubtful if the Geraldine Lucas place can be purchased during the lifetime of Mrs. Lucas. The Bar B C and J Y Ranches, proper, have rather heavy investments but it would probably not be necessary to purchase them. If, however, at a later date, it was decided that they must be taken, we feel that there would be no difficulty in making satisfactory arrangements, as they are owned by the right kind of conservationists.

"We have done considerable disinterested visiting in that territory since we saw you and gathered a great deal of information without exciting any curiosity. From figures and information we have obtained, we believe the average cost of the 14170 acres would be approximately $28.00 per acre, or $397,000.00. Some of it can be purchased as low as $10.00 per acre, and we know of several bona fide cash offers ranging as high as $100.00 per acre.

"There is no question that this is the most difficult and expensive block of the Jackson Hole country to buy and that it would require careful, slow and skilful handling. I am convinced also that if the big plan for saving this wonder spot of America is to be carried through, the proper place to begin is in this particular block. Using the last two years as an indication, the price of land in this neighborhood will increase each year. If it were only possible to start operations during the winter season while the natives are undergoing their annual attack of cabin fever it would be splendid. Any other information I can gather I will be glad to send and I will be glad to have any suggestions from you."

Mr. Winger is an educated man, formerly owned the little paper in the Jackson Hole and recently has been engaged in the contracting business. I am naturally very disappointed that his figures, both as to acreage and values, should have run so high and I am afraid the project may strike you as one that is impossible of further consideration.

Of course, I think that you agreed with me that it would be desirable to let the Bar B C Ranch and the J Y Ranch remain in private hands in view of the fact that they are very well operated by people who are devoted to the preservation of the wilderness character of the Teton region. Mrs. Geraldine Lucas I do not know but I understand that she came out from the east and homesteaded under the Tetons because she wanted to spend the rest of her life within sight of these mountains. She is a lover of beauty and nature and I am very certain that she would not allow her property to be put to any objectionable commercial use.

A considerable portion of the land discussed in Mr. Winger's letter lies above and below the J Y Ranch. Perhaps I neglected to tell you when we were at the J Y Ranch that the proposed south boundary of the Grand Teton Park would be some five miles south of the J Y place. I doubt, however, whether we would want to go within one mile of Wilson, which is the town at the point where the highway turns west to cross the mountains.

I am writing to Mr. Winger to give me other estimates on the land values, mile by mile, between the J Y Ranch and the line that he took in making the study on which he has just reported. Perhaps these further figures will give us a more favorable prospect. The thing that I regret most about this Teton project is that we could not get Congress and the heads of the Interior Department to listen to us ten years ago when we asked first, to have the park extension made; second, to stop homesteading in the Jackson Hole country, particularly on the west side of the Snake River, and third, to make some arrangement to buy out the few ranches that then existed. In those days the land could have been bought for two to five or six dollars an acre for uncultivated land and thirty to fifty dollars an acre for cultivated land. Each year as travel increases those Teton lands are going to become more and more expensive as Mr. Winger says and his prediction is based on the experience of the last five years although, as I have already confessed, I never dreamed that values had increased so much.

I will be glad to have your comments on what I am submitting in this letter and also your advice as to whether I ought to go further with the investigations and prepare a report with maps and pictures, showing completely the situation of the area in which we are interested.

Sincerely yours,
HORACE M. ALBRIGHT

Richard Winger. Jackson Hole rancher. Sometime publisher of a newspaper in Jackson, Wyoming. He was active in the Snake River Land Company and in the operation of the JY Ranch.

November 1, 1926

Dear Mr. Rockefeller:

I wrote to you some two weeks ago in regard to the Jackson Hole land matter and your secretary told me under date of October 4th that you would be away for some weeks. Later on I found that, owing to the exceptionally fine weather, we were going to be able to do a great deal more clean-up work this fall than I suggested in my letter of September 16th and I wired on October 27th, stating that we had used up the $5,000.00 under your commitment of September 23rd. I asked that you let us go on with our work to the extent of about $3,500.00 additional. Miss Adams wired back that you were still out of town and would not be back until the end of next week. I did not know exactly what to do in this situation and tried to make a decision in the light of our conversation in regard to the clean-up project while you were here.

I remembered how enthusiastic you were over the roads along the Lake Shore and along the river to Grand Canyon and that you and I had agreed that the next project to be undertaken should naturally be the Grand Canyon - Yellowstone Lake section which would, with the Government work on the new Lake Shore road and on the Inspiration Point road, give us perfectly clean roadsides all the way from Inspiration Point and Artist Point on the rims of Grand Canyon through to West Thumb Junction, where we ate lunch in the ranger station the second day you were here. We had expected to make good progress on this section during the fall but when I wrote you on September 16th, I had in mind the possibility of encountering storms and other obstacles that would delay the work or cut it off entirely. As a matter of fact, we did have some storms in late September and during the first week of October and we had a hard time keeping men but then the weather turned warm and clear and I do not believe I have ever seen such beautiful fall working conditions. We were able to get more men and recruit our crews to suitable strength.

With this good organization we move along very rapidly and as I write this letter, we have completed about ten miles of clean-up; 3 1/2 miles between West Thumb and the beginning of the new Lake Shore road, 2 miles around Lake Junction and North of that point, 3 miles from the southern end of the Inspiration Point road, that is the end near the hotel, to the beginning of Hayden Valley and about a mile and one-half of the heavy work remaining to be done between Mammoth and Norris on our original project. The total cost of the fall work will be about $9,500 of which $953.29 we had on hand from last spring. This made our average cost per mile about $950.00.

WORTHWHILE PLACES

We had between three and four miles of extremely heavy or difficult clean-up work, owing to canyons, in these fall projects. In connection with this estimate I have to confess with considerable regret that we have not been able to finish the Mammoth-Norris section within our original estimate of $14,430.00. More difficulty with the Obsidian Creek swamp and the exceptionally heavy logs that had to be handled, caused us to over-run the estimate about $800, and we will still have a little work to do at Roaring Mountain to carry out your suggestion that even heat-killed trees should be cleared. As a matter of fact, we had to go over Obsidian Creek section between the thirteen and fourteen mile posts north of Mammoth, the heavy section which I left for you to see, two or three times in order to make a finished job because as soon as we would remove one tier, so to speak, of dead and down timber and debris, another would show up in its place. This was one of the most baffling and exasperating sections that we have yet had to contend with.

Had it not been for this extremely difficult piece of work remaining to be done on the Mammoth-Norris section, we would have made an exceptionally fine showing on the unit cost per mile of the work this fall.

I sincerely hope that you will approve my going on with the work in view of the fine weather conditions. I am sure that you intended that we should go on with it next spring anyway, and that was another factor that guided me in deciding to continue the work now.

To finish the entire project from Canyon to West Thumb will require $7,700.00 including the $3,000.00 fund which you said we could count on for assistance in cleaning up our new Lake Shore road. On our new Lake Shore road we have already spent approximately $6,000. We will still have to spend $1,000 on this project in addition to the $3,000 that you are going to let us have. I believe that we will be able to do much of this work next spring. In fact, we think that we will be able to complete the project before the opening of the season.

We are sending you under separate cover a very interesting map showing the status of the roadsides throughout the park. All of the work that has been done with funds placed at our

66

disposal by you is carefully plotted, using separate colors to show when it was done. We have also shown the work that we have done with Government funds in connection with the reconstruction of roads, meadow lands where no clean-up is needed are indicated, the work which still remains to be done with private funds, assuming that we cannot get Congress to take over this work as it ought to do, and the roads that do not have any color or other marking are those that we must reconstruct within the next few years and clean up as we go with our own funds under the newly established policy of making complete roadside clean-ups as road construction proceeds.

I am attaching to this letter for your perusal if you are interested in the details of our work, a complete report of what has been accomplished or will have been accomplished during 1926. As soon as the crews are in, we will make up a final financial statement and submit it to you.

I have been called to Washington and am leaving tonight, going by way of Denver and Chicago. The clean-up work has been left in the very capable hands of my resident engineer who will bring it to a close in the course of the next week or ten days in accordance with the estimates of work set forth above. I sincerely hope that all of this meets with your approval. I could have stopped the work and perhaps you will think that I should have done so but it did seem a shame to do so when we had such exceptionally fine weather and good crews making excellent progress without the interference of traffic or other conditions that make progress expensive.

I will be in Washington on the 11th and before I return west, I understand that all of the superintendents are to visit Palisades Interstate Park. When I am in New York I will give myself the pleasure of calling at your office. I hope it will be at a time when you are in town. If I have time, I also want to get up to Lafayette Park and see the road and forestry work that has been done there under your personal supervision. In fact, I would rather go to Lafayette Park than devote much time to the Palisades Park as the latter park is bound to be more of a civilized affair than our national parks will ever be; at least I hope that is the case.

WORTHWHILE PLACES

Hoping that all of the above will meet with your full approval and that what we have been able to accomplish this fall will be as pleasing to you as our past results, I am

Sincerely yours,
HORACE M. ALBRIGHT

Ann Adams. Personal secretary to John D. Rockefeller, Jr.

Palisades Interstate Park. Created by the states of New York and New Jersey and dedicated in 1909. Originally intended to preserve the face, shore line, and rim of the Palisades along the west bank of the Hudson River, the park, in 1988, had 25 areas with over 79,000 acres of land extending from Fort Lee in New Jersey to Storm King Mountain in New York.

John D. Rockefeller made an early contribution to the governing body, the Palisades Interstate Park Commission. Rockefeller, Jr., gave 700 acres on top of the palisades on the New Jersey side of the Hudson River to protect the area and provide space for a parkway from the George Washington Bridge to Harriman State Park.

Laurance S. Rockefeller was appointed to the Commission in 1939 and served until 1979. He was secretary, vice president, and was president for seven years, 1970-1977. His son, Laurance, is currently president of the Commission.

Lafayette National Park. In 1916, President Woodrow Wilson created the Sieur de Monts National Monument of 5,000 acres from the land donated to the government by the Hancock County Trustees for Public Reservations. In 1919, the name was changed to Lafayette National Park. In 1929, the name was changed again to Acadia National Park.

November 9, 1926.

Dear Mr. Albright:

Your letter of September 29th is received, regarding the Jackson Hole situation. The boundaries that we talked of last summer are no longer fresh in my mind. A simple map showing them clearly would be helpful. Perhaps a fuller and more detailed statement might be desirable after I have studied the matter. In the meantime, it may be that I shall see you here in New York and we can discuss the subject together.

Very cordially,
JOHN D. ROCKEFELLER, JR.

November 27, 1926.

My dear Mr. Rockefeller:

Referring to your letter of November 9 in regard to the Jackson Hole lands, I am having a special map made up in the Washington office which will go to you in a few days. We did not have an opportunity to discuss this matter the other night and I am wondering perhaps we had not better hold the problem in abeyance until I get back here in January. I am due in Washington on January 12 and will be here until about March 1. My address for the next month will be 2501 Ashby Avenue, Berkeley, California.

I look back with the keenest pleasure on the delightful evening we spent at your home last Saturday. It was so fine to see Mrs. Rockefeller and the boys and you again. Once more let me thank you for letting us have this most interesting and enjoyable evening with you and your splendid family.

Sincerely yours,
HORACE M. ALBRIGHT

WORTHWHILE PLACES

November 28, 1926

Report of Roadside Clean-up

Autumn-1925

This is a brief report on the results of roadside clean-up work in Yellowstone National Park for the autumn. It is not as satisfactory a report as I wish I could make. We have not been able to get the results I expected and promised you. The cost, too, have been higher than expected. There may have been defects in our plans and organization but I cannot see how we could have done better under the conditions we encountered.

....Neither Chief Engineer Burney nor I calculated correctly the difficulties to be encountered in cleaning Obsidian Creek, along which the road runs for a mile north of Obsidian Cliff. The moment man or horse stepped off the road on the creek side, he found himself in a swamp. As there was a tangled mess of dead trees and debris in the creek and swamp, it seemed necessary to clean it, and we did, but our original estimates of the time and costs of cleaning this section were soon worthless.

Costs of the Project

The cost of the work done so far is as follows:

1924	$3,491.72
1925	$4,734.25
	$8,225.97

The Lake Shore Road

This brings me to a discussion of our own clean-up work this year. Under new road appropriations, we nearly completed our new Lake Shore Road from West Thumb to Bridge Bay, eliminating the 18% grade over the hill between these bays of Lake Yellowstone. This is a beautiful new road following the route of an old road built in 1891 but abandoned in 1901. By July first next, we will have cleaned up all of our own debris incident to road construction, and we have also disposed of much old slashings of the original road.

January 4, 1927.

Dear Mr. Rockefeller:

Your wonderful Christmas letter with the check, a gift from Mrs. Rockefeller and yourself, reached us yesterday having been forwarded from Yellowstone, and after lying in the postoffice here over the New Year holiday.

Any mere words that Mrs. Albright and I might write or speak to you could never really express the happiness that your letter and gift gave to us, and the letter means even more than the gift, as much as the latter helps in a direction, we must admit, where need has been great. However, your words regarding my work are, and always shall be, deeply appreciated and cherished. We send to Mrs. Rockefeller and you our heartfelt thanks.

The check is going into safe bonds as an addition to the savings we have been able to accumulate for the education of our children. It came just when we were discussing ways of changing our budget in order to save more this new year than the pitifully small amount we managed to put away in 1926.

As soon as I can get the services of a stenographer, I want to write you in regard to progress on the policy of roadside cleanup in parks I have recently visited. You will be greatly pleased to learn that the U.S. Bureau of Public Roads officials are enthusiastically interested in this work.

When I returned from a recent trip to Yosemite, they asked me, at once, how I liked their work on the roadsides. They seemed more interested in this than in the fine new road construction itself.

I am leaving for Grand Canyon Park tomorrow, and will reach Washington about the 18th. I will be working in and out of Washington until March first.

With many more thanks for your thoughtfulness and kindness, and with all good wishes to Mrs. Rockefeller, the boys and yourself, I am

Faithfully yours,
HORACE M. ALBRIGHT

February 16, 1927.

Dear Mr. Rockefeller:

I think I am now in a position to give you a definite program of action on the Teton Mountain and Jackson Hole land question.

I have been unable to consult with Mr. I. H. Larom, who can not reach here until February 27th, and Mr. Henry Stewart of the J.Y. Ranch, says he can not see me until next week. Mr. Struthers Burt, of the Bar B C Ranch came here last week, and spent a day with me. He has since written a very interesting letter, a copy of which I attach for your information.

There has also come to my attention a little pamphlet entitled "Investigation of Elk Conditions in Jackson's Hole, Wyoming", by Mr. Dall DeWeese, of Canon City, Colorado, an old time sportsman and hunter. At his own expense he studied the elk problem, for the Izaak Walton League, last autumn. I do not know Mr. DeWeese, nor do I vouch for all his conclusions as to the size of the elk herd. His booklet I hope you can get the time to read. A copy is enclosed herewith.

I have also received two letters from Mr. Winger who gets my confidential information for me. He says that the spirits of the people on the east side of the Snake River are at low ebb, but the great increase in tourists last summer west of the river have made landowners over there sufficiently optimistic to still feel fairly happy over prospects even now as the snow gets deeper and deeper. Recent news reports from the southern part of the park and the Jackson Hole tell us that the snowfall, and water content thereof, is heavier than it has been for years past.

Should you feel that this is a matter that you would like to proceed with, I am sure it can be handled with excellent results along the following lines:

1. Say nothing, at the present time, about the larger or ultimate plan of acquiring all of the private holdings in the Jackson Hole.

2. Confine all activities to acquisition of holdings west of the Snake River in the area colored on the map you had, and which I return herewith.

3. Buy in this area, through an agency or agencies, under a plan to organize a recreation and hunting club. If there were more grazing lands on the west side of the river, I would advocate operating as buyers for a land and cattle company, but obviously there is no room on that side for cattle. A cattle company to operate on the east side later would be an ideal agency.

4. Employ a firm of attorneys in Salt Lake City to coordinate buying operations and disburse funds. I have in mind the firm of Fabian & Clendenin, men of unimpeachable integrity and judgment. They are sportsmen, very public spirited and intensely interested in Yellowstone. Mr. Clendenin I have known from childhood. We were classmates in college, and closest chums. He and his partner would act in this matter on a very narrow margin of cost.

I could go to Salt Lake City as soon as possible and put them in possession of all necessary facts and papers. They could deal with my Jackson Hole operators, one of whom I would have meet me in Salt Lake City. They could also coordinate the efforts of "dude ranchers" like Burt and Stewart. I could be in constant and confidential touch with them, and they could also communicate with your confidential agent in New York.

5. Through these attorneys, acting for "a recreation and hunting club", or some other hypothetical organization if a better one can be found, the lands could be acquired for cash, but on a policy of getting a month's time to get work back and forth between the interested parties.

6. As soon as possible, the National Park Service and General Land Office will plat on maps all of the other private holdings in the Jackson Hole. I have the list of holdings as of December, 1923. There were then 402 owners of a little over 100,000 acres of land. The situation has not materially changed since then. That land, which includes the west side of the Snake too, is worth on an earning basis, perhaps $1,000,000, including value of improvements. I can not say what it could be acquired for, but investigations of value can be quietly secured this coming summer.

By October, 1927, we would have for you a complete report with maps, pictures, data on animal life, plans for future utilization, etc.

There are three objections to any purchasing at all:

1. We have to rely on Congress for the final policy of their administration, and none may be adopted. The answer to this is that within a reasonable time, if action is not taken, the holdings can be sold, and there can be no possible doubt about their growing more valuable every year.

2. After purchase, the lands would remain subject to taxation, until Congress takes them over. I believe, as Struthers Burt has suggested, that we could operate them at a profit sufficient to meet all taxes and other expenses. This applies to hay lands especially, and those adapted to recreation resort utilization without expensive additions to buildings and equipment.

3. It would attract undue attention to absolutely prohibit, suddenly, the taking up of other vacant public lands, and so, while we buy improved properties, others, now lying untaken and unused might be settled. The answer is that practically every tract susceptible of cultivation has been taken up under homestead laws, and that without the lakes under the Tetons to use as reservoirs, new irrigation works cannot be constructed. Practically, settlement has reached its limits considering national forest and other permanent withdrawals from permanent occupancy.

These objections may impress you as serious obstacles, and I hope you will ask for more details if you regard them as controlling.

My judgment is that we have two distinct projects, one of which includes the other:

1. The west side of the Snake region is involved only in what we may call "The West Side Plan". It is naturally a part of the Teton National Park project. Should these west side lands be acquired, they would round out and complete the Teton Park, preserve the foreground of the mountains, and put into the park an interesting glaciated region of great recreation and scientific value. Standing alone, this plan is a tremendously worthy one, and could be consummated without reference to the larger project.

2. The proposal to turn the entire Jackson Hole back to Nature as the greatest scenic and wild life preserve (including, of course, the Yellowstone Park), on the face of the Earth. This project, we might call "The Jackson Hole plan." It is immensely bigger, and includes "The West Side Plan", but most of the lands involved are far less valuable.

Under the larger plan, all fences would be removed, except in places where hay should be cultivated for elk, antelope and buffalo, and the region would be turned back to Nature. With the purchase of each ranch, cattle grazing rights, or rather privileges, on the adjacent national forest lands would be extinguished, thus enlarging the winter feed range of the wild life. Perhaps in the lower part of the "Hole" one ranch might be kept for cattle as a sort of museum exhibit of the old West, equipment of the ranch, costumes of cowboys, etc. being maintained in accordance with traditions of old Wyoming. At headquarters there would be a collection of relics of the trappers and traders, Indians of the region, buffalo hunting days, early ranch days, etc. Furthermore, abundant wild life - elk, antelope, buffalo, mountain sheep, deer, moose, and fur-bearing animals would constitute what Mr. Burt calls "a museum on the hoof".

There would be, including Yellowstone Park, about 10,000 square miles of wild territory, with native animals, birds, flowers and forests, a region useless for any other purpose, and therefore destined for perpetual preservation as a wilderness country.

The only important flaw in the final picture would be Jackson Lake with its unsightly shores. Perhaps, however, even that could ultimately be cleaned up under pressure of public opinion.

I have written at length, Mr. Rockefeller, not with any idea of trying to urge favorable action, but just to give you this big park and wild life preserve plan as we have visualized it. I think if it could be consummated, it would go down in history as the greatest conservation project of its kind ever undertaken, and never again could another be undertaken as there would be no place for it to start.

However, I realize that it has many angles, and that its present status is not ideal as a foundation on which to build.

I shall await, eagerly, your impressions of this preservation. I will be here until March 6th.

> Very sincerely yours,
> HORACE M. ALBRIGHT

I. H. Larom. Jackson Hole rancher.

Henry Stewart. Owner of the JY ranch in Jackson Hole. Rockefeller purchased the ranch and used it for his family and friends. Laurance S. Rockefeller later donated most of the land to educational and medical organizations. These organizations sold the land to the Federal Government for addition to the park. A reduced section of the ranch remains in the family's possession.

Struthers Burt. Owner of the Bar B C ranch. Author of western stories.

February 28th 1927

Dear Mr Woods:

The buying up of all of the land not held by friendly Dude Ranchers in the entire Jackson Hole Valley with a view to its being ultimately turned over to the Government for joint or partial operation by the Department of Parks and the Forestry Department, is a proposition which I have been studying for some months past.

Were this plan carried through, it would mean the extending of the Yellowstone Park to include the Teuton Mountains, Jackson Lake, the several other exquisitely beautiful little Lakes to the South of it, and the Valley and Foothills of the Jackson Hole country. It would involve the readjustment of Park boundaries and all boundaries as between Park and Forestry lands.

The two reasons which have moved me to consider this project are:

1st: The marvelous scenic beauty of the Teuton Mountains and the Lakes at their feet, which are seen at their best from the Jackson Hole Valley; and

2nd: The fact that this Valley is the natural and necessary sanctuary and feeding place for the game which inhabits Yellowstone Park and the surrounding region.

I am told that only through the preservation as a sanctuary of the Jackson Hole country can the Buffalo, Elk, Moose and other animals be permanently maintained and preserved from extinction in the West.

To carry out this purpose involves the purchase of something like 100,000 acres of land, which at $10 an acre, the lowest probable average price, would mean an investment of at least a Million Dollars.

The purchase divides itself naturally into two parts:

1st: The purchase of the land to the West of Snake River-some 14,170 acres in total, valued at an average of $28 an acre, or a total cost of $397,000. This data is taken from Mr. Albright's letter to me of September 29th, 1926.

2nd: The purchase of the balance of the land lying to the East of the Snake River, which is largely cattle-land, little in demand at present and of much less value.

The fourteen thousand odd acres to the West of the Snake River is owned by some 400 people. Many unsightly and some disreputable places are being built on it to attract the increasing summer visitors. These places are rapidly marring the beauty and attractiveness of the country. To prevent their increasing and to terminate their existence is a matter of first importance. It is believed that this Western tract should be bought during the next few months, if at all.

The tract to the East of the Snake River can be considered another year.

I am prepared to embark on this project of the acquisition of the entire Jackson Hole country, having in mind its ultimate addition to the Yellowstone Park.

The purpose of this letter is to authorize the expenditure of what may be required to carry out this project, understanding that it will be not less than a Million Dollars ($1,000,000) - possibly a little more. The immediate expenditure will be probably not over $400,000 - the amount involved in the purchase of the fourteen thousand odd acres West of the Snake River.

I desire to place this entire matter in your hands, to plan, organize and carry out. I am turning over to you certain maps and letters bearing on the subject. Mr. Albright is ready to see you at once to plan the campaign with you.

Very sincerely,
JOHN D. ROCKEFELLER, JR.

Arthur Woods. Rockefeller associate. Former New York City Police Commissioner. His office handled several Rockefeller projects such as Jackson Hole, Williamsburg, and the proxy battle with Colonel Stewart.

The $1 million in 1927 is the equivalent of $6,900,000 in 1990.

May 26, 1927.

Dear Mr. Rockefeller:

In conference with Mr. Chorley about ten days ago, he told me that you would be leaving in the near future and would not be at your office for several months. I am taking the liberty of writing to you about Yellowstone matters in which you have been interested.

In the first place, the Jackson Hole project is proceeding as fast as it can considering the many problems that have arisen in connection with getting the plans finally worked out. Unfortunately, I have been over-whelmed with a multitude of official duties, relating not only to Yellowstone Park but to several of the other big parks in the west and I have not been able to devote as much personal attention to the program as I would like to have done. I feel, however, that Colonel Woods and his associates have the plans well developed and are moving along as fast as is possible to proceed.

You have doubtless noticed in the newspapers that the lake formed by the slide in the Gros Ventre River broke the Dam and caused great loss to ranchers in the Jackson Hole. This calamity is bound to have a very depressing effect on these people who have already had more than eight months of winter. The Jackson Hole is still snowbound and we believe it will be July 1st before we can get through to that country from Yellowstone Park.

As to the cleanup work, I am afraid that we are not going to be able to continue this work this spring. Most of the roads are still under snow and it is melting very slowly. The tourist season will be upon us before we have the highways cleared of the big drifts. I do feel, however, that we could go ahead with the cleanup work in late August and I would like to recommend the following program for next autumn's work:

Complete one and one-half miles on the southern end of the West Thumb - Lake Junction road near Arnica Creek and do the work on the new Lake Shore drive between these two points, in which you said you would be glad to assist. This work will probably require $5,000 altogether.

Then I would also like to suggest that we start a new project on that section of the road system lying between West Yellowstone and Old Faithful. This section of highway will not be reconstructed and, therefore, there does not seem to be any prospect of adequate cleanup being done. There are not many places on this section of road where heavy cleanup work is required and from Madison Junction up the Fire Hole River five miles, we have already completed the work as a part of reconstruction projects we have been carrying on during the past two years. Many miles of roadsides require extremely light work. We could spend approximately $3,000 on this project next autumn, making $8,000 in all.

Before leaving New York, would you care to authorize the continuation of this cleanup work, the projects to be started in late August? Before asking for funds - provided the projects are authorized - I would submit estimates covering the work to be done, mile by mile. During the winter and spring I have been giving great amount of attention to the national park road program and I feel reasonably certain that after the completion of the West Yellowstone - Old Faithful section, there will not be many miles of Yellowstone roads that cannot be cleaned up as a part of construction and reconstruction work to be carried on by the Government. In other words, it seems to me that we are nearing the time when we can tell you that the Government road construction program can take care of Yellowstone roadside cleanup work.

Since I saw you in February, I have visited Grand Canyon, Sequoia, Yosemite, and Mount Rainier National Parks and I have had extensive conferences with the superintendents of Zion, Crater Lake, and Glacier Parks and with the highest officers of the Bureau of Public Roads resident in the West. I inspected new road work in Grand Canyon, Sequoia, Yosemite, and Mount Rainier Parks and I was tremendously pleased with the interest that has been taken in roadside cleanup and the results already obtained in the improvements of the roadsides. Everywhere I went I found the keenest interest displayed in the protection of the roadsides.

In Grand Canyon Park a particularly fine job was made on roadside clearing; in fact, perfect work was done there. In the regional Office of the Bureau of Public Roads, where I made my headquarters for a time in San Francisco, many engineers came in to see me and it was interesting to hear their questions about what I thought of the roadside cleanup work that had been accomplished.

I feel that we owe all of this interest in the improvement

of our highways to your help in the Yellowstone. You started one of the most important movements ever undertaken in the national parks and the results obtained have attracted so much attention that there has been no difficulty in getting roadside cleanup recognized as an exceedingly important part of future road construction programs to be carried on by the Government. I only wish I could put down on paper and thus convey to you the interest and enthusiasm that I observed among park superintendents and road engineers for this roadside improvement work.

I am sorry that you are not coming West with your family this summer but shall hope that your 1928 plans will bring you this way again. In the meantime, the knowledge of your interest in our work and the inspiration of the projects you have approved, will continue to powerfully stimulate my own enthusiasm and capacity to accomplish results in the Yellowstone to show you when you come again.

With all good wishes to Mrs. Rockefeller, you, and the boys in which Mrs. Albright joins me, I am

Sincerely yours,
HORACE M. ALBRIGHT

Kenneth Chorley. Rockefeller associate. Worked in Arthur Woods office. Worked on several Rockefeller projects including Jackson Hole and Colonial Williamsburg. He was president of Colonial Williamsburg from 1935 to 1958 and vice president of Jackson Hole Preserve, Inc. from 1954 to 1964.

June 3, 1927.

Dear Mr. Albright:

Your letter of May 26th is received. The Jackson Hole project has assumed such large proportions that it gives one pause. Just what it is wise to do in the matter I have not yet decided. We are to have a conference today.

I note what you say about the clean-up work in Yellowstone Park, and authorize the additional expenditure for early fall work of what may be required up to $8,000 for the areas set forth in your letter. That you believe when this work has been done there will be little remaining which the Government itself cannot take care of, is gratifying. I am glad that the interest in roadside cleaning is so rapidly increasing.

Very cordially,
JOHN D. ROCKEFELLER, JR.

June 8, 1927.

Dear Mr. Rockefeller:

I am grateful to you for your letter of June 3rd which reached me today. I am delighted to know that we can count on continuing the cleanup work during the late summer and early fall.

As to the Jackson Hole project, I realize that this is developing into something considerably larger than I ever had any idea it would be. I have been particularly disappointed in the land values which have risen far higher than I dreamed they would during the past two years. Naturally, I hope that as it appears now, it does not seem to you to be impracticable. I know that if it can be carried out, it will be the greatest achievement in the conservation of big game animals ever attempted in this country as well as a project involving the conservation of scenery on a grand scale. I have never been so enthusiastic over anything in my life as I am over the possibilities of this project, should it appear to you to be feasible from your standpoint.

Sincerely yours,
HORACE M. ALBRIGHT

October 18, 1927

Dear Mr. Rockefeller:

I attach hereto a report on roadside clean-up accomplished since my last report, and an outline of what we are doing now. If this meets with your approval I would appreciate it if you would advance us $5,000, check to be made payable to Leroy Hill, our disbursing officer.

We think we have been getting excellent results, and the comments by everyone who observes the work that is being done are all highly favorable.

I inspected Crater Lake Park this summer with Director Mather, and found that Superintendent Thomson's road side cleaning activities were being carried on with splendid results. His work this year was contracted, and his contractor has been very slow in his progress, and has had to be watched very closely. Both Mr. Thomson and I are convinced that we can only do this road side work with our own crews and under our own direction.

Reports from Glacier Park are to the effect that some good work was done this year in cleaning up the lake front, the roads and forest near Many Glaciers Hotel. I know you were interested in that situation.

With many thanks for your continued interest in our parks, and for your aid, and with all good wishes, I am

Sincerely yours,
HORACE M. ALBRIGHT

March 16, 1928

Dear Mr. Rockefeller:

We are building some very beautiful bridle paths in Yosemite Valley, particularly among the oaks on the talus slopes between Yosemite Falls and Mirror Lake.

We have succeeded, we think, in getting one of the most beautiful bridle paths that exists in any National Park.

Knowing your interest in this sort of thing, I am taking the liberty of sending you a few pictures which will give you a slight conception of the way these trails have been built and the attention that has been given to the preservation of the landscape. While I have not had the opportunity to see the trails of Lafayette National Park, I hope that what we have accomplished here in Yosemite Valley is comparable, in some respects at least, to the wonderful bridle paths and trails that were so carefully constructed under Mr. Dorr's able direction.

I am leaving for the East tonight, and expect to reach Washington March 25.

With all good wishes, I am

Faithfully yours,
HORACE M. ALBRIGHT

July 7th 1928

Dear Mr. Albright:

With reference to the Clean-up Work in the Yellowstone National Park in which I have had a part, my office records show the following:

There were six projects: To Cost

A. Mammoth Hot Springs to Norris Junction $14,430
B. Lake Junction to Bridge Bay, ... 1,200
C. Yellowstone Lake-Grand Canyon, Artist
   Point, east side of Canyon, & Five miles
D. West Thumb and south end New Lake Shore R'd 8,500
E. New Lake Shore Road, ... 3,000
F. Southern half West Thumb, Lake Junction
   Road, near Arnica Creek 2,000

G. Section of road between West Yellowstone and
Old Faithful, light clean up work, ... 5,000

$32,130

Since you did not intend to ask for the $5,000 author-
ization, listed above as "G" - I suggest that we cancel this
item, which is covered in my letter to you of June 3rd, 1927,
and leave it for consideration when you are ready to present
the matter again. This would reduce the total authorizations
to $29,130.

Due to increase in wage costs, I understand, you have
over-run your original estimates for the work covered by projects
A and F to the extent of $789.45, and that you have used
funds provided for other items to meet these costs. I also
understand that approximately $3,600 will be required for the
completion of all of the work on the East Side of the Park,
and am willing to provide this additional sum. This would bring
the total Authorizations to $32,930., against which payments
of $30,590.65 have been made, leaving a balance subject to
your call of $2,339.37.

Very truly,
JOHN D. ROCKEFELLER, JR.

August 13, 1928

Dear Mr. Rockefeller:

Mr. Gumbel transmitted to me your letter of July 7th, setting
forth the status of the roadside cleanup funds which you made
available to Yellowstone National Park. Your record of these
funds, as stated in your letter of July 7th, is exactly in accordance
with the financial records of Yellowstone National Park.

Some time ago I suggested to Mr. Gumbel that I thought
it would be a good idea if we arranged in tabular form the

various cleanup projects and the funds allotted to them. For convenient reference, I am including the table here.

ROADSIDE CLEANUP AUTHORIZATION AND COSTS
YELLOWSTONE NATIONAL PARK - TO MAY 1, 1928

PROJECT NAME (NEW)		No.	AUTHORIZATION AMOUNT	EXPENDITURE	
			$	$	$
1	Mammoth-Norris	A	14,430.	14,430.00	
	20 miles	B		44.47	
		C		600.28	
		Total	14,430.	15,074.75	15,074.75
2	West Thumb-Arnica	C	5,000.	3,518.64	
	Creek	D	3,500.	2,038.12	
		F		106.58	
		Totals	8,500.	5,663.34	5,663.34
3	Lake Shore Road	E	3,000.	1,184.14	
	(Fixed limitation)			1,184.14	
4	Bridge Bay-Lake	B	1,200.	1,155.53	
	Junction-Canyon	C-D		2,619.45	
		F	2,000.	1,893.42	
		Totals	3,200.	5,668.40	5,668.40
5	West Yellowstone-Old Faithful 19 miles				

Total Authorization $29,130.
Total Expenditure. $27,590.63

At the end of the summer, when we are in a position to report fully on our own construction work including roadside cleanup as well as on the work done under funds granted to us by you, I will extend the above tabular statement with estimates of costs of the West Yellowstone-Old Faithful section, as well as one or two other sections which you may want data on in view of possible long time delay in completing the cleanup of the Grand Loop road under our Government construction program.

What I mean is this: As stated in previous letters, I conscientiously feel that we ought not to present to you any other project than what remains of the roadside cleanup between West-Yellowstone and Old Faithful because all of the other roads are scheduled for reconstruction with Government funds. On the other hand, take the Old Faithful-West Thumb section,

86

for instance, which crosses the Continental Divide, as near as we can figure now, it is going to be eight or ten years before we can reconstruct this piece of road. I doubt whether we could ever get funds diverted to clean up this section before we begin reconstruction.

I just thought that when I make my next report, I might bring in matters of this kind for such consideration as you would care to give them, not at all with the expectation that you would want to approve any cleanup on any of these other pieces of road that will ultimately be cleaned up by reconstruction by the Government, but because there lurks in my mind the feeling that with most of the roads in the park thoroughly cleaned, you might not want to see certain remaining sections that can not be touched for quite a long period of time left in an unsightly state.

As to work done during the past spring, we can not make a final report at this time because we are still carrying on this activity as weather conditions permit. For instance, every time it rains, we divert part of our maintenance crews to roadside cleanup and have made good progress during the summer in this way. On August 1st, we had approximately $580. left from the fund of $3,000. placed at our disposal in May for the completion of Projects 3 and 4, as listed above. This balance with the amount available from previous authorizations as given in your letter of July 7, 1928, namely, $2,339.47, seems entirely sufficient for the completion of the roadside cleanup of the roads on the east side of the park. We will be unable to initiate Project 5 (West Yellowstone-Old Faithful) this fall as it will require our entire outfit to carry on construction programs that we have under way this year, including roadside cleanup projects, which are a part of road reconstruction.

As we have pointed out before, it is quite difficult to find foremen for roadside cleanup work and it seems as though we must utilize the few we have to finish our uncompleted projects this fall.

I hope all of the above is satisfactory to you. You have been most generous in your acceptance of our reports and I am pleased that they seem to meet your approval.

WORTHWHILE PLACES

I am awfully sorry that you could not come out this summer and see the results of our roadside cleanup work. The park has never been more beautiful. Where the roadsides have had two or three years to get entirely back to nature, the wild flower displays have been unusually beautiful and hundreds of people have commented on the marvelous displays of wild flowers along the roads: Even this late in the season, the wild flowers are growing in greatest profusion where in 1924 and later years there were tangled labyrinths of dead and down timber. Right now, the Golden Rod and Fireweed are making a very spectacular roadside exhibition.

Sincerely yours,
HORACE M. ALBRIGHT

September 27, 1928

Dear Mr. Rockefeller:

I am enclosing the page from the magazine "California Highways and Public Works" regarding Mrs. Rockefeller's campaign to improve the architectural character of refreshment stands along public highways. I had another clipping along this same subject which I wanted to send to you but it was misplaced and has not yet come to light. It was a clipping from the Jackson Hole Courier containing both an article on this campaign and an editorial heartily endorsing Mrs. Rockefeller's work. I thought you both would be particularly interested in this recent clipping, because I think it was on the trip to Jackson Hole that Mrs. Rockefeller first mentioned the possibility of bettering "hot dog" stands and similar establishments through competitions such as she has since inaugurated. As I remember it, the dance hall and other unsightly structures which so greatly impaired some of the views of the Tetons were the very things that prompted Mrs. Rockefeller's plan.

The Yellowstone is closing now after entertaining 230,000 people, more than 30,000 in excess of the number we had here last year and almost 50,000 more than were here in 1926.

An article which I wrote for the Saturday Evening Post on our road policies has appeared in the current issue. Thinking that perhaps this might come to your attention and that you would be disappointed in the omission of the Lafayette National Park, I want to explain that I had Lafayette quite thoroughly covered in my original manuscript and was greatly disappointed when my statement in regard to that park was omitted. As a matter of fact the editor eliminated all reference to about five of the national parks, including Crater Lake and Lafayette, both of which have particularly interested you.

With all good wishes, I am

Sincerely yours,
HORACE M. ALBRIGHT

In 1928, Abby Aldrich Rockefeller initiated a series of four competitions for bettering the appearance of roadside stands which, it was said, through ugliness of conception or carelessness of construction, were beginning to menace the beauty of American highways. She contributed $7,000 to the Art Center of New York which administered the competitions in association with the American Civic Association of Washington, D.C. The first awards were made in December 1928. They ranged from $50 to $300 and were made for refreshment stands in New Jersey, New York, California, and Nova Scotia. The second and third competitions were held in 1929. A fourth competition was in the nature of annual awards over a term of years for the good appearance and upkeep of stands which had been built as a result of the early contests.

CHECK FOR $5,000.

December 31, 1928,

Dear Mr. Albright:

I have heard of the new position which it is probable you will shortly enter into. In recognition of the able and unselfish service which you have rendered through your various relations with the National Park Department during a considerable period of years, I trust you and Mrs. Albright will indulge me by accepting the enclosed, which brings to you the best of good wishes from Mrs. Rockefeller and me for a happy, healthy and properous new year.

Looking forward with confidence to the further service which those who know you are counting on your rendering in the position to which we are all hoping you will be appointed, I am,

Very sincerely,
JOHN D. ROCKEFELLER, JR.

Albright became Director of the National Park Service in January 1929.

January 15, 1929

Dear Mr. Rockefeller:

The day after you sailed for the other side of the world, I found your letter in my accumulated mail. I was overwhelmed by the gift from Mrs. Rockefeller and you which it contained, and I was deeply touched by the kind words of your letter.

I have delayed acknowledging this wonderful letter, thinking that I might find the words to adequately express my thanks, and tell you too what an inspiration your references to me and my work were to me. I do sincerely thank Mrs. Rockefeller and you, and Mrs. Albright would join me in this expression of gratitude were she with me. I have left her in California until I can find a home for her and the children here.

When I arrived in Washington, the Secretary of the Interior made me acting director, and then when Mr. Mather resigned a few days later appointed me to his place. I took the oath of office on January 12th.

I think the place would have gone to Mr. Cammerer just as easily and naturally as it came to me but he insisted that on account of his wife's health, his own physical condition and his unfamiliarity with far western conditions, I should succeed Mr. Mather. I have never before witnessed such unselfish, broad-visioned conduct as characterized Mr. Cammerer's course in this emergency. I have the highest admiration and affection for him, and we shall carry on our work as partners, rather than as chief and subordinate.

Your gift, Mr. Rockefeller, is going to be of great aid to me in getting a home out on the edge of the city where my children can have opportunities for outdoor life such as they have been accustomed to in winter times.

In the summer, I hope to keep them in or near some national park.

I am wondering what your plans are for the coming summer. Mr. Cammerer says you are planning a western trip. I hope you will include Yellowstone and the parks in Southern Utah. I would like to be of assistance in arranging the trip, if you will let me help.

I am glad to tell you that Colonel Thomson has been appointed superintendent of the Yosemite National Park. He welcomes the larger opportunity and Yosemite needs him.

At Yellowstone my place will be filled by Superintendent Roger W. Toll of Rocky Mountain National Park, one of our ablest and most public spirited men.

We accomplished excellent results in roadside cleanup work in the Yellowstone this fall.

You will be interested in the fact that the State Highway Department of California has just set aside $250,000 for roadside cleanup for this year alone.

With all good wishes for a restful and happy trip, and again thanking Mrs. Rockefeller and you for your kindness, I am

Faithfully yours,
HORACE M. ALBRIGHT

In 1929, the Secretary of the Interior was Roy O. West.

Rockefeller's gift to Albright in recognition of his work in the National Park Service was not unique. Stephen T. Mather devoted much of his private fortune as well as all of his energies during the last eleven years of his life to developing the Park Service. He willed $25,000 each to Horace Albright and Arno B. Cammerer, Albright's successor as Director. Others followed his example. George Wright, a man with an independent fortune, worked in the Park Service without salary for a while and paid the salaries of some of his staff when Congress failed to make funds available. Roger Toll, an engineer from Denver who followed Albright as superintendent at Yellowstone, was another who made personal contributions to the Service.

March 25, 1929

Dr. W. A. R. Goodwin,
George Wythe House,
Williamsburg, Va.

Dear Dr. Goodwin,   PERSONAL-CONFIDENTIAL

You so stirred my imagination with your plan for a Great National Historical Park that on my way back, I saw in Washington, Mr. Horace M. Albright, who, besides being a great friend of mine, is the director of National Parks and in other words is the head of the National Park System in this country. I talked with him of your general plan and he was most enthusiastic about it.

I am trying to get him to come down to Williamsburg with me on April third, the day before our meeting. I should like to take him to Jamestown and Yorktown and go over Williamsburg with him and we would, of course, like very much to have you accompany us.

I think perhaps it would be best, if no one but yourself knew that Mr. Albright was coming and who he is. Perhaps you could arrange so that we could borrow a car, which I could drive, so that the three of us might go to Jamestown and Yorktown and discuss the matter by ourselves. I am not yet certain that Mr. Albright can get away so as to be there by the third, but as soon as I know definitely, I shall write you.

Sincerely yours,
KENNETH CHORLEY

W.A.R. Goodwin. Rector of Bruton Parish Church in Williamsburg, Virginia. He had the dream which Rockefeller converted into the reality of a restored colonial village.

March 27, 1929.

CONFIDENTIAL:

Mr. Kenneth Chorley,
Room 3006, 61 Broadway,
New York, N.Y.

Dear Kenneth:

Here is a curious coincidence.

The last time I saw you you confidentially broached the Jamestown, Williamsburg, Yorktown idea. Now, this morning, I received a letter from Mr. W. E. Carson, the head of the State Commission on Conservation and Development, in which he makes an almost identical proposition, except that he is not bringing in the idea of connecting roads or parkways.

I am so enthusiastic over this proposed historic park that I can hardly restrain my imagination. Unquestionably it will become the most famous park in the world almost immediately upon its establishment. I can not think of a more interesting and worth while object to work for than this idea. Of course, I shall continue to keep absolutely silent on the subject, but give me a hunch as to what I should say to Carson.

Sincerely yours,
HORACE M. ALBRIGHT

June 15, 1929

Dear Mr. Albright:

For several years I have been talking with Mr. Cammerer about the desirability of developing a type of architecture which would be appropriate for the park buildings in Lafayette National Park. Mr. Cammerer has been most sympathetic with this idea. I have asked Mr. Grosvenor Atterbury, a New York architect of wide experience, to visit various of the national parks this summer, in the interest of such a study. Mr. Atterbury was hoping to see Mr. Cammerer before going West, but has now arranged to see his assistant in Washington next week, since Mr. Cammerer is away for several weeks.

If you are in Washington when Mr. Atterbury makes his visit, I hope very much you can spare him a few minutes. My thought was that Mr. Atterbury should visit only those parks where outstandingly attractive and promising park architecture has been developed. I had in mind the hotels on both the north and south rims of the Grand Canyon, the little restaurant at the head of the Hermit's Rest Trail, the rangers' hut on the edge of Yellowstone Lake, at which we stopped for lunch one day and of which Mr. Atterbury has a photograph, the rangers' social house given by Dr. Mather in the Yellowstone Valley, and some new houses in Bryce's Canyon, I think. There may be and doubtless are others that will occur to you.

This study is, of course, being made confidentially, and yet Mr. Atterbury should have such credentials from the Park Department as would enable him to get all the information desired without revealing his relationship to me.

I am sending Mr. Atterbury a copy of this letter for his information.

Very sincerely,
JOHN D. ROCKEFELLER, JR.

Grosvenor Atterbury. Architect, town planner. He did architectural work for Rockefeller in Cleveland and New York as well as in the national parks.

July 18, 1929

Dr. Stephen Mather
National Park Service
Washington, D. C.

Dear Dr. Mather:

My absence in Europe last winter prevented my carrying out a purpose that has been in my mind ever since I heard that you had found it necessary to retire from the directorship of the National Park Service. That purpose was to give myself as a citizen of the United States the pleasure of telling you of my admiration and appreciation of what you have done in building up the parks and the park service during the years of your leadership of that department. Before I came to have the pleasure of knowing you, I had met a number of the superintendents of national parks - among the first, Mr. Nusbaum, later Mr. Albright and others. Thus some years ago I had come to realize what extraordinarily fine, able, unselfish men had been brought into the park service. Knowing how meagre the salaries which these positions carry, I wondered that men of such high calibre had been attracted to them. This was made clear to me when I came to know you and to learn something of what you have been doing in the department of parks these many years. These young men have been drawn into the service because of their admiration and affection for you and because of the fine example of unselfish public service which you have set them. They have come to realize that the National Park Service offers an opportunity for a man of ability and idealism to make a very real contribution to the development of his country. Thus, coming into the department, as they have, with almost a missionary spirit, one understands their devotion and singlemindedness. I fancy too, from an occasional word that has been dropped, that in other ways than through your fine example and friendship you have helped to make the life interesting, worthwhile and easier for your colleagues. I may add also that I know, although probably in small part, how exceedingly generous you have been with your money as well as your time, in promoting park interests. The result of all this has been that there is perhaps no other department in the national government run on so high a plane and so wholly in the interest of the public which it serves as the Park Service.

For several years I have feared that you could not stand the heavy load which you were carrying and have wished that your burden might be lightened. Often, however, it is easier to stop altogether than to slow down one's pace when one's task is so absorbing and worthwhile as yours has been. While I am sure you miss the work, as you are so greatly missed by your former associates, it must be a tremendous satisfaction to you to realize the change in the Park Service since you took hold of it and to see the fine personnel which you have left to carry on after you so loyally and efficiently.

Please know, therefore, of my great admiration for what you have done and my sense of personal gratitude as a citizen of the United States as I reflect upon all that you have accomplished. May I also express the hope that your health may soon be fully restored so that in the many years to come you may have the satisfaction of seeing the continuing and ever broadening results of the efforts which you have put forth.

With warm regards, I am,

Very sincerely,
JOHN D. ROCKEFELLER, JR.

March 11, 1930.

Dear Mr. Rockefeller:

I take pleasure in handing to you herewith a report by the Acting Superintendent of Yellowstone National Park on roadside clean-up work accomplished during the season of 1929 in Yellowstone Park with funds contributed by you, and also the work accomplished with Government funds in connection with road construction and reconstruction. There are some very interesting pictures submitted in connection with this report. Also, a useful map has been included in order that you may see at a glance just what the present status of the roadside clean-up projects are. I feel that we are now in a position to carry on this work ourselves and for that reason we do not present any more projects to you.

In this connection, I want to point out, as I have one or two times in the past, that there remain in Yellowstone two roads which cannot be rebuilt for some time, the sides of which are very unsightly. These are the road between Canyon Junction and Norris Junction, a short cut used very largely by commercial traffic serving the hotels, lodges and other utilities but also serving a very considerable number of tourists; the road connecting the Old Faithful region with Yellowstone Lake by way of the Continental Divide. It may be from five to eight or ten years before these two roads can be rebuilt. We feel, however, that we ought not to undertake the cleaning up of the roadsides in these cases because of the likelihood that large sections of these highways may be abandoned when reconstruction is undertaken. On the other hand, we hope that you will visit Yellowstone again this summer and view the work that we have done with your own eyes and after observing conditions on the ground give us the benefit of your advice as to what ought to be done on these two remaining roads which we must admit are now altogether out of harmony with the remainder of the highway system. In making these statements regarding the two old roads I am consistently maintaining the position which I stated to you when you were in the park in 1926.

We have inquired as to what disposition you want us to make of the balance of the funds remaining in our contribution account. Prompt remittance will be made in case you want this balance returned to you. You will note from the report that there was a certain amount of burning and other finishing touches on the work that was done last fall before the work under project No. 5 may be regarded as completed. Of course, this finishing work will require but a portion of the remaining balance.

At the risk of boring you by repetition of statements formerly made, I want to say again that I feel that the various roadside clean-up projects which you made it possible for us to carry through in the Yellowstone have done more to improve the park landscape than anything else that has been done in the history of the park. Also, we shall never forget that your undertaking of this work is directly responsible for our now generally accepted policy which contemplates the clean-up of all the roadsides in all the national parks in connection with the construction of new roads or the reconstruction of old highways. I hope that this final report is acceptable to you and I hope, too, that it gives you as much happiness and satisfaction as it has given to me.

Sincerely yours,
HORACE M. ALBRIGHT

P. S. We have just received from Acting Superintendent Daum, copy of Mr. Gumbel's letter of February 28, advising that the balance remaining in the donation fund may be retained until the work has been entirely completed and then any remaining amount may be returned to you.

H.M.A.

April 5, 1930.

Dear Mr. Rockefeller:

Mr. Cammerer has just told me that you expect to be in Washington Tuesday and that you will be at the Department. I am greatly disappointed that I am not going to be able to see you as I am going that morning with the full Committee of Public Lands of the House of Representatives and several members of the Appropriations Committee to Jamestown, Yorktown and Williamsburg. These gentlemen and their wives are going down as the guests of the State of Virginia and I have been asked to accompany the group because nearly all of them are Western men with whom I am closely acquainted.

I wanted particularly to have the opportunity to thank you personally and also on behalf of the whole National Park Service for your generosity in contributing one-half of the funds necessary to acquire the great sugar and yellow pine forest of Yosemite and its extension, thus eliminating from the park nearly 12,000 acres of privately owned lands, and making it possible for us to protect this beautiful exhibit of original California mountain forest. I do want to express this thanks of the Service and my own appreciation of this great gift and inasmuch as I cannot be here when you come to Washington I take this means of conveying our feelings of gratitude.

Secretary Wilbur asked me yesterday if Mr. Cammerer would not bring you to his office while you are in the building as he particularly wanted to see you.

WORTHWHILE PLACES

Yesterday, the President approved estimates for funds to cover the Government's half of the Yosemite timber purchase and later in the afternoon I appeared before the Senate Committee on Appropriations to explain the estimates. The membership of the Committee was well represented by Senators from all sections of the country and they were deeply interested in the story of the acquisition of these great timber holdings. Several of them expressed their personal appreciation of what you did in making possible the perpetuation of these outstanding forest tracts, and there is no question but that the estimates as finally considered today will have the unanimous approval of the Committee, and that the item will be carried in the Interior Department Appropriation bill which has already passed the House of Representatives.

With all good wishes, I am

Sincerely yours,
HORACE M. ALBRIGHT

In 1929, Rockefeller agreed to provide one-half of the funds needed to buy about 15,000 acres of yellow and sugar pine lands fronting on Yosemite Park in California, to save them from lumbering. Congress appropriated the other half of the needed funds. Rockefeller gave $1,645,955.77 in 1930.

April 29, 1930.

Dear Mr. Albright:

This is just to thank you for your most considerate letter of April 5th in regard to the part I have had in the purchase of the Yosemite timber lands. I am delighted that this long and difficult negotiation has at length been brought to a satisfactory conclusion and that these thousands of acres of virgin timber will now be for all time preserved for the enjoyment of the public. I am constantly impressed by your own patience, foresight and breadth of vision in matters of this kind. My congratulations on what you have accomplished.

I am sorry not to be in Maine when you and Mr. Cammerer are there the end of this week, for I know you will greatly enjoy seeing Acadia National Park. I only regret that so limited a time is available for your visit.

Very cordially,
JOHN D. ROCKEFELLER, JR.

June 10, 1930.

Dear Mr. Rockefeller:

Mr. Cammerer and I returned to Washington Sunday from our visit to Acadia National Park. I thought I would be able to write you at once my impressions of the park, but one thing or another has prevented my getting around to my dictation until today.

As you know, I had never been in Acadia National Park, and, for that matter, even in the State of Maine, until this trip. Mr. Dorr met Mr. Cammerer and me at Bangor and drove us over to Mt. Desert Island, so we got a very good idea of the land approach to the park.

During the afternoon of the first day we were there, we covered the new road which was built east of Eagle Lake and Jordan Pond, visited your own beautiful home and other places about Seal Harbor, then returned via the radio station, to the Homans house and the ocean drive.

The following day, Thursday, we covered all of your carriage roads except in the Amphitheatre district, and we also visited Somes Sound, and, in a motor boat, went out to Northeast Harbor and back to Mt. Desert or Somesville. In the afternoon, with Mr. Olmsted, we tramped over the route

101

of the new roads in the vicinity of the great meadow and on up past The Tarn. We then went around The Beehive and climbed to its summit in order to get a comprehensive view of the route of the road from The Tarn around to the ocean and then around the whole shore to Otter Point. We were on the preliminary line of the road coming up and going down the lower parts of The Beehive. Later we went nearly out to Otter Point along the line for the new road that is being considered there.

The following day, Friday, and this was the last day we were there, we took a boat to Schoodic Head and made a study of the proposed location of the radio station on Big Moose Island. We went clear around the shore of the island and then back to the boat arriving at Bar Harbor for luncheon. That afternoon, we tramped the line of the new road all around Otter Point, and gave further consideration to the possibility of moving the radio station to another point not far from where it is now located but back in the timber. Before making this last trip we went to the Amphitheatre and covered the roads in that neighborhood.

You can appreciate the fact that we were very busy all the time that we were in or near the park. I was tremendously impressed with the beauty of the island and particularly of the park. I had never seen such shore lines as one can observe on Mt. Desert Island, Schoodic Head, and the other islands in the mouth of Frenchman's Bay. The forests and lakes were very lovely. The work that you have done is particularly interesting to me. I like the roads, both motor and carriage, that you have constructed and naturally I was deeply impressed with the roadside cleanup work and the bridges and culverts that have been built in connection with the roads. I had to see your magnificent accomplishments, in order to visualize correctly all that Mr. Cammerer and Mr. Dorr had told me about your program during the past few years. I can best emphasize my love of the park by telling you that already I am making tentative plans to spend a month there next year, beginning about August first.

As to your own plans for the future, I went over them quite thoroughly with Mr. Olmsted. I feel that you have a program that means everything to the park and to the National Park Service. We shall cooperate in every feasible way. Already we have discussed the radio station problem with Congressman Cramton who in turn has taken it up with Mr. Britten of Illinois, who is head of the Naval Affairs Committee and with Mr. Burton L. French of Idaho, Chairman of the subcommittee of the House Appropriations Committee handling the appropriations of the Navy Department. We are all agreed that the expenses in connection with moving the radio station should be met by the Government as a logical Government park activity as well as a measure of appreciation of what you are doing in and for the park. I feel also that we should undertake any road construction that is deemed necessary on the Schoodic Peninsula. I have asked Mr. Dorr to send us his program for roads in that section of the park.

I did not start out to write you as long a letter as this and I hope you will pardon my going into things at so much length.

Again thanking you for your kindness to us in New York, I am

Sincerely, yours,
HORACE M. ALBRIGHT

In 1930, Rockefeller was planning to extend the carriage and motor road systems in Acadia.

Frederick L. Olmsted. Landscape architect. Son of Frederick L. Olmsted who designed Central Park in New York City as well as many other outstanding parks. The younger Olmsted headed up a firm operating out of Boston.

The radio station stood on land which was needed to permit the proposed shore road, or Ocean Drive, to hug the coast along Otter Cliffs, a particularly scenic section of the proposed drive.

Louis Cramton. Congressman from Illinois. A strong friend of the Park Service.

WORTHWHILE PLACES

Private and Confidential

Dear Mr. Albright:

Since our conference in my office the other day about Acadia National Park mattters, it has occurred to me that the following steps should be taken as soon as they conveniently can:

1. My deeding to the Government the lands on Otter Creek Point and ocean front as agreed. I am waiting only for the necessary map to accompany such a letter of gift.

2. Preparation of a map showing the proposed motor road.

3. Map showing the proposed horse road on the Bar Harbor side.

4. Map showing the Amphitheatre Road.

5. It occurred to me that these proposed roads could all then be shown on the new pathmap which is coming out this summer and which shows all existing horse roads and motor roads on the Island; that if it was your pleasure this map could be published showing the roads, horse and motor, which the Park had approved and was prepared to build as the necessary lands and money were made available.

6. That I might write you a letter, offering to build the motor road, and, for the present, make no mention of an offer to build the two horse roads in the Bar Harbor section or the Amphitheatre road.

The effect of this procedure would be that the park's sanction of these several roads would be publicly indicated, the public on Mount Desert Island would thus be given notice of what the Government proposed ultimately to do, any criticisms could be made, and all without my having appeared as the donor of the roads other than the motor road. Then whenever it seemed wise, either late this summer or another year, I could make my offer to build any of the horse roads as I desired, and the offer would not need to be considered by the public, for the road project itself would already have been thus considered. How does this method of procedure strike you? I am sending a copy of this letter to Mr. Cammerer.

Very truly,
JOHN D. ROCKEFELLER, JR.

Rockefeller's plans for a motor road circling the eastern section of the park along the coast had evolved from his earlier stand against motor cars in the Park. In 1923 he wrote:

> *I think you can feel quite comfortable about the automobile problem, so far as my property and the Lafayette National Park are concerned. I cannot imagine a day ever coming when I should be willing to admit motors over our own roads, and the Park authorities, both local and in Washington, are thoroughly committed and on record as permanently opposed to the admission of automobiles into the Park, except on the one or two roads to be built especially for automobiles, namely the one to the top of Green Mountain and the other running from the Green Mountain Road to Bubble Pond and finally out to the south side of the island.*

Green Mountain is now Cadillac Mountain.

The carriage roads he wished to build in 1930 were short extensions of the over 48 miles of such roads he had built between 1915 and 1930.

Private motor cars were slow gaining entrance into the national parks. There were no cars in Mount Rainier until 1908; General Grant until 1910; Crater Lake, 1911; Glacier, Yosemite and Sequoia, 1913; Mesa Verde, 1914; and Yellowstone, 1915.

WORTHWHILE PLACES

June 16, 1930.

PRIVATE AND
CONFIDENTIAL:

Dear Mr. Rockefeller:

Mr. Cammerer and I have been discussing your letter of June 12th, which just arrived, and, responding to your invitation, have the following suggestions to lay before you:

The sequence of matters as discussed and agreed upon in your office and covered in points 1 to 4 is as we understand them. The formal deeding by you of the lands on Otter Point and the ocean front is understood of course to depend upon the successful prosecution of the plan for the removal of the radio station from its present location, either to Schoodic Point or some other location satisfactory to you and us, and either entirely or one-half at Government expense, to provide room for the new motor road you plan to build there. I have already committed myself unreservedly to the removal of the station to Schoodic Point as being soundly in the interest of the park itself in case the motor road is built, and later Congressional cooperation to effect that removal, preferably entirely at Federal expense, appears assured at this writing.

Under 5 as I understand it you suggest that the three road projects covered in points 2 and 4 inclusive should be shown as proposed road projects on the new pathway map coming out this summer, thereby complying with the policy of publishing such projects before Secretarial approval is secured by me, and you not appearing as donor of any of them except the new motor road, the proposed horse road on the Bar Harbor side and the amphitheatre road to appear as park road projects. That, after that map has been published and thereby the publicity given all these road projects and any criticism drawn forth for the Secretary's consideration, they could upon the Secretary's subsequent approval be taken as definitely approved future road projects, depending solely upon the availability of funds for the construction, but you, under your number 6 offering funds for the immediate construction of the motor road only.

I am so convinced of the value of these roads to the park, based on my own and Mr. Cammerer's recent inspection and such professional advices as I have been able to contact, that I would today recommend approval of their construction to the Secretary were it not for the policy of publication prescribed by Secretary Work, and which I think you and I agree it is wise for Secretary Wilbur to follow from the standpoint of both the park and yourself.

I am wondering, however, whether upon reflection you might not agree that it would be wiser, in view of the past history of things, that you adhere to your first plan of combining the offer to build the motor road with one to build the amphitheatre road, or in fact make the offer at one time to construct the motor road, the amphitheatre road, and the Bar Harbor horse road. Being on park land, the last two roads would necessarily be park road projects even though your participation would inevitably be assumed locally. And once the approval of the Secretary to this program, after due publication, had been secured, then to begin the construction of the amphitheatre road coincidently with the work on the motor road so that you may be assured that, should the present Secretary suddenly step out of office, some future Secretary might not defer construction of the former for reasons of local pressure which have been recognized in the past. I am as keen as you are that nothing should interfere with your public-spirited plans, and am not inclined to take a chance on any of our arrangements going wrong later on. You will remember that the road plan recommended by Mr. Cammerer in 1922 and approved by Acting Secretary Finney was later suspended in part until offers of funds were definitely in hand.

To reiterate, I believe it would be more advantageous for you to make the offer of the construction of the several roads contemplated, and begin construction coincidently of the amphitheatre road and the motor road as soon as Secretarial approval has been secured. Don't you agree?

I have one further suggestion and that is that you have Mr. Olmsted prepare a report on your Mt. Desert program and have him embody in that not only his observations and comments on the program itself but also on any other phases of the development of the park that he feels ought to be treated in such a report.

I expect to leave Washington for Denver on the afternoon of next Saturday, the 21st, and will be in Rocky Mountain Park until about the 29th, after which I will go to Salt Lake City and Zion National Park. Mr. Cammerer will spend the summer in Washington and can be reached here at any time.

Sincerely yours,
HORACE M. ALBRIGHT

Ray Lyman Wilbur, Secretary of the Interior, 1929 to 1933.

June 19, 1930.

Private and Confidential

Dear Mr. Albright:

I am enclosing herewith a map showing the four tracts of land on the Ocean Drive and extending down to the southern part of Otter Creek Point which I have talked with you about deeding forthwith to the Government. Tract 1 is the Derby property which I own, on the west and north sides of the Bar Harbor highway. Tract 2 is the Roberts property which I own, on the west and north sides of the Bar Harbor highway. Tract 3 is the Leffingwell property which I own, on the west and north sides of the Bar Harbor highway. Tract 4 is the Bingham property which I own, on the west and north sides of the Bar Harbor highway.

As soon as I looked at this map, which I have just had prepared for your information, I realized that I should add at this time the property which I own on the western half of Otter Creek Point south of the Radio Station, which is roughly shown by the section with a pencil cross and a number "5". I have wired the engineers to add this tract to the map immediately and will send you a copy thereof as soon as it is received. Please, therefore, destroy the map enclosed herewith when the corrected one is received.

In your letter of June 16th, covering the various matters referred to in my letter of June 12th, you refer to my purpose to deed to the National Government these four (now five) tracts, as follows: "This action to depend upon the successful prosecution of the plan for the removal of the Radio Station from its present location to either Schoodic Point or some other location satisfactory to you and us and either entirely or one-half at Government expense, to provide room for the new motor road you plan to build there." I had not quite understood the situation as you outline it. I had assumed it would be necessary for the Government to own this land as a part of Acadia National Park in order to be in a position to deal with the Navy Department, and I was prepared to deed the land to the Government, irrespective of whether the Radio Station was moved or not. This was my plan. Do you think it unwise? Is it not, on the other hand, rather the wisest course? Would it not be unfortunate for me to be in the position of making conditions to the Government, and would it not bring me into the picture of the trade between the Navy Department and the Department of the Interior, as I would not be brought in were I to deed the properties above mentioned without condition forthwith?

Please give me the benefit of your further thought on this matter at your early convenience. I shall be in my office for three days only before leaving for the West; those days will be this coming Tuesday, Wednesday and Thursday. We leave that night for the West, and if possible, I should write the letter offering these properties before I go.

If you are away when this letter is received, perhaps Mr. Cammerer, to whom I am sending a copy of the letter for his information, will reply on your behalf.

Very truly,
JOHN D. ROCKEFELLER, JR.

WORTHWHILE PLACES

REVISED AND FINALLY ACCEPTED FORM OF ORIG-
INAL LETTER OF JUNE 27, 1930. Copy 2.

June 27, 1930

The Director,
National Park Service,
Department of the Interior,
Washington, D.C.

Dear Sir:

I am enclosing herewith plan showing the line of several
proposed roads, some for motors, some for horse use only,
in Acadia National Park and certain adjacent private lands on
Mount Desert Island.

No.I. (the red line) shows the proposed motor road
connecting the present Park motor road with the Ocean Drive.
This road is 13 1/6 miles in length; it traverses Park lands
for about 3 1/3 miles and private lands nearly 9 3/4 miles.
The construction of this road would involve, I the consent of
the Town of Eden (a) to the realignment of the present Gorge
road just north of the Tarn and its going in an underpass beneath
the proposed Park road; (b) to the abandonment of a certain
portion of the Ocean drive the same to be made a part of the
proposed road; (c) to the closing of a Town road laid out
extending from the Ocean drive at Otter Creek westerly to the
shore of Otter Creek south of the Salisbury Cove Biological
Laboratory property; II some permanently satisfactory
arrangement for the passage of this road (a) over the property
occupied by the Radio Station at Otter Creek, (b) over the
nearby property owned by the Salisbury Cove Biological
Laboratory; III the consent of the War Department to the
construction of a causeway over Otter Creek inlet. So far as
this road is concerned the offer made below is conditioned upon
the satisfactory adjustment of these items I, II, III.

No.2 (the green line) shows the proposed horse road loop
connecting the Eagle Lake horse roads and Norrell Park. This
road is 6 1/4 miles in length. It traverses Park lands for 2
miles and private lands for 4 1/4 miles. Its construction would

110

involve the consent of the National Park Service to two underpasses underneath the present Park motor road.

No.3 (the yellow line) shows the proposed completion of the Jordan (Penobscot) and Sargent Mountains' horse road. This proposed road, with its connection, is 2 1/2 miles in length and traverses Park land only. Its construction will complete a road some 15 miles in length, which will then completely circle Jordan (Penobscot) and Sargent Mountains.

I hereby offer to build the above-mentioned roads without expense to the National Park Service, the motor road to be built according to the specifications of the present Park motor road; the horse roads to be built according to the specifications of the present Park horse roads; both to include the usual roadside cleaning, planting and forestry. As to the horse roads, it is understood, as is true of all other horse roads in Acadia National Park, that these roads, if constructed, would be open to use only by horses, horse driven vehicles and pedestrians, but not to motor traffic.

If work upon any one of these three roads has not been begun within a period of five years from the date of this letter or during my lifetime in the event of my earlier death, there shall be no further obligation upon me if living or upon my heirs in the event of my decease as regards such particular road or roads.

If work has been begun upon any one of these three roads or upon a section of any one of them, which section is connected at each end with a public highway or an existing park road, the completion of that particular road or section shall be regarded as incumbent upon me if living or otherwise upon my heirs, unless some adjustment of the matter satisfactory to the National Park Service can be made.

Mr. Frederick Law Olmsted, the well-known landscape architect, has spent many weeks in laying out and studying these roads. I think I may say without qualification that, in his judgment, they all represent desirable and important additions to the present Park development. I shall hope within a few days to place in your hands Mr. Olmsted's report and recommendation in regard to these projects.

Very truly,
JOHN D. ROCKEFELLER, JR.

WORTHWHILE PLACES

Dear Mr. Rockefeller:

This is just a hurried acknowledgment of your letter regarding your summer trip, which reached me at Moran. Naturally I am very greatly pleased with the kind remarks you have made about the cooperation of our organization, particularly our superintendents, in carrying out your itinerary during the past summer. As soon as I return to Washington, I am going to write them telling them of your letter and expressing my own appreciation of their efforts. I want you to know, however, that they and I enjoyed the opportunity of being with Mrs. Rockefeller, the boys and you and of being of some little service to you.

I visited Glacier early in September, then went with Secretary Wilbur to Bryce, Zion and the North Rim of the Grand Canyon, then joined the special Senate committee on the conservation of wild life in the Jackson Hole. Mr. Fabian, of course, was with me, and we have just finished four days of inspection of your great project and conferences regarding it. I am glad to say to you that the committee is tremendously interested in the project, and has pledged its support in carrying it through. I am sure that very shortly you will hear from several of the committee members, giving their own impressions of the Jackson Hole country and of the great work you have authorized.

The committee, Mr. Fabian and I were all pleased with the cooperation we received from the responsible citizens of the Jackson Hole, who apparently are now going to cooperate with us to the fullest extent. We were also fortunate in meeting at Moran Ex-Governor Robert D. Carey, who will be the next U. S. Senator from Wyoming, Honorable Vincent Carter, the lone representative of Wyoming in Congress and Governor Frank C. Emerson of this state. All of these men told us that, inasmuch as the Jackson Hole people seemed to be heartily in accord with what we are trying to do, we could count on them for their support. Of course, the thing that we have to do now is to tie the Jackson Hole sentiment into a written report or petition, and Mr. Fabian is staying over a few days more to work on this phase of our problem.

Two of the senators, Chairman Walcott and Senator Key Pittman of Nevada, are staying in the Jackson Hole for further inspection of the high country, and I am here in Yellowstone with Senator Peter Norbeck of South Dakota, and am going with Senator Norbeck to the Black Hills at his request.

I am due in Washington on October third.

With all good wishes, I am

Faithfully yours,
HORACE M. ALBRIGHT

Harold P. Fabian. Salt Lake City lawyer. Member of the firm of Fabian and Clendenin. He handled legal matters for the Snake River Land Company, the Rockefeller firm which purchased the land in Jackson Hole. Fabian later became president of the company and a trustee of the private foundation created to hold the land, Jackson Hole Preserve, Inc.

October 30, 1931.

Dear Mr. Albright:

In my letter of the other day, I forgot to tell you with what pleasure I observed the beautifully graded banks along certain of the roads in Yellowstone Park which are now being built. Your people there have already gotten onto the idea and are as pleased with what you have done as I am. I am sure you will feel in the long run that the little extra cost involved is worth while.

Very sincerely,
JOHN D. ROCKEFELLER, JR.

WORTHWHILE PLACES

October 31, 1931.

Dear Mr. Rockefeller:

Your letter of October 27, in regard to your visit to Jackson Hole with Mrs. Rockefeller, reached me yesterday.

Nothing during the entire year has given me more happiness than your cordial, appreciative letter about your visit to Yellowstone and Grand Teton Parks. Naturally, your kind references to Mr. and Mrs. Woodring gave me especial pleasure because they have both been so closely associated with me for many years and have been very loyal and faithful. Mrs. Woodring was my stenographer for six or seven years and Mr. Woodring was my Chief Ranger during the ten years that I was Superintendent of Yellowstone.

It seems to me that the situation is rapidly improving in Wyoming and I am absolutely sure that your visits to Jackson have already made a very great difference in the outlook of the opposition.

With gratitude for your fine letter and with all good wishes, I am

Faithfully yours,
HORACE M. ALBRIGHT

February 4, 1932

PERSONAL AND CONFIDENTIAL

Dear Mr. Rockefeller:

I want to make grateful acknowledgment of your letter of February 2 to Mr. Cammerer, recording your willingness to contribute not exceeding $200,000 toward the Shenandoah National Park project, which ensures putting that project through on the acceptable temporary minimum basis brought

114

to your attention. The bill cutting the original area down to 160,000 acres was rushed through Congress and will doubtless be before the President for approval tomorrow. The Virginia Commission has called its meeting for next Tuesday to assure the actual transfer of the million dollar authorization into funds in the Treasury, which will be just before the general state budget gets on the floor of the legislature for discussion; such action having been taken, I am informed, will forestall any efforts that might be successfully made to divert the authorization and appropriation to other channels. Under the circumstances again your public-spirited interest has ensured that for posterity which otherwise doubtless would have failed. The inspiration you have given us to carry on in our work by your thoughtful and kindly cooperation has meant more than I can tell you, but on the other hand there is no one who can thank you adequately for what you have been accomplishing through your generous interest in still conserving a few of the outstanding beauty spots of the country for the enjoyment of the countless millions of the future. I have real satisfaction in knowing that your share in the creation of the hundreds of square miles of the Great Smokies National Park will stand as long as this country will stand as a memorial to someone who was very dear to you.

Most sincerely yours,
HORACE M. ALBRIGHT

In 1893, the North Carolina Press Association presented a memorial to Congress urging the creation of a national park in the southern Appalachians. This first attempt failed, but in 1923, Stephen Mather, Director of the National Park Service, and Hubert Work, Secretary of the Interior, endorsed the idea of a second national park east of the Mississippi. A committee was appointed to study the question, and the idea was soon brought to Rockefeller's attention. John D. Jr., contributed $500 toward the cost of the study.

Representative Henry W. Temple from Pennsylvania introduced a bill in Congress, in 1926, providing for the establishment of two national parks, Great Smoky and Shenandoah.

Tennessee and North Carolina authorized $3,500,000 in bonds to be used for the purchase of land in Great Smokies and donated additional land for the park. But in 1927, the Park Service estimated that $4,500,000 to $5,000,000 in additional funds was needed to complete the project. John D. Rockefeller, Jr., President of the Laura Spelman Rockefeller Memorial, convinced the philanthropy to donate $5,000,000 in memory of his mother.

Rockefeller personally contributed $160,000 to round out the purchase of land in Shenandoah National Park in Virginia.

February 4, 1932.

PRIVATE AND
CONFIDENTIAL

Dear Mr. Rockefeller:

    I returned this morning from a week's visit to the Great Smoky Mountains and Hot Springs National Parks and I found on my desk your letter of February 3, in regard to the Otter Cliffs Radio Station problem. I think I ought to write you a little more fully just what happened in Washington the day I telephoned to you through Mr. Chorley.

    Secretary Wilbur sent for me. Upon arrival in his office I found there with him Senator Hale, Representative Nelson, and Mr. Dorr. I had not been previously advised of the contemplated conference; in fact did not know that Mr. Dorr had come to Washington. The group wanted to discuss the possibility of going ahead with the road project without any reference to the Otter Cliffs Radio Station. They said they first wanted to get our views as to whether the radio station could be by-passed for the time being by a temporary short cut, also whether the road could be built by moving the radio station a little to one side. I told them that these proposals had been thoroughly considered when your plans were being formulated

116

and that they had been discarded as being too much in conflict with the ideal project; that you were interested there in Acadia Park as elsewhere in achieving an ideal or in executing a plan in as nearly an ideal manner as might be humanly possible.

I pointed out that I felt that through my own discussions of these alternate proposals with you I could inform them then and there that you could not favorably consider them and that little would be gained by discussing them with you. However, they insisted that I communicate with you and try to arrange for them to see you here on your way back from Williamsburg. I asked if there was any other mattter that they wanted to take up with you besides these alternative proposals because I felt that if there were no other plans to discuss that you would not feel anything could be gained by stopping. They said no, that they merely wanted to discuss these ideas with you. I therefore told Mr. Chorley frankly what they wanted to see you about and that they had nothing else to present. When your message came stating that you would be unable to stop over in Washington on your return from Williamsburg I communicated with the delegation and also with Secretary Wilbur.

Before leaving the room Senator Hale said that he had been in touch with Secretary Adams and that the Navy were considering the possibility of moving to a point on Mt. Desert Island somewhat south and west of the old Sea Wall Station. They said that the old Sea Wall site itself was not satisfactory but it might be that a site somewhat beyond might be satisfactory and that tests would be conducted to find out about the availability of that site. I ventured the opinion that any site in that section of the Island would be quite satisfactory to the National Park Service and to you although I was careful to point out that I had no power whatever to speak for you. So much for the conference in Secretary Wilbur's office.

That same afternoon the Interior Department Appropriation bill came out on the floor of the House of Representatives and we were greatly disappointed to find that the Appropriations Committee had decided not to insert the authority in our road item authorizing the removal of the Otter Cliffs Radio Station at National Park Service expense and to a place to be agreed upon by the Secretary of the Interior and the Secretary of the Navy. In order that you may see how I expected this to work out I attach the wording of our road item. The underlined matter relating to the Otter Cliffs Radio Station was our suggestion for meeting the situation. I am assured by some members of the Committee that they were favorably disposed to inserting this item but there was a general policy adopted by the Democratic leaders that nothing should be included in any appropriation bill that was not recommended by the Bureau of the Budget. This matter therefore was not considered on its merits but merely fell afoul of a general policy. Senator Hale could get this item inserted in the Senate as he is on the Appropriations Committee and I tried to get him to say that he would do so but he would not commit himself at the time he was with us in Secretary Wilbur's office. It seems to me that we would be in a very strategic position if we could get an item like this in the Appropriations Bill and then have the Navy Department find that the new site in the neighborhood of the Sea Wall area will be satisfactory for the new Otter Cliffs Station. Rest assured that we are going to keep at this as long as there is any opportunity to make headway.

I too look back with lots of pleasure on our visit with you at the Dodge Hotel. Mr. Cammerer and I feel that we took too much of your precious time. However, we are profoundly grateful for your patient attention to our discussion.

Sincerely yours,
HORACE M. ALBRIGHT

Charles Francis Adams. Secretary of the Navy, 1929-1933.

Albright's suggested wording for the road appropriation for Acadia was: "Provided further, That in connection with the construction of the Acadia National Park motor road, not to exceed $350,000 shall be available for the complete removal of the present Otter Cliffs radio station on Mount Desert Island, Me., and its relocation and reconstruction on Schoodic Peninsula within the Acadia National Park. . . ."

February 11, 1932

Dear Mr. Albright:

Your letter of February 4th making mention of the recent visit which Mrs. Rockefeller and I made to the George Washington Birthplace National Monument was duly received. This visit we made in motoring from Washington to Williamsburg. We found the drive most delightful and were pleased beyond expression at the beauty of the country from Fredericksburg on. We were not prepared to find the sight of Wakefield so beautiful as it is. The day was warm and balmy and the point of land so heavily wooded with evergreens and with charming views of the river on both sides seemed to us most entrancing. The house which has been on the old site certainly suggests to the lay mind very vividly the kind of house that might have originally stood there. As to how accurate it is in detail of design and construction we of course could not tell but it impressed us most favorably.

We visited the little cemetery of the Washington family and there met the representatives of the National Park Service who courteously introduced themselves and offered any assistance we might require. The whole layout at Wakefield we found delightful and most attractive and congratulate you on what has been done there in the public interest.

We then visited Stratford for the first time and were charmed with the extraordinary house which still stands there in its delightful setting of fine old trees.

While at Williamsburg we sought to go over the new park highway from Yorktown but the time available for that purpose was immediately following a heavy rain storm and your representative there advised Mr. Chorley that the road would not be safe. This we shall hope to do on our next visit.

May I take this opportunity of acknowledging with thanks your gracious letter of February 4th in regard to my pledge to the Shenandoah National Park project. Not only because this project is deemed to be a really important and worthwhile park project, but also quite as much the deep interest which you and Mr. Cammerer have had in it and your anxiety lest at the last moment it fail to go through, led me to make the pledge that I did.

Very sincerely,
JOHN D. ROCKEFELLER, JR.

George Washington Birthplace National Monument. On the Potomac River, 38 miles from Fredericksburg. Rockefeller contributed $118,000 for the purchase of additional land surrounding the building site. Established as a monument in 1930. In 1937, Rockefeller gave the Park Service three Morgan horses which were kept at Wakefield for several years as part of a living museum.

March 1, 1932.

Dear Mr. Rockefeller:

As Mr. Cammerer has been ill at home for over a week and his physicians are keeping him incommunicado for the present, your letter of the 18th last concerning your contribution to the Shenandoah National Park project has been brought to me.

I can readily see from your letter that the situation, as it faced us, is not altogether clear to you. Mr. Cammerer's letter to you of January 25 last as to the irreducible minimum park area states the facts as we knew them at that time and as they exist today. Had we been able to know last December when we had our bill introduced with what amounted to a guess of 160,000 acres minimum that the irreducible minimum beyond which we finally found we could not go was 192,754 acres, we would have substituted that figure for the 160,000 acres mentioned in the bill. In any event the latter figure was a safe one where we were fighting against time. In laying out a national

120

park we must observe definite standards and physical requirements, such as you mention in your last paragraph, without which a park is impossible, and these were the standards by which the total acreage, and consequently the total minimum amount found necessary, were measured. It included thorough survey of scenic spots, roadways and protection of entrances, and the President's Camp, such as you advert to; in fact, the consideration of those elements without which the park would have been unacceptable to the Government, and which were communicated to the Virginia authorities, as a sine quo non for the park. This appears to me to have been covered by Mr. Cammerer's letter to you of January 25 last.

The fact is that entirely irrespective of the funds then in hand or solicited, the final results for a boundary acceptable to me and the Secretary and the President, from which all possible cutting had been done through information then available, were turned in on the afternoon of January 25 as 192,754.09 acres and formed the basis of the last paragraphs of Mr. Cammerer's letter to you of that date. Of course, in an area about 80 miles long and an average of 4 miles wide, with irregular boundaries, some adjustments must be found necessary in study on the ground, but these, if made, will not increase the total acreage.

I had the maps on which we were placing boundary lines with me at our conference at the Dodge Hotel several weeks ago in order to show you our problem and how we had to work it out. I am very anxious that it be very plain to you, and, if necessary, would be pleased to call in person to go over this matter with you, or to have Mr. Cammerer do so after he has returned later on.

While I have not stated so to you in conversation or by letter, nor do I believe has Mr. Cammerer, the fact remains that without your pledge, as the finances stood and the Virginia political situation existed, the national park project would have been an utter failure. The studies we were making proved that a park of less than 192,000 acres in round numbers was entirely unacceptable from a Government standpoint. If the funds necessary to acquire that amount were not forthcoming, the project appeared doomed. That must have been what Mr.

Cammerer had in mind by his words "if the funds will be available".

Cordially yours,
HORACE M. ALBRIGHT

March 7, 1932.

Dear Mr. Albright:

Your letter of March 1st, regarding the Shenandoah National Park project is received. You may be right in your interpretation of the following quotation from Mr. Cammerer's letter of January 25th:

"In other words, while a minimum of 160,000 acres is prescribed in the bill now before Congress, an area of 192,754.09 acres will be secured if the funds will be available."

On its face it seemed clear that anything above the minimum of 160,000 acres prescribed in the bill, up to 192,754.09 acres, would be secured if the funds were available, but not otherwise, and that in the latter event the minimum project would not be jeopardized. However that may be, the amount I should be called upon to pay on my recent pledge is to be determined, as stated in my letter to Mr. Cammerer of February 18th, in accordance with two measurements: First, the minimum outside contribution that would hold the appropriations and pledges made by the State of Virginia and by the people of Virginia; secondly, the minimum number of acres which the Federal Government, on the advice of the National Park Service, would be willing to regard as adequate for a national park. On the latter point your letter seems final in its statement that the 192,754.09 acre area is the minimum which the National Park Service was willing to accept as embracing those features which it regards as irreducible in a national park. If this is the case and if, irrespective of the willingness of the Virginia authorities to stand by their commitments on the basis of 160,000 acres, the National Park Service would have let the project fail rather than recommend a park of less than 192,754.09 acres, then a contribution from me of $189,813. is the least amount that would have saved the project, and that is what I set out to do, within the limit of $200,000.

If you assure me that the above statement represents the facts in the matter, I shall regard myself as obligated under my recent pledge to the extent of $189,813., payment of which will be available whenever called for.

Very truly,
JOHN D. ROCKEFELLER, JR.

March 7, 1932.

CONFIDENTIAL:

Dear Mr. Rockefeller:

The following comes to me by an "underground route" and probably cannot be substantiated. It seems that when the Director of the Budget and his associates were discussing with the President the authority for the removal of the station and the expenditure of $250,000 for so doing there were data available either from the records of the White House or the Bureau of the Budget to the effect that the Chief of Naval Communications had recommended the abolishment of the Otter Cliffs Radio Station from the Naval Communication System. It seems that the President thought this would be a good idea. I am giving this to you for what it is worth. If true, it would seem that there may be a possibility of getting rid of the station entirely. I am going to try to follow up this clue and see whither it leads me.

Faithfully yours,
HORACE M. ALBRIGHT

March 10, 1932

Private and Confidential

Dear Mr. Albright:

Your two letters of March 7th in regard to the Radio Station at Otter Creek, are received. The shorter letter passing on to me a rumor which you have not been able to confirm, is exceedingly significant. If this rumor is confirmed it will afford a very easy solution to a difficult problem. I shall be interested to hear if confirmation is had.

As to the other letter, I am glad to find you feel I have accurately analyzed the attitude of the Navy Department. That the passage, both in the Senate and the House, of legislation including an appropriation of $250,000. for the removal of the Radio Station, is so likely is most gratifying. That will give you the whip hand and completely alter the situation. I agree with you that the original estimate of $350,000. for removal is probably an outside estimate and that it undoubtedly could be greatly reduced. If relocation rather than permanent removal is the thing finally decided upon, I am much pleased to have you say that you still feel the Schoodic Head site can be adopted, for from my point of view that is distinctly the best location under the circumstances,

Thanking you for keeping me advised of this interesting situation, I am,

Very truly,
JOHN D. ROCKEFELLER, JR.

April 11, 1932

Dear Mr. Rockefeller:

I am glad to inform you that on March 30 the President signed the proclamation adding to the George Washington

Birthplace National Monument the land you recently conveyed to the United States.

Your public-spirited and far-sighted action in thus rounding out the area necessary to maintain and develop for posterity the birthplace of George Washington as a great national shrine is one of the many fine things your interest has impelled you to do. I am confident that as time goes on the vital effect of this will be more and more appreciated by the people of the country, and that you yourself will derive in increasing measure the satisfaction that your generous donation deserves.

Sincerely yours,
HORACE M. ALBRIGHT

June 13, 1932.

Dear Mr. Rockefeller:

I am leaving for the West today and am attaching hereto, for the use of your office in the event that for any reason you want to get in touch with me, a copy of my itinerary. This is only tentative and may be changed from time to time. I am inclined to think, however, that it will be followed pretty closely until I reach Glacier National Park.

I want to tell you again how much I enjoyed my day with you in Acadia National Park. It was one of the most interesting days of my national park career. The unfolding of your plans for Acadia Park very greatly broadened my view of the whole project. I came back from Acadia this time with greater enthusiasm than ever for this exquisitely beautiful park.

The importance of the Cadillac Mountain Road looms larger every day. I have taken all feasible steps to program its further improvement through roadside clean-up and we are shortly sending to Acadia Park two of our very best men,

Assistant Chief Engineer O. G. Taylor and Landscape Architect Zimmer, who will spend considerable time there studying the problems that need more attention.

In August, Assistant Director Harold C. Bryant, who is in charge of our educational work and who was a member of the original educational advisor committee financed by the Laura Spelman Rockefeller Memorial, will go to Acadia Park for an extended stay. It is likely that Dr. Bumpus will join him there. They will devote attention to the Cadillac summit with a view to working out a plan for trails and such educational structures and equipment as will provide the visitors with facilities not only for enjoying the beauty of the scenes spread out before them but also to tell the story of the forces of nature that constructed these superb scenic features.

Mr. Dorr doubtless told you before you left Acadia that the boathouse at Eagle Lake will be removed at once and that with the cooperation of your trapper the beavers will be taken from park waters.

Secretary Wilbur has just told me that he expects to visit Acadia Park late this month, going thence from Dartmouth College. I understand he is to speak at Dartmouth on Commencement Day and is to receive the honorary degree of Doctor of Laws.

I hope to go back to the park in September to review the accomplishments during the summer and to bring to a head, I hope, all matters relating to the removal of the radio station. In the meantime, if in the economy provisions of the legislative appropriation bill there is retained a measure to reorganize the Government activities it may be that the radio station will be abandoned.

I hope you will pardon this rather lengthy letter.

With all good wishes for a restful summer, I am

Faithfully yours,
HORACE M. ALBRIGHT

Dr. Herman C. Bumpus. Director, American Museum of Natural History.

September 26, 1932.

Dear Mr. Rockefeller:

Last Saturday night in the Shenandoah National Park area Mr. Cammerer and I had a long final conference with the Virginia State authorities in direct charge of the State's program for the acquisition of that park. We all believe that matters are now in such shape that they are ready to proceed with the work of acquiring the land.

In an earlier letter I wrote you that I was not willing to accept less than 192,754.09 acres for that park at an estimated cost of $1,745,869.58, barring minor adjustments here and there that might raise or lower that amount slightly. Included in that estimate were timberlands belonging to two lumber companies for which they, as seems customary with lumber companies, wanted an exorbitant price. As they were going to fight their cases to the highest courts, it presented a picture of interminable delays, possibly over a period of years. The President and Secretary Wilbur both have expressed the wish that these holdings be eliminated from the park area, at least for the present, so as to do away with all these complications. This I, therefore, reluctantly did, fully concurring in the wisdom of the move, but it necessarily involved some boundary adjustments that do not alone reflect the acreage and value of the timberlands. It, however, brought the total acreage down to 176,710 acres at an estimated cost of $1,719,687.63, or a reduction of $26,181.95 below the original figure. This presents a reduction in that amount of your pledge, or from $189,813 to $163,631.05.

Will you kindly forward your check to Mr. Cammerer at this address for that amount, payable to John F. Purcell, Treasurer of Virginia, For Credit to the Shenandoah National Park Fund, so that Mr. Cammerer as Executive Secretary to the Virginia organization collecting these funds may transmit it to him with remittances made on other pledges?

While there probably will be a number of instances where final court action over a course of months, or even years, may increase the base estimate somewhat, the State authorities say that the State may be depended upon to appropriate any additional small amounts that in such events may be found necessary.

Sincerely yours,
HORACE M. ALBRIGHT

October 24, 1932.

Dear Mr. Rockefeller:

It was thoughtful of you to ask me to take breakfast with you at your home next Friday morning. There will be a number of interesting things to review and real progress to report in most instances.

Mr. Cammerer and I agreed that you ought to have before you a copy of Mr. Taylor's excellent report on the Little Cranberry Island site for the radio station, and accordingly a copy was sent to you, which I hope you will have an opportunity to glance through before my arrival.

We have also received from Mr. Dorr a report on the visit of Senator Hale and Captain Hooper to Acadia Park last week. You know, of course, that the Navy Department has completely capitulated and now favors the Schoodic Head site. We are wondering, however, whether it would not be best for us to press our advantage and insist on the removal to Little Cranberry Island.

With reference to our correspondence last spring about Point Lobos in California, I am very glad to tell you that it appears that the State has just completed arrangements for the purchase of Point Lobos for a State Park. The attached clipping gives you the latest information that has come to me about this interesting project. I had an opportunity to visit Point Lobos last summer and was very fortunate in having as my guide Ferdinand Burgdorff, an artist of Carmel, who has painted some exquisite pictures of this extraordinary piece of land. I was so impressed with Point Lobos that I was prepared to recommend its acquisition by the government as a national monument if the State found it impossible to acquire it for a park. Both the sea coast at the Point and the exceptional tree growth make it one of the most unique as well as one of the most beautiful landscapes in the country.

I was at Williamsburg last week and was surprised at the progress that has been made during the summer in the restoration of the Capitol, the Royal Governor's Palace, and many other buildings.

Mrs. Albright and I were pleased to receive the invitation to John's wedding. We hope we can attend this lovely affair. I have not had the pleasure of meeting John's fiancee but I have known her father for quite a number of years.

Looking forward to seeing you, and with all good wishes, I am

Faithfully yours,
HORACE M. ALBRIGHT

Point Lobos. A dramatically scenic spot on the coast of California near Carmel. Now a state reserve.

October 28, 1932.

Dear Mr. Albright:

I do not seem to find the copy of the Navy report on the removal of the Otter Creek Radio Station, from which you read me extracts this morning and which I understood you were going to leave with me. Perhaps you took the report by mistake; if so, would you be good enough to return it to me at your convenience?

May I take this opportunity of recording for our mutual convenience the statement which I made to you this morning as a result of our discussion of the radio station removal problem. That statement was as follows:

The removal of the radio station to either Schoodic Point or Little Cranberry Island will be satisfactory to me. I would not be prepared to consider any other location that has thus far been suggested, until and unless I had been fully convinced that for reasons which I might regard as adequate neither of these locations was practicable.

Very sincerely,
JOHN D. ROCKEFELLER, JR.

November 25, 1932.

Dear Mr. Rockefeller:

Your letter of November 22, answering mine giving you the latest information on the Otter Cliffs Radio Station reached me this morning.

Referring to Mr. Lynam's suggestion in his letter to you of November 16, in view of the fact that our appropriation expires June 30, next, it will be necessary for us to build the new radio station, together with power, water and sewer lines, between now and the end of the fiscal year or we must have the whole project under contract by that time. The building of the road, of course, could come later. In fact, it would not be possible to complete the road prior to beginning work on the new radio station.

Senator Hale telephoned me Wednesday saying that he had been in touch with Admirals Pratt and Robinson, respectively Chief of Naval Operations and Chief of Bureau of Engineering, and that they had agreed to the proposal that the National Park Service design and build the new radio station structures. This decision must still be conveyed to the Interior Department in a formal letter from the Navy Department.

To bring you up-to-date, I am inclosing copy of Secretary Wilbur's letter of November 21, to the Secretary of the Navy

130

and a copy of a letter from the Secretary of the Navy confirming the promise not to erect towers in excess of 200 feet in height.

Doubtless, you have noticed in the newspapers that U. S. Senator Hale of Maine has succeeded to the Chairmanship of the Appropriations Committee filling the place left vacant by the recent death of Senator Jones of Washington.

I am also attaching copy of a letter from Mr. Dorr of November 22, which came to my desk after I dictated the above.

I will be in New York, Hotel Pennsylvania, Tuesday and Wednesday of next week in the event that you may wish to discuss any of these matters with me.

With all good wishes, I am

Sincerely yours,
HORACE M. ALBRIGHT

Albert H. Lynam. Bar Harbor attorney.

January 28, 1933

Private and Confidential

Dear Mr. Albright:

One of the subjects which I am hoping to discuss with you next Wednesday is my relationship, present and future, to the National Park Service in the matter of the proposed motor and horse roads in Acadia National Park. The present situation is that you have told me informally, and I think have so written me, that the consent which the Government gave to my building these roads as approved by it was not regarded by your Department, nor could it be regarded, as a legally binding contract on me that was enforceable. You did request, - and with perfect justice - and the request has been incorporated in our correspondence, that if any section of the proposed road were undertaken, I would agree to complete that particular section so that it would be usable and not left as a blind end.

In view of the opposition to the road building project I have asked the Government to relieve me from my obligation in the road building matter. At the instance of the Secretary of the Interior I agreed not to press that request for a year and have extended that agreement for a second year which expires this coming summer. In the meantime, the Secretary of the Interior will have gone out of office and his successor will have been appointed. If it seems wise on both sides and is practicable, I feel that some adjustment of this situation should be made before that change comes about. This is the adjustment I have in mind, that if the matter can be covered in letters or agreements to our mutual satisfaction, any obligation on my part to build these roads shall be cancelled at the same time I continuing to have the right to build the roads in whole or in part at my pleasure. Such a right should, of course, be limited by the stipulation of a definite period of years, which period might be extended if before its expiration I had constructed some portion of the system. If this thought can be satisfactorily worked out, it would be my plan to write the Secretary forthwith somewhat as follows: "First, I understand the removal of the Radio Station is practically assured. Secondly, I am hopeful that the acquisition of Mrs. Ogden's property in the not distant future is more probable. Third, I believe the opposition to the roads is materially lessened and practically negligible. Under these circumstances I feel justified in saying at this time that I will no longer ask to be relieved from the gentlemen's agreement entered into with the Department in regard to the construction of the roads but am willing to definitely contemplate their construction if, as above suggested, it can be so arranged that to undertake this construction will be wholly at my option and in no way a binding obligation on me or my heirs."

I am writing this hasty note to lay before you the main features of what I have in mind so that you can be giving them consideration before I see you Wednesday. I shall hope in the meantime to have drafted a possible form of letter

132

to cover what is in my mind that we may together consider my suggestion in that concrete form.

Very sincerely,
JOHN D. ROCKEFELLER, JR.

The opposition to the Rockefeller road-building plans came primarily from the summer residents. Many of them felt that the island should be kept as wild as possible with no interference from mankind. They enjoyed the footpaths to the little springs and bogs to which few had access. Most of the year-round residents looked on the roads as a source of work and looked forward to the opening of the island.

In 1933, the Secretary of the Interior was Ray L. Wilbur. He was succeeded by Harold L. Ickes of Illinois on March 20 of that year.

Rockefeller's concern about the location of the naval radio station at Otter Creek resulted from two problems; the station stood on land needed for the proposed road addition, and the antennas were unsightly.

February 10, 1933.

Dear Mr. Rockefeller:

I have just received the following telegram from Superintendent Dorr:

> "Meeting held today voted unanimously to purchase Ogden land at price set by family stop This removes last obstacle to Rockefeller road."

Confirming what I said to you personally in our interview, Tuesday, the road to Big Moose Island on Schoodic

Point is to be advertised in a few days and the bids will be opened on February 28. This means that a contract for the road, parking spaces, etc., will be signed prior to March 4. It is likely also that we will be able very soon to enter into contracts for the installation of power and telephone facilities for the new radio station.

As to the radio station itself, as I explained to you, I had a conference with Naval officers Tuesday morning, this including the executives of the Naval Communications Branch as well as engineers of the Bureau of Engineering of the Navy. The Naval officers all assured me that they were working on the preparation of plans and that absolutely no conditions had arisen in the Navy Department to interfere with the progress of these plans. They predicted that there would be no new situations arise that would unduly delay the removal of the radio station. The officers of the Navy thought that before March 1st they would be able to let contracts for certain new equipment, including the new steel towers. They say floor plans for the new radio station will be ready for us next week.

As a matter of record, I acknowledge your letter of February 6, to which you attached copies of letters addressed to Messrs. Stetson and Lynam by Mr. David O. Rodick, as well as Mr. Lynam's letter of February 1 to you.

I have not yet received information from Mr. Dorr that he has been successful in getting Congressman-elect Utterbach of Bangor to visit the park and study on the ground the road and radio station problems in which we are so deeply interested.

Sincerely yours,
HORACE M. ALBRIGHT

David O. Rodick. Bar Harbor attorney. Member of the firm of Deasy, Lynam and Rodick.

February 11, 1933

<u>Private and Confidential</u>

Dear Mr. Albright:

Under date of February 6th Mr. Lynam writes me with reference to the transfer of the present Otter Creek Radio Station property to the Park, as follows:

"I did not know what procedure, if any, was necessary to exchange the lots. If a transfer is necessary and it were done (the Navy Department retaining the use of the present lot for a term of years) our now strong case would undoubtedly be strengthed".

I take it from what you said the other day that the transfer of this property prior to the removal of the Radio Station is entirely out of the question. If, on the other hand, the transfer were possible under some agreement between the two departments, it would strengthen the situation.

Mr. Lynam writes me that he has directed Mr. Rodick, his partner at Bar Harbor, to send deeds to the property at Winter Harbor which has recently been purchased to connect the proposed Park road with the Winter Harbor highway to Washington at once. I assume the deeds and abstracts have already been received by you. Mr. Lynam points out that there is often delay in getting deeds accepted by the Government. I told him I would ask you, or in your absence, Mr. Cammerer, to take such steps that might be necessary to see to it that the early acceptance of these deeds was had. You have undoubtedly already had the matter before you.

My last advices from Maine are that the Bar Harbor Town Meeting was held on Monday to condemn Mrs. Ogden's property, that the meeting, apparently by agreement with Mrs. Ogden's family was adjourned to this Friday at which time the meeting will be asked to authorize not the condemnation of the land but its purchase from Mrs. Ogden. Thus it seems as though this matter were about to be successfully dealt with.

I saw Admiral Byrd in New York on Wednesday and took advantage of the opportunity to explain to him the road building

135

proposal on Mount Desert Island, the offer made the Government of all of the land on the Otter Creek Point for certain conditions fulfilled, and the relation to these two proposals of the transfer of the Radio Station at Otter Creek to Schoodic Point. The Admiral had never had any slightest knowledge of these proposals nor of their significance. He was immensely impressed with their far-reaching importance and volunteered the opinion that nothing should be allowed to interfere with the carrying out of the program.

It was a pleasure to have such a leisurely talk with you the other night and I was greatly interested to know what you told me.

Very sincerely,
JOHN D. ROCKEFELLER, JR.

Mrs Ogden. A summer resident of Seal Harbor. Opposed Rockefeller's plans for roads in the park.

Admiral Richard E. Byrd. A friend of Rockefeller's. Rockefeller contributed to Byrd's expeditions to the North and South Poles. Byrd became president of the National Economy League, a nonpartisan citizen's organization formed in 1932. It sought to eliminate waste and unnecessary government expenditures. Its primary target was "the non-disabled veterans legalized racket" and the payment of the bonus. Byrd resigned from the League in April 1933.

February 13, 1933.

Dear Mr. Rockefeller:

I have your private and confidential letter of February 11, in reference to the transfer of the Otter Cliffs Radio Station property to Acadia National Park.

The only way that this property can be taken over by the National Park Service is by act of Congress in the same way that we secured control of the Seawall Radio Station. I attach a copy of the Seawall act. The Navy presumably will never agree to a transfer of the Otter Cliffs land to the park as long as their radio station there is still in use and completely under their control. I will verify this by conversation with Captain Hooper and perhaps add a postscript to this letter.

We have received the deed covering the tract of land south of Frazier's creek which was forwarded from Bar Harbor by Mr. Rodick on February 7, and are proceeding to clear this through the Solicitor's office so that the deed may be accepted as early as possible. The deed covering the land purchased north of Frazier's Creek, however, has not been received up to this writing. We were advised in a telegram from Mr. Dorr, received Saturday, the 11th, that the additional deed and abstract of title would probably be forwarded that night so that it should have reached us today. I am wiring Superintendent Dorr to check up on this second deed at once. By making these cases special there seems to be no reason why we can not get the deeds accepted by the latter part of this week and you can depend on this office doing everything possible to expedite acceptance.

I am glad to note that an agreement has been reached for the purchase of the Ogden property and trust this will also be cleared up at an early date.

The news about your conference with Admiral Byrd is most interesting. This leaves our opponents, whoever they are, without any recourse to the National Economy League.

I, too, tremendously appreciated the opportunity for a leisurely talk at the Dodge Hotel the other night.

Sincerely yours,
HORACE M. ALBRIGHT

March 10, 1933

<u>Private and Confidential</u>

Dear Mr. Albright:

Your letter of March 8th is received. I am glad to have a copy of the telegram you sent the municipal officers of Bar Harbor at Mr. Rodick's request and also to know that all of the matters which Mr. Rodick was handling in the Town Meeting have been carried through satisfactorily.

I was talking with Mr. Atterbury on the telephone last night about other matters and he mentioned having spent the day with your two architects on the Schoodic Point Radio Station layout. Mr. Atterbury is eager to be of any help possible. He feels that his position in the matter is not clear. He, of course, would be loath to be regarded as in any way responsible for the final outcome of the plans unless he has commensurate authority in directing what that outcome shall be. Mr. Dorr, in his recent communication to Mr. Atterbury, was vague about what authority or responsibility Mr. Atterbury was expected to have and also as to whether his services were to be entirely gratuitous or not. Mr. Atterbury said he had not heard from you for several months. Whether he is paid or not, whether he is given authority or not, Mr. Atterbury is only too glad to do what he can but properly does not want to be put in the position of being held in any sense responsible for the plans without having commensurate authority to influence their development. He said that generally speaking the layout seemed to him good and that generally speaking the suggestions which he made seemed to be acceptable to your two architects. He felt the question now was largely one of the design of the buildings and that that was a very difficult question to deal with without knowing how much money was available for them. On that point he said the architects seemed very vague.

I am writing you thus fully and confidentially, not at Mr. Atterbury's request or with his knowledge but simply because you had talked with me about the matter and because I am deeply interested in the situation. If you have not any funds with which to pay Mr. Atterbury or if you supplement those funds to the extent of $1,000 would be helpful, you can draw upon me to that extent. Mr. Atterbury felt that better results could be obtained were one of your architects able to stay in New York and work in his office for a while actually working out the plans in collaboration with him. You will know, however, whether that is possible or not.

Very truly,
JOHN D. ROCKEFELLER, JR.

March 11, 1933.

Confidential:

Dear Mr. Rockefeller:

Answering your private and confidential letter of March 10, in regard to the planning of the new radio station to be established on Schoodic Point, I want to express my appreciation of the very fine offer you have made to assist us in securing Mr. Atterbury's services in connection with the design of the new station buildings.

Our architects returned last night from New York and reported fully to me on their visit with Mr. Atterbury. I did not realize until my talk with them that there was apparently some confusion in Mr. Atterbury's mind as to what his relation to this project should be.

About December 1, I was in New York and had a conference with Mr. Atterbury. In fact, we went over to the Century Club and spent several hours together. I told Mr. Atterbury of the plan for the removal of the radio station and expressed the hope that the design of the new buildings on Schoodic Point could be brought quite completely into harmony with his plans for structures on Mount Desert Island. He said that he was very much interested in our Schoodic Point Project and would be glad to help us in any way that he could. I explained to him that our funds were very limited and that we had no authority anyway to employ an architect on the usual professional basis. He said he recognized this and would be glad to place his services at our disposal gratis provided we were able to arrange visits with him so as not to interfere with his professional work. He asked me to have the plans brought to him and said he would be glad to look them over from time to time as they progressed toward completion provided definite appointments were made and plans brought to him for criticism and there was no "running in and out" with them. I told him I would see that he was bothered as little as possible and that if it became necessary for him to spend some time on them I felt that we could reimburse him by a rather limited per diem with a total payment of something over $500. There is a provision under Civil Service Rules and Regulations by which we can employ services up to a total of $540 without reference to the Civil Service list of eligibles.

I thought the arrangement with Mr. Atterbury was quite definite and for that reason I did not take up the matter a second time which apparently I should have done.

Our architects say that Mr. Atterbury was pleased with their general outline and that they are to see him again before long. On the other hand they were somewhat disturbed by his attitude, feeling that he was uncertain of his status. Mr. Dorr agrees too that it seems desirable to have a more definite arrangement with Mr. Atterbury. I shall proceed at once to interview Mr. Atterbury either personally or by telephone and see if we cannot bring him more definitely into our counsels. If I find that I need to draw upon you within the limits of the fund you have generously made available, I will advise you. I can, as mentioned above, provide $540.00 from our funds.

I do not think there is any question but that our architects have caught the spirit of Mr. Atterbury's planning and that they, are well on the way toward the development of just the right thing for the new radio station. Just the same we ought to have the new station very closely in harmony with the Acadia type of architecture which you have been instrumental in making available to us. For that reason we need as much of Mr. Atterbury's assistance as he feels he can let us have.

Again expressing my appreciation of your interest in this important matter, I am

Faithfully yours,
HORACE M. ALBRIGHT

P. S. The Navy Department has just changed its idea again and has withdrawn all buildings from the coast of Schoodic Point to the interior of Big Moose Island. This greatly simplifies our problem (if another change does not occur), and will result in some important economies.

Horace

March 11, 1933.

Private and
Confidential.

Dear Mr. Rockefeller:

The latest word that comes to me is that the new Assistant Secretary will probably be Mrs. Nellie Tayloe Ross, former Governor of Wyoming. When Mrs. Ross was Governor of Wyoming I was Superintendent of Yellowstone and am accustomed to transacting official business with her. She takes a great interest in national parks. Her son was employed in Yellowstone for several seasons before he became a Rhodes scholar at Oxford and she can be counted upon to be very sympathetic to the national park cause.

I have not yet had a conference with the new secretary, Hon. Harold L. Ickes, but I am very much impressed with his approach to his new work. He has a magnificent personality. He tells me that he has been around Yellowstone Park on horseback, making two trips of this kind with the late Howard Eaton, the real founder of the "dude" ranch.

I expect to be in New York several days beginning the 21st. Before I leave here I hope to have a full conference with the Secretary so that I can report something definite to you as to whither the Park Service is headed. Reorganization is just now worrying us more than the possibility of a change in the directorship. Extremely drastic consolidations of bureaus seem to be under consideration. I am afraid that we may wake up some morning and find that we are a subordinate division of some other bureau. This would be the most disastrous thing that could happen to us because any change from the present independent status of our organization would be almost certain to bring it under the domination of western agricultural or other utilitarian interests.

Faithfully yours,
HORACE M. ALBRIGHT

Nellie Tayloe Ross. Elected Governor of Wyoming in 1924 to replace her deceased husband. She was the first woman to govern a state. Eight other women have served as governors, five of them elected in their own right.

March 23, 1933.

<u>Private and Confidential</u>

Dear Mr. Albright:

I have your letter of March 17th, also a copy, sent here, of your letter of March 20th, for both of which I thank you. I have examined with interest the plans of the radio station which you sent me, and am returning them to you today.

142

The two small buildings are picturesque and will, I think, be pleasing. I was rather surprised to see the large apartment building, for several reasons. First, I had not supposed so many married men would be at the post; second, I see no provision for the single men; third, I had somehow in mind that there would be a number of small buildings. Obviously a large building will be less expensive to heat and care for than a number of small buildings. It will, of course, be much more conspicuous and difficult to conceal to any extent by planting. I presume it will give the effect of a summer hotel. The general style of the building, in so far as the elevations suggest it, is simple and pleasing; it is of course not only difficult but impossible to make so large a building picturesque or particularly natural or at home in such a location as Schoodic Point. That it will be a vast improvement over the best of the buildings at the present radio station, goes without saying. In fine, if a large apartment building is the desirable thing from the service point of view, the building as shown is probably as good looking, as convenient and as inexpensive to operate as any building of that character could be.

I am sorry not to have been able to consider these plans with you and Mr. Atterbury in New York, as you had suggested. Our return may be delayed a few days in order to give Mrs. Rockefeller an opportunity to more completely recover from her cold, which has hung on some weeks. While we had expected to reach New York this coming Tuesday, it may be that we will not arrive until later in the week or early the following week.

I note with interest your statement that you and Colonel Woods have had a very satisfactory talk with the new Secretary of the Interior; the Colonel has also written me to that effect. I am glad to learn that the Secretary wants to have a lawyer as Assistant Secretary. I have never heard of Dr. Isiah Bowman, head of the American Geographical Society, who you say is mentioned as a possible Director of National Park Service.

Very sincerely,
JOHN D. ROCKEFELLER, JR.

P.S.-Mrs. Rockefeller has wondered whether the rear elevation of the apartment building was not simpler, more harmonious and therefore more attractive then the front elevation. This may be because all of the windows of the rear elevation are square top as well as the doors, while the windows of the second floor of the front elevation are round tops, as well as the first floor doors. I assume the architects have made this change, thinking to give variety and interest to the front facade. Perhaps they have succeeded; I just raise the question.

Of course, we do not know what style of architecture the building is supposed to follow. It suggests primarily Georgian. However, the round top windows and doors may be to introduce a French touch. Possibly it may be confusing.

Another question Mrs. Rockefeller raises, namely, whether French windows, while attractive, may not be impractical so far as weather conditions are concerned, in so exposed a location. Could not the same effect be gotten with double gung windows, and with greater protection against the weather?

These are merely passing suggestions that may have no value.

March 25, 1933.

CONFIDENTIAL:

Dear Mr. Rockefeller:

Your letter of March 23, from Ormond Beach, reached me this morning.

I am very greatly pleased to have the comments of Mrs. Rockefeller and yourself on the first draft of the radio station plans which were sent to you in New York and forwarded to you by Mr. Gumbel. Many of your suggestions in reference to the plans are very like questions raised by Mr. Atterbury whom I saw in New York on Tuesday and Thursday of this week. I am taking the liberty of quoting the suggestions in your letter, both your own and Mrs. Rockefeller's, in a communication to Mr. Atterbury.

I discussed your letter this morning with my own staff and it is clear that we must have one large building because of the views of the Navy Department. We, of course, would much prefer to have several smaller buildings. We too question the need for so many apartments but the Navy insists on exactly the floor plan that you have seen in the blue prints sent to you. Mr. Taylor, our engineer, is very certain that the building will not be visible from our Schoodic Point road and parking space. He believes that it will be necessary to get out to sea a short distance before the building will appear in the landscape. It will be located in a place which is quite heavily forested and the clearing will not be any more extensive than necessary to make the installation.

I have now arranged with Mr. Atterbury to assume the preparation of all the plans and specifications for the radio station. I have arranged to appoint Mr. Atterbury and his own associates, Tompkins and Devorak, as consulting architects to the Director of the Park Service under a certain provision of the Civil Service Rules and Regulations which permits employment of this type of service provided the cost thereof for any one individual does not exceed $540 per annum. In other words, three of the Atterbury organization will receive $540 per annum. In addition to that, under Civil Service Rules and Regulations, we will provide him with all necessary drafting services. Furthermore, we will be able to meet out of our funds all incidental costs, such as supplies, blue prints, etc.

Mr. Atterbury is much interested in the project and it will receive his personal attention.

Mr. Atterbury feels that he can make the building, to use your own expressions, "picturesque" and "natural" and "at home in such a location as Schoodic Point." The principal criticism that he made of the preliminary drawings of our own men was that the building would be "institutional" in appearance. He told me in general he liked the elevations. I should say also that he hopes to reduce the height of the building at least three feet.

I am awfully sorry to hear about Mrs. Rockefeller's prolonged cold. We are having a similar experience in our home,

Mrs. Albright and our little daughter both having had a difficult time of it for a couple of weeks. I hope Mrs. Rockefeller's recovery will be rapid and complete.

Again thanking you for your fine letter, and with all good wishes, I am

Sincerely yours,
HORACE M. ALBRIGHT

P.S. I ought to explain the reference to "$540 per annum." This means that no more than $540 per annum could be disbursed to any one of these architects but each will get $540 for the work they put in on the plans. This money will come from the general funds available for the project. I have said nothing about your offer of cooperation and I hope it will not be necessary to ask you for assistance. However, there may be incidentals that cannot be readily obtained because of some Government rule or regulation and in emergencies such situations might be met through your aid.

H.M.A.

April 8, 1933.

Dear Mr. Rockefeller:

I have considerable good news for you.

The Director of the Bureau of the Budget has definitely cleared our Schoodic radio station program. A letter from the Director to the Secretary fully releases the funds that were made available for this project.

Mr. Atterbury has submitted not only the new floor plans but also the new elevations for the radio station buildings and this morning Mr. Taylor secured the approval of these plans and elevations by the proper Navy Department officials. Furthermore the Navy Department has agreed not to send these plans to the Boston Commandant for his perusal and approval.

Therefore Mr. Atterbury is free to go ahead with the working drawings which means that we ought not to have to jump any more hurdles between now and the time for the calling for bids.

Again thanks for your interest and support of this radio station problem.

Sincerely yours,
HORACE M. ALBRIGHT

April 11, 1933.

Confidential

Dear Mr. Rockefeller:

Last Sunday, Secretary Ickes and I rode with the Presidential party to the Hoover camp on the Rapidan. While making the trip the Secretary discussed quite frankly the position of Assistant Secretary and told me that he was not going to appoint the gentleman mentioned in our correspondence. He said he had made his decision definitely and finally. Both the First Assistant Secretary and the Assistant Secretary will be western men with legal training.

You will be glad to know that the President took me in his car on the return trip from the Rapidan and I had a visit with him extending over a period of about three hours. I had an opportunity to explain the whole Acadia park project to him and found too that he was most interested in the Williamsburg Restoration, the Great Smoky Mountains and the Shenandoah projects. There was no opportunity for me to bring up the Jackson Hole plan. Secretary Ickes, however, is thoroughly familiar with our great western project.

Faithfully yours,
HORACE M. ALBRIGHT

WORTHWHILE PLACES

May 10, 1933.

Mr. Kenneth Chorley
Room 2601, 61 Broadway
New York, N.Y.

Dear Kenneth:

Answering your letter of May 9, I am sending you, as
I intended to do anyway, a copy of Secretary Icke's radio speech
which he made at 9:30 on the night of May 8. This address
went out from the National Broadcasting studios in Washington-
WRC. I am also sending copies to Van and Harold.

You will note that there is a very great deal in this address
about Mr. Rockefeller's assistance in national park projects. The
Secretary a week or more ago asked for a list of the projects
in which Mr. Rockefeller was interested or had assisted in
completing. He used this list in preparing his radio address.
Monday morning he read the national park section to me and
I suggested changes that would have eliminated in some cases
and modified in others the references to Mr. Rockefeller's gifts.
He did make one or two changes but the other suggestions he
did not adopt. Both Cam and I realized that this address might
not strike Mr. Rockefeller as favorably as we would like but
on the other hand it is in accordance with the Secretary's own
ideas and he conscientiously wanted to give Mr. Rockefeller credit
for his great work. Of course, we also had the feeling that there
was no possibility of any harm being done and, taking into
consideration Senator Carey's attitude, it seemed that it might
be helpful so far as the Jackson Hole Project was concerned.
I might say further that Congressman E. T. Taylor of Colorado
inserted the address in the Congressional Record and it is to
be found on page 3139 of the Appendix in yesterday's Record.

I expect to be in Williamsburg with the Secretary this
weekend. We will reach there Saturday evening and will stay
there Sunday. For that reason I hope you can come down
Saturday night. I will wire you again a little later in the week.

Sincerely yours,
HORACE M. ALBRIGHT

148

May 24, 1933.

Dear Mr. Albright:

I tried to get you at the Roosevelt Hotel last night but was told you had not yet arrived. I am sending you this note to see whether by any chance you could dine with Laurance and me at 10 West 54th Street tonight at seven o'clock. Mrs. Rockefeller is in Providence with her sister and Laurance and I are alone. If you are free, come in your business clothes, and I shall quite understand your leaving immediately after dinner to keep any other appointment you may have. It occurs to me that this will perhaps be the best chance we may have to talk over for a brief time the various matters of interest. Perhaps you will telephone my office if we may expect you, or if this note does not reach you until late in the day, to my house (Telephone Circle 7-0026). Come at the last minute if you can.

I am delighted to know the Secretary of the Interior is going to Acadia National Park this weekend with you. Nothing would please me better than to be there at the same time, but unfortunately I am unable to get away. My usual Maine trip was planned for two weeks ago, but had to be abandoned because of the pressure of other things. Please tell the Secretary how sorry I am not to be there to welcome him and to have the opportunity of both meeting him and going about the park with him.

I am delighted with what you told me about your visit to Williamsburg with the Secretary, and have already received a most gracious note from him in regard to the restoration work. How fortunate it is that the Secretary is so genuinely interested and sympathetic with the work in the National Parks to which you have devoted yourself so many years.

I am sorry not to be able to sign this note myself.

Very sincerely,
JOHN D. ROCKEFELLER, JR.

149

WORTHWHILE PLACES

Dear Mr. Rockefeller:

I had expected to write you this letter in my office Monday afternoon after returning from Acadia National Park. As you know, the Secretary and I flew up to Bangor and spent Sunday afternoon and night in Acadia Park. Leaving Bangor Monday morning we were due at our desks in Washington not later than three o'clock that afternoon but about 1:30 we had to land on Staten Island on account of fog and we returned to Washington by train. As the next day was a holiday and I faced a terrific accumulation of mail yesterday this has been my first opportunity to tell you of our trip.

We left Boston at six o'clock Eastern Standard time Sunday morning and flew along the coast to Rockland, thence across Vinal Haven, on to Deer Isles, to Southwest Harbor, thence over your home at Seal Harbor, the Black Woods and the Otter Cliffs, thence to the new radio station site on Schoodic Point. After circling around Schoodic Point so we could see the road work that was going on we flew to Bar Harbor and on to Bangor. We returned to Bar Harbor by automobile and Mr. Dorr had Mr. Olmsted join us for luncheon.

Afterwards the Secretary, Mr. Olmsted, Mr. Dorr and I got in an automobile together and drove to the summit of Cadillac Mountain. While the day was dark we had fine visibility. Mr. Olmsted with his maps explained both the motor and horse road systems. We also pointed out to the Secretary all the principal features of the park. Furthermore we spent some time studying the teahouse site near the summit of Cadillac. Leaving the mountain, we took the motor road to Seal Harbor, stopping for a glimpse of the gatehouse below the Jordan Pond teahouse, Mr. Ralston kindly arranged for us to enter the grounds of your home and enjoy the view from your front porch. We then drove to the Black Woods, the Otter Cliffs radio station and out to the end of the road work.

While we were walking on the road the cars went back to Bar Harbor and out to the north end of the Shore Drive improvement. We walked through the new work to the car.

We next visited the Homans' house and then made a study of the routes for the motor road, explaining fully to the Secretary the land situation as it affects the road project, - the Potter Palmer property, etc. We went on around the mountain to the Sieur de Monts Spring and to Great Meadow. We then went to Eagle Lake and out on the horse roads. We covered a considerable part of this road system, including the Amphitheatre Road. On this trip we also saw the second gatehouse. The Secretary was very much impressed with the park, the beauty of the mountain and forests and the extraordinary views of land and sea, particularly the panorama from Cadillac Mountain. He was delighted with the opportunity to learn about your road systems and was greatly pleased to have the chance to study them with Mr. Olmsted. He fully approves the plans and feels that you are undertaking a work of very great importance to the park and to the people who for generations will visit and enjoy the park. It was wonderful to get the Secretary so early in his administration to get such a very comprehensive view of Acadia's problems, and to get fully in his mind the scope of the road program.

Early Monday morning we drove back to Bangor and flew to Staten Island, as I have said, and then to Washington by train. The trip was a very happy one and one that we will long remember.

I hope there will be an opportunity for us to see you on your return from Williamsburg. I know the trip there will give you much pleasure and satisfaction. I have written Mr. Chorley my suggestion about your return through Washington by Charlottesville and Shenandoah Park.

Sincerely yours,
HORACE M. ALBRIGHT

Mr. S. F. Ralston. Superintendent of the Rockefeller properties in Maine, 1924-1943.

WORTHWHILE PLACES

Confidential:

Dear Mr. Rockefeller:

The President has approved an allotment of $1,550,000 to round out the Great Smoky Mountains National Park. In accordance with your understanding with Mr. Cammerer $500,000 of this fund will be used to match the balance of funds made available by you through the Foundation. This will complete the park of 427,000 acres originally authorized, one-half the cost of which will have been contributed by you in memory of your mother.

With the additional funds the park will be further extended and when completed will have in the neighborhood of 460,000 acres. It is possible even more land will be bought in that neighborhood for park purposes, first, because we want to keep Civilian Conservation Corps camps in operation through the winter, and, second, because now that the Government has undertaken to develop the entire Tennessee River valley the Great Smoky Mountains National Park becomes of even greater importance as a Federal project than it was in the past. You are doubtless aware of the fact that the whole Tennessee River watershed is being carefully studied by the Tennessee Valley Authority under the direction of Dr. A. E. Morgan, of Antioch College. He has appointed a planning board headed by Mr. Earle F. Draper, an outstanding architect and planner of Charlotte, North Carolina, one of my most intimate friends. Dr. Morgan and Mr. Draper regard the Great Smoky Mountains National Park as one of the most important parts of the River project, especially viewed from the standpoint of social welfare.

I do not know how far we will be able to proceed with additional purchases under the further appropriation before the change in the administration of the Service takes place on August 9. Doubtless very little can be accomplished. However, Mr. Cammerer is more familiar with conditions in the Great Smoky Mountains National Park than I am and the completion of this project will become a problem of first importance to him and one to which he will give his personal attention.

Sincerely yours,
HORACE M. ALBRIGHT

The foundation Albright refers to was the Laura Spelman Rockefeller Memorial. John D. Rockefeller established it in 1918, in memory of his wife.

August 10, 1933.

Dear Mr. Rockefeller:

My work as Director of the National Park Service ends today and I am turning over my office to Mr. Cammerer. I want to write just one more letter to you while I am still here and tell you again how grateful I am for all the interest you have taken in National Park affairs during my administration and for the enormous help that you have extended to the Service in many extremely important projects.

The privilege of enjoying your friendship and your confidence, and the inspiration of your character and ideals have meant more to me personally than I can ever express.

I expect to continue my interest in public affairs, particularly in the work of the National Park Service, and I shall always be available to assist in any enterprise in which you are interested. If at any time I can be of assistance to you, please do not hesitate to call upon me. It has been impossible for me to repay, even in small measure, my indebtedness to you for your very great contributions to the success of my administration, and I deeply regret that our Jackson Hole project which you adopted on my representations has brought you difficult problems to solve. Again I assure you that I will always be available to help carry this project through to a successful conclusion.

WORTHWHILE PLACES

With heartfelt gratitude and sentiments of highest esteem, and with all good wishes to Mrs. Rockefeller, the young folks and yourself, I am

Faithfully yours,
HORACE M. ALBRIGHT

Albright told an interviewer in 1960 that he left the government for financial reasons. He felt he was leaving a strong organization in the national park system. There was a cadre of professionals to take his place and continue the work he and Mather had started in 1916. His new employer, the United States Potash Company, was a young firm. It had offices in New York City and a mine in New Mexico. Albright had legal training and a lifelong interest in mining. The Potash Company told him they wanted him to keep active in conservation matters and promised time as well as extra help to keep this interest active. He joined the firm as vice president and general manager. The president, Henry McSweeney, was 90 years old and inactive. Albright ran the company and later became president.

October 10, 1933.

Dear Mr. Albright:

Your letter of August 19th, written as you terminated your work as Director of the National Park Service and speaking so appreciatively of these happy years of cooperative endeavor in the public interest which it has been my privilege to share in a very modest way with you, gave me the greatest pleasure. Surely, no man knows better than you the abiding satisfaction that comes from worth-while service well rendered. The spirit of unselfish devotion to high ideals of service which has characterized your public life ever since I first knew you is an inspiration to all who have had the privilege of being associated with you.

154

As I look back over this period which is now ending for you, the things that have been accomplished, so largely through your efforts, seem almost unbelievable. While relatively few people will know that it is you who have been chiefly responsible for the development of the national parks, there are hundreds and thousands, yes, millions of people whose lives have been made happier, richer, better because of you, their unknown friend, have opened to them nature's treasure store of beauty. This you have done at the sacrifice of your own advancement, ease, comfort, even health, and other personal considerations.

It gives me the greatest satisfaction thus to review your public service and to speak this word of gratitude, admiration and friendship. And now that you have turned to a new field of endeavor, I hope you may have the opportunity of realizing your desires and dreams for yourself and your family to a degree that has not heretofore been possible. I am glad that you are to be in and about New York, and shall look forward to seeing you from time to time. But whether we meet often or not, please know that I shall always retain for you the highest esteem and warmest friendship.

Did they know I am writing you, I am sure Mrs. Rockefeller and all the boys would want to join me in these expressions of regard, and in extending to you, Mrs. Albright and your young people their best wishes.

> Always truly your friend,
> JOHN D. ROCKEFELLER, JR.

October 28, 1933.

My dear Mr. Rockefeller:

I can never find adequate words to express my appreciation of the letter you so kindly wrote to me in reference to my retirement from the National Park Service.

WORTHWHILE PLACES

It was generous of you to place such a high value on the achievements of my administration and my part in building this record. What you have said about my work gives me the greatest happiness, yet I realize and will never forget that, in the four years and seven months of my service as director, I constantly received the aid of an extremely capable and faithful corps of assistants within our organization, and that, in nearly all our great projects of really permanent value to the Nation, I had your interest cooperation and very generous financial support, without which I could not have gone far toward the attainment of my ideals and ambitions for the advancement of the National Park Service.

The Colonial Historical Park, the great Yosemite sugar pine forest preservation project, the educational program of the Service with its museums, the purchase of lands at George Washington's Birthplace, the Acadia road plan and Mr. Atterbury's studies there, the Jackson Hole-Grand Teton project, the Yellowstone roadsides improvement which brought new national standards in road-building specifications, and finally the establishment of Shenandoah and Great Smoky Mountains National Parks, all were outstanding achievements of my administration, and all I owe, directly or indirectly through the Foundation, to you.

I can never repay you even in a very small way for your magnificent support and for your words of encouragement and advice, nor for your recent letter referring so thoughtfully and kindly to my work, but I am keeping in close touch with Colonel Woods and his staff, and I am ready always to devote time and effort to assisting in the completion of your national park projects that are still unfinished.

I shall give special attention to the Jackson Hole-Grand Teton problem at all times.

Mrs. Albright joins me all good wishes to Mrs. Rockefeller, the boys and yourself, and in thanks to you for your letter which means so much to us.

Faithfully yours,
HORACE M. ALBRIGHT

PART II
1934 – 1943

Acadia National Park, Colonial Historical National Park, Indian Pueblos, Jackson Hole National Monument, Public Highways Beautification.

WORTHWHILE PLACES

August 18, 1934.

Dear Mr. Albright:

Thank you for your letter of August 10th. Mr. Chorley gave me your message about your visit to Acadia National Park. I am so sorry that we are not in Maine this summer when you are there. This is the first summer in twenty-five years we have not been in Seal Harbor.

You kindly offer to take up any matters in the park that I might suggest as needing attention. I am glad to take you at your word and suggest the following as subjects which you may find it possible to consider with Mr. Dorr or others on the ground, without its being known that I have mentioned the matters:

1. Mr. Chorley told me you thought it not impossible that the Government could build some portion at least of the approved automobile road. This I suppose could not be done unless the Government owned all of the land which the road traverses. If funds were available and the ownership of the land is the only obstacle, it would be perfectly possible for me to give the land involved to the Government forthwith. Certainly this could be done with some sections, reserving the right to me to build within a given period of years the horse roads already approved by the Government that traverse such lands, in spite of the fact that the lands might have passed from me to the Government. Were this possible, I would suggest to begin with the construction of the link of the automobile road from the Eagle Lake end of the present road to the Sieur de Monts Spring. If this were done, the Ocean Drive now having been finished on the sea side of Newport Mountain range, there would remain only the connecting link between the Sieur de Monts Springs and the Ocean Drive at Mr. Satterlee's sand beach.

As you know, there has been discussion as to whether the road should go south through the gorge and over the mountain near the Beehive, which route the Government has approved, although it was bitterly opposed by some of the summer people, or whether it should go around the north end of Newport Mountain, which is from every point of view the better route. This latter route was favored by Mr. Olmsted from the outset. He agreed to the other only because at that time we thought that the property holdings on the northern route would make its consideration a waste of time. Since then we have found that there are only two, possibly three property owners on this route, namely: The Livingstone place, only a corner of which would be traversed by the road; the land adjacent, owned by the Potter Palmers, which they have flatly refused to sell for the park road; and the land adjacent to the Potter Palmer's property, which I bought from Mr. Richard Hale under an agreement not to build a road through it for twenty years. If the other two property owners could be handled, I think Mr. Hale could be influenced to alter his condition.

Mr. Hill, my engineer in Bar Harbor, is fully familiar with all the details of these two routes. Mr. Lynam knows about the steps that have been taken to try to get the northern route adopted. Mr. Dorr is less fully informed on either of these points. You could talk freely with both Mr. Lynam and Mr. Hill if you so desired. That there is anything you can do about this situation, I doubt.

2. I have finished the Ocean Drive. Mr. Dorr is building a path parallel to it and between it and the ocean. Paths from this path to the rocks in various places have been agreed upon. His men are doing good work. I hope they can be encouraged to continue it and to complete this path construction, also the planting, grading and forestry work which should be done in this entire area in connection with the paths and the parking spaces on the Ocean Drive. I have written Mr. Dorr a letter to this effect.

3. You will recall that I gave to the park a year or two ago the Brown Mountain Lodge house and the property adjacent thereto. One of the landscape men now directing the C.C.C. work is, by arrangement with the park, living in the house. When he moved in Mr. Dorr said one advantage of his residence would be that he would do further planting around the lodge and get the place in good shape. Mrs. Farrand has done the planting there for me to date, and I think has done it well. I am not myself concerned whether more planting is done here or not, but I do think the park

should keep the place up if possible. The present occupant asked Mr. Ralston if he would mow the grass for him this summer, which Mr. Ralston agreed to do. In other words, neither the park nor the occupant of the house seems to be doing anything to maintain the premises.

This is a little matter and of no particular consequence, but with the facts above set forth in mind you may hear something in your talks with Mr. Dorr that bears on the subject.

These are the only matters which occur to me. None of them need take your time and thought other than incidentally and as you are going about. If it does not prove easy and convenient to consider any of them, I will entirely understand.

Very sincerely,
JOHN D. ROCKEFELLER, JR.

Mr. and Mrs. Potter Palmer. Bar Harbor summer residents. They objected to the building of roads across their land.

Mr. Richard Hale. Bar Harbor summer resident. He also objected to roads being built across his land.

June 26, 1935

Dear Mr. Rockefeller:

While I was in Washington last week I had a very interesting talk with Secretary Ickes about Acadia problems. He asked me to assure you that he was going to construct just as many sections of the motor road as he can possibly get funds to undertake. He agrees that the signed map should be sent to you together with any clarification of the acceptance of your proposal that the situation requires. The National Park Service has arranged to have a new map prepared based on the map you submitted together with information subsequently submitted in letters written since your return from Europe. This map will be brought to New York in early July, probably within the next two weeks by Mr. T. C. Vint, Chief Landscape Architect, who will review it with me. I think, it would be fine if we could have an interview with you in order that you may also check it before it goes back to Washington to be placed in final form for the signatures of the Secretary and the Director.

So much for your land and road problem.

The Radio Station legislation is now in pretty good shape, and almost certain to pass both Houses very soon. In fact it should pass the Lower House today. Secretary Ickes asked me to see his legislative representative, Mr. Poole, which I did. Mr. Poole has this bill on the "must" list for this session of Congress.

I hope you have fully recovered from your cold. These summer colds are always hard to shake off. I am terribly sorry about Mr. Chorley.

Faithfully yours.
HORACE M. ALBRIGHT

May 14, 1936

Dear Mr. Albright:

You will recall that when you and Mr. Cammerer met in my office some months ago to discuss Acadia Park matters, we felt it was necessary to have a legal opinion as to the rights of fishermen on the Otter Creek Inlet waters, their rights to reach the water over private land and the right of the Government to build the causeway over navigable state waters. I have only recently gotten from Mr. Rodick his opinion on these two matters and am sending you herewith his letters of May 5th and 6th with the opinion which accompanied the latter. His judgment as to the Government's right to build the causeway is rather upsetting.

WORTHWHILE PLACES

It occurred to me that you would want to study these papers rather carefully and that it would be well if you and I could discuss them with Mr. Debevoise at an early date. Next Wednesday would be my first opportunity. Perhaps you will arrange with Miss Warfield as to what hour during the day would be convenient for you.

In the meantime, as I have been studying this whole situation, it has seemed to me that the simplest thing to do with reference to boats and fishing on the Inlet would be to have a permanent underpass road to the shore of the Inlet, which would permit the public to get to the shore without crossing the Park motor road. I remembered that there now exists what was formerly a public road to the shore just north of the Radio Station property. This road was abandoned at our instance several years ago. I have had the matter studied on the ground and believe that such an underpass road is entirely possible. For your information I am sending herewith a letter from Mr. Ralston, also a letter from Mr. Hill on this subject, together with a blue print that illustrates the situation. Perhaps we could also discuss this matter when we meet next week. Will you be good enough to bring back all this material at this time?

Very sincerely,
JOHN D. ROCKEFELLER, JR.

November 13, 1936

Dear Mr. Rockefeller:

Last Sunday in one of the New York papers there was a discussion of road building, road-side improvement, etc. Among other things it was stated that during the year 1936 approximately $7,000,000 will be expended in road-side beautification and other improvements. Whether or not you saw this article I know you must feel considerable gratification that the work you began in

Yellowstone National Park in 1924 has led to national recognition of the importance of protecting and beautifying the road-sides whereas at the time you undertook the Yellowstone experiment Congress and Legislatures regarded the whole idea as mere embroidery that could never be afforded.

Next I bring to your attention a mimeographed statement by Associate Director of the National Park Service in regard to parkways. It was to carry out this program that Congress authorized $10,000,000 per year for two years, and it is from these appropriations that we wish to secure funds for continuation and completion of the Colonial Parkway.

Now let me say that I have very encouraging advices from Mr. F. A. Delano that the National Park Service will be given the kind of protection we discussed when I was in your office the last time.

Finally, of course you saw that Senator Carey was defeated in Wyoming. His successor, Hon. H. H. Schwartz, is a man of broad sympathies toward public projects and has a deep understanding of problems of the public domain. At one time he was in the Department of the Interior. It would seem that Mr. Carey's defeat by Mr. Schwartz is distinctly favorable to early consummation of our Jackson Hole project.

Sincerely yours,
HORACE M. ALBRIGHT

Frederic A. Delano. Uncle of Franklin D. Roosevelt. Businessman, member and president of the National Capital Park and Planning Commission.

September 16, 1937

Dear Mr. Albright:

Your letters of the 8th and 10th were most welcome. How fortunate that you should have seen Mr. Cammerer just after receiving my several letters about Acadia Park matters and thus have been able to discuss them with him. I have within the last day or two received a preliminary letter from Mr. Cammerer confirming what you say and telling me that he will write further after an early conference with Mr. Vint.

As to progress here on right of way, we have been less fortunate during the last week. For your information I am enclosing a copy of the letter I wrote Mr. Potter Palmer and of his reply. With Mr. Palmer's temperament and type of mind, any attempt at explanation or argument would seem to be hopeless and, much as I regret it, condemnation seems the only way out.

I spent a couple of hours with Mr. Dorr the other day, told him of the Dane situation and of my letter to Mr. Palmer. I had not then received Mr. Palmer's reply. I asked Mr. Dorr how he wanted to handle the properties to the northwest of Newport Mountain through which the road would need to pass, one or two of them being owned by the Wild Gardens of Acadia and, at least the piece above the quarry, by him. I thought he might say whether he would sell the property needed or give it to the Park or whether he was only willing to part with a right of way. I could not get him to discuss the matter at all. He said he would have to think the whole thing out very carefully as a single proposition and that that would take time. He did consent, however, to my having his engineer make an accurate plan showing the exact boundary lines of these several properties and locating exactly the proposed line of the Motor Road. This is being done. It will form the basis for further discussion and will enable me to reopen the question with Mr. Dorr, although now that Mr. Palmer has refused to cooperate, Mr. Dorr will probably want to let the matter lie until Mr. Palmer's land is acquired.

I have gone with Mr. Grossman over the line of the road on the east side of Newport Mountain from the Satterlee sand beach and am in entire agreement with the proposed line close to the mountain, which I find all the engineers favor. This will be worked up and completed this fall, as also the line on the west side around to the little pool where muck was being taken out with a steam shovel.

Mr. Grossman's engineers are working on the Dane underpass problem and will have a solution within a few days. Mr. Candage, who owns the quarry that had a right of way over the Jordan Pond Road and my land, is most cooperative and is willing either to part with his quarry on very reasonable terms or to definitely contract now to do so within three or five years, in which event I should think the Park would not be unwilling to have him get what little access to the quarry he requires over the Park Road, thus avoiding the necessity of a new entrance for him and a right of way therefor over Mr. Dane's land.

I did not think it wise at any time to take up the Williamsburg underpass with the Secretary. On several occasions I mentioned Williamsburg purposely and certain things there in order to give him an opportunity to raise the underpass question but, since he did not do so, felt it unwise to myself bring up the issue.

I think the Secretary was genuinely appreciative of the courtesy shown him by Mrs. Rockefeller and me. I think he really enjoyed our two horse drives, on each of which we were together for two hours or more and, naturally, in a very informal, friendly way and I think he is most anxious to push forward the completion of the Motor Road in Acadia Park. I discussed on several occasions the delay in accepting the Black Woods deeds and pointed out that bids could not be sought until that legal formality had been taken care of. He communicated with his Washington office the following day and asked for a report on the situation immediately on his return. I even suggested to him that I would be glad to spend two or three thousand dollars in paying the salary for a few months of a special attorney who could give all his time to clearing these deeds in the Department if that would be acceptable to him and would facilitate matters. This suggestion he received with complacency, did not seem at all to object to it and said he would look into the matter and let me know. He was very pleased with Mr. Dane's cooperation, hoped Mr. Palmer would also come along but on several occasions spoke with finality as to his readiness to condemn and was going to look up just what powers the Federal Government had.

Very sincerely,
JOHN D. ROCKEFELLER, JR.

Mr. Ernest B. Dane. A summer resident on Mt. Desert. Owned Wildwood Farm.

Mr. Leo Grossman. National Park Service road engineer.

June 27, 1938

Dear Mr. Rockefeller:

Land problems

I have just returned from a trip to Acadia National Park. I spent Saturday and Sunday there. This report is being hastily dictated, and perhaps will not be as orderly and as coherent as it should be. However, it will include in it all of the important matters that I discussed while down there.

In the first place, let me say that I found Superintendent George B. Dorr in poor health. He is almost totally blind. It is a mystery how he manages to get around his house, and up and down stairs as well as he does. He is growing thinner. He has angina pectoris, and the presence of this coronary trouble was confirmed recently by a Boston heart specialist. It is causing him some discomfort and at night rather serious sweating, which breaks up his sleep. His associates believe him to be in rather serious state, and I think he himself regards his own condition as quite hopeless. Two or three times he told me that he would not be here long, and might go at any moment. Another time he humorously referred to having his valise packed.

He has his affairs in good shape; that is they are in as good shape as it is possible to put them when all his property is covered by a $46,000 mortgage. I gathered from my discussions with Mr. Dorr Saturday night, which ran well toward 2 a.m. Sunday, that his income, except his salary of $3,000., had been cut off through the total loss of securities in New England industries such as the Amoskeag mills, and others, the securities of which years ago were gilt edge. In other words, he must have lost that part of his inheritance which was represented by stocks and bonds.

In building up the park and carrying on his various activities perhaps including the nurseries, he got heavily in debt. Your purchase of 123.2 acres of the Great Meadow and adjacent territory for $100,000 must have enabled Mr. Dorr to greatly reduce his indebtedness but it is probably true that he used some of that money to buy other lands for the park.

When the Park Service undertook the recreational demonstration project in the western part of the Island it bought some 5,000 acres of land, and included a number of tracts that Mr. Dorr had. From the sale of these tracts Mr. Dorr realized a little over $20,000., over $17,000. of which was applied on mortgages held by the local bank. The remainder went into clearing titles of other lands, which the Government was acquiring, the money being spent on the Government's behalf since its funds could not be used for title clearing. In other words, Mr. Dorr made further sacrifices out of his own funds to facilitate land acquisition in the western part of the Island.

He now has about 206 acres of land including Oldfarm, the nurseries, the quarry tract, the Bear Brook Pond tract, etc., and they are all pledged to the bank to secure outstanding mortgages totalling about $46,000. It is perfectly clear, therefore, that Mr. Dorr cannot under any circumstances donate the lands that are necessary for the continuation of the motor road around Champlain Mountain. It is probable that in these times of depression the whole of his property if sold would not realize $50,000. There is no possibility of selling the big old summer mansion Oldfarm. The little house he lives in is not valuable. Of course, he has a good many antiques, book, etc. but even to suggest selling these would be a death blow to the old gentleman.

WORTHWHILE PLACES

His land holdings are roughly divided as follows:

76 acres in the Oldfarm and adjacent land excluding the
   nurseries, 22 acres - nurseries,
9 acres - the Bear Brook Pond tract,
7 acres - the quarry tract.

Then he has 25 acres in the gorge beyond the tarn. On
the western part of the Island he has about 89 acres lying between
Echo Lake and Great Pond. The tracts on Great Pond are
right at the southern and most valuable end of that body of
water. He has control of the situation there. He also has a
few lots on Strawberry Hill. It is probable that there are some
other small miscellaneous lots but I have listed most of his
holdings.

It has been Mr. Dorr's ambition all these years to donate
the Bear Brook Pond tract and the quarry tract, and I feel
that whatever is done about clearing up the mortgages some
way should be found to make it possible for the old gentleman
to donate these tracts. Roughly his holdings should be divided
in, four parts.

The first should include all of the lands south of Oldfarm,
part of the nursery lands, the gorge tract, and the tracts on
the western side of the Island, which should be purchased for
say $50,000 or at least enough to liquidate the mortgage.

The second group would include the Bear Brook Pond
and the quarry tracts, which would be freed from the mortgage
so that Mr. Dorr could donate them to the Government for
the right-of-way of the road.

The third group should be enough land to continue the
nursery, which would be operated if possible at a profit to the
Dorr Foundation but which would always be handled as
exhibition gardens. Mr. Dorr hopes that here may be carried
on his plans for the Acadia Wild Gardens.

The fourth tract would simply include the water front of
Oldfarm, the gardens of the old houses, the houses themselves
with their furnishings. These would continue in the ownership
of the George B. Dorr Foundation, which has already been
established, and which will be operated by a Board of Trustees,

two of whom are to be Serenus Rodick and Ben Hadley. I did not ask the names of the other trustees.

It seems clear that Mr. Dorr has made arrangements for the disposition of everything he has upon his death, and that everything goes to the public, assuming of course, that some way can be found to liquidate the mortgages. Should that not be possible everything will have to be sold to satisfy the bank. The George B. Dorr Foundation will administer Oldfarm, the homes, antiques, books, fine glassware, and other heirlooms, which Mr. Dorr has. The income, if any, will be used to print a history of the park, and other essays and papers that he has prepared. Apparently he has been working on them during the winter for several years. These statements have been well prepared and are very interesting. I put in a number of hours reviewing them, of course, reading only here and there in voluminous manuscripts. It is doubtful, of course, whether there will be enough income from the Foundation to carry out Mr. Dorr's wishes but I am quite sure that the Foundation has authority to sell property necessary in order to do certain things.

Next Mr. Dorr wishes the nurseries to be operated, if possible, for the benefit of the Foundation but open to public inspection, and he hopes that attention will be given to carrying out the Wild Gardens idea. The nursery lands, of course, would be greatly limited because of the necessity for selling as much land as possible in order to liquidate the indebtedness hanging over all the property.

Next Mr. Dorr would give the Quarry and Bear Brook Pond tracts, thus completing his gifts to the park. Finally but really the first thing to be done is the sale to the Government, if possible, of the other lands about Oldfarm, in the gorge, and between Echo Lake and Great Pond. I am taking up the question of the sale of these lands in Washington, and hope that there is still money available which might be matched with outside funds under the old authority granted to the Park Service in 1929 and 1930. If that authority is still available the fund of $23,000 or $25,000 to be matched dollar per dollar by the Government would clear up this situation and at once free the lands for the right-of-way.

The only further question that arises is whether Government appraisers would agree on a value for the lands back of Oldfarm, in the gorge and between Echo Lake and Great Pond that would justify a total expenditure of $50,000. I am afraid that the per acre cost would be regarded as too high. There might be added to the land to be sold the quarry itself, leaving only the lands above the quarry to be donated by Mr. Dorr. It seems that the quarry is an exceptionally fine one, has superior granite, and of course, it is easily accessible. As a quarry it may have considerable value. To regard those rocks as quarry rocks is like thinking of board feet in a noble sugar pine. When I once remarked that a sugar pine contained 25,000 board feet Secretary Wilbur said it sounded as bad as if I spoke in war times of the amount of lard in a German soldier. Nevertheless, it may be necessary to have the quarry tract sold although I had hoped that this might be avoided so that Mr. Dorr's donation ambition might be carried out.

I am afraid I have taken too much space to explain the land situation but I hope I have made it clear. I have asked Messrs. Hadley and Rodick to prepare a map, showing these various tracts in different colors, and told them if they did not hear from me in the next week to see that you got a copy of this map when you arrived in Seal Harbor.

Mr. Dorr's health and the necessity for getting the road project on its way require quick and positive action. I do not know whether you would want to consider taking control of the situation by buying the mortgages, leaving it to us to work out next fall some kind of a basis for Government participation in this acquisition with you or with you and others working together; or whether you would prefer to let the whole matter stand until I can get back from Europe the latter part of August. The great danger in delay is, of course, that Mr. Dorr may not live until the end of the summer.

Road Problems

I inspected all the roads in the Park except the horse roads. I never saw the roadside more beautiful. The wild flowers were blooming in abundance everywhere. The Kebo Valley road is completed except for the bridge, which will be finished next month. This is an exquisitely beautiful section of the highway. The town's people and summer people have been using each end the road to the bridge, and apparently for the first time they have come to fully realize what the motor road means in giving access to the beauties of the park and the beautiful views from it without encountering village streets, telephone lines, etc. I went over the improved surveyed lines of the extension of this road to the quarry. I believe that the engineers have at last solved all the problems.

I wonder how you still feel about the horse road in the Kebo Valley. If you are still certain that it ought to be built would you want to consider letting the Park Service undertake all or part of its construction, possibly in connection with the clearing up of this land problem, continuing the application of the theory that it would be best for you to round out the park lands while the Park Service rounds out the road improvements. I have not refreshed my memory with the correspondence with Secretary Ickes about the taking over of road building by the Government, and I cannot recall what commitment you made in reference to the continuation of the horse road system. There would seem to be several good grounds on which the Government might build this one section of the horse road. In the first place, it would tie the system into headquarters, and in the second place the Hemlock Road is already available for inclusion in the horse road line. In the third place, it would be a public demonstration of the Department's strong interest in recreation of horseback riding and horse driving. I realize this suggestion may not be of any value, and is simply placed in this report for any consideration that you think it deserves. Of course, it is possible that the Department would not consider building any horse roads at all. There are two underpasses for the horse roads that should be built when the extension of the Kebo Mountain road to and around Champlain Mountain is undertaken.

The Day Mountain Connection to Jordan Pond Road

Sunday morning I met Mr. Simpson and with him and Mr. Hadley I walked over the line for the temporary connection along the north end of the Candage property. I found the line extraordinarily good. The brook is in a deeper gorge than I expected to find but it turns eastward along the Candage line inside the Candage property so that there is practically no likelihood of Candage disturbing what must be the northeastern corner of his property. It is only a short distance from the brook to the Jordan Pond road, and the timber and brush is very thick along the line, so keeping back 25 ft. will give ample protection to the new road. As a matter of fact, the engineers plan to build about a 24 ft. road, which is ample, on the northern part of the 65 ft. strip, that is 40 ft. road right-of-way plus the 25 ft. protective strip. Assuming a 24 ft. road is to be built, therefore, there would be a protective strip of 41 ft. The connection into the Jordan Pond road is going to be quite satisfactory.

I discussed standards with Mr. Grossman, and he said he thought it would be best to use a wooden trestle over the little gorge, first in order to avoid excavation, second in order to avoid a fill which might later have to be removed, and third, in order to keep the new line more frankly temporary. Finally to keep the cost as low as possible. I agreed with all these points.

Mr. Simpson showed me where the new Dane approach project underpass would be built. It occured to me there on the ground that you ought to push this new approach road to the Wildwood Farm as fast as possible, making it available for Mr. Dane before he leaves in the autumn. By that time the new park road would not yet have reached the underpass, and it might be that he would see how utterly foolish it will be to have two entrances to the Wildwood Farm road, and would not object to the connection with the Jordan Pond road along the permanent line. This is simply a suggestion for you to give such consideration as it merits. I predict that Mr. Dane is going to be tremendously pleased with the approach road that you are going to build for him.

Unfortunately the Bureau of Public Roads has been short of engineers, and has not made satisfactory progress in getting ready for the extension of the motor road to the Day Mountain pass including the underpasses. It looks now as if it will be August or September before contract for this section can be let. I am again writing to Washington urging that Mr. Grossman be given sufficient help to drive this project through. I should tell you that last winter Mr. Grossman took topography on the Camplain Mountain road and ran a line across the Potter Palmer and Livingston properties. That whole road project now clear around to a connection with the ocean drive is in such shape that it can be made ready for contract very quickly once the right-of-way problems are solved.

Mary Roberts Rinehart.

The famous writer, Mrs. Rinehart, who lives in the late Dr. Abbe's house now owned by Atwater Kent, invited me to luncheon with her yesterday. She has been ill and is just now beginning to see people. She has bought the Phillip Livingston place and will move into it this fall. She is tremendously enthusiastic over everything that has been done in the way of road and trail building.

She knows the National Park System through many visits in the West. She has ridden horseback in Glacier and Yellowstone Parks. She and her boys are enthusiastic riders. She says her sons and their families have used your horse roads and think they are the finest they have ever seen. She wants to be helpful in carrying out your projects, and those of Mr. Dorr. I told her about the Atwater Kent Meadow, and its importance to the Park. She believes that she can be very helpful in working out this problem. She says Atwater Kent is having trouble with his wife and is pretty "low" now. She seemed to think that if something could happen that would give him a little favorable publicity it would be a good thing for him. I told her a gift of this property or assistance on his part in arranging for its transfer to the Park would get him some magnificent publicity. I told her, however, not to do anything about this until she heard from you.

I would strongly suggest that when you return, Mrs. Rockefeller and you meet Mrs. Rinehart. I feel that you can talk freely with her about all your hopes and plans for Acadia. She has the greatest admiration for you and your works.

She says that Potter Palmer is an uncertain person but that his wife is a lovely woman and thinks that if we want to get anything out of Palmer we should work through her. I did not discuss the details of the Palmer problem. I merely said there was something for him to do in connection with carrying out the park plans. Mr. Dorr says that Potter Palmer is entirely under the influence of a man named Charles Pike, who has always been a trouble maker. Pike lives near Palmer. It is rumored that Pike has cancer and cannot live. Arthur Train told Mr. Dorr this a few days ago, and also said that Palmer will object to the road as long as Pike does. Mr. Dorr's final words were "Pike is a pig-headed fellow. He married a daughter of R. A. Alger, former Secretary of War, and she has not been any help". I do not know whether this gossip is of any importance or not but it may offer some leads which can be followed up.

This has been a very long report, and I regret that I have had to go into so many details. There are many other things that I picked up that would be worth passing on to you but I do not feel that I should trouble you with them while you are on vacation. Perhaps when I am on the ship next week I will have an opportunity to write them out for you to peruse before you go to Acadia.

Laurance was on the train with his wife and baby going down to Bar Harbor. He has a lovely family.

I have a note from Secretary Ickes in which he says that he had the pleasure of meeting Mrs. Rockefeller and you in Europe.

We finally got the Colonial Historical Park Bill through both Houses, and it has been signed by the President.

With all good wishes, I am

Faithfully yours,
HORACE M. ALBRIGHT

Mary Roberts Rinehart. Author. Supporter of the National Park Service. Wrote a book on her travels through Glacier National Park.

Atwater Kent. Inventor. Manufacturer of radios.

Charles B. Pike. Seal Harbor resident. Opposed Newport road.

Arthur C. Train. Opposed motor roads in park. Conservation activist.

July 12th 38

Dear Mr. Albright:

Your letters of June 27, 28 and July 1 have been received. How I wish we could talk over the matters of which you wrote. But since that is impossible I will give you as briefly as I can my reaction to the several questions that need early consideration.

1. While it is none of my business I cannot see that any useful purpose would be served by the establishment of the George B. Dorr Foundation. The same to own Mr. Dorr's houses and their contents, all to be operated for the interest of the public. Everyone who knows Mr. Dorr loves him. When he is gone the houses in which he lives will have value only in proportion to their intrinsic merit and not because they were once owned by Mr. Dorr. It would therefore seem to me, although you may think it heartless for me to say so, that the public interest would best be served in the long run were the homes and possessions of Mr. Dorr to be sold.

2. What I have said in "1" applies equally to any effort to perpetuate the nurseries. There again I feel no worth while public service will be rendered.

3. In view of the above I should feel, from a cold blooded point of view, that ultimately it would be in the interest of the public not to retain any foundation for exhibition purposes the Dorr houses, their contents, the surrounding lands and the nurseries, but rather that they should be sold, the monies derived therefrom after paying the debts of the estate to be used for thē other purpose of the Dorr Foundation, which as I understand it has to do with the development and upkeep of the Wild Gardens of Acadia.

4. As to the Wild Gardens of Acadia, their perpetuation and development from any other point of view than merely

dded to the park, seem to me of no great value,
me time of far greater value than the retention
tion of the houses and nurseries in the Foundation.
ng the views above expressed, my feeling is that the
that are of interest to the Park are the following:

he Bear Brook Pond Tract
the Quarry Tract
. the 25 acres in the Gorge beyond the Tarn
d. the 89 acres between Echo Lake and the Great Pond
e. Possibly the lots on Strawberry Hill.

Of this group, the most important pieces of properties
are the Bear Brook Pond Tract and the Quarry Tract. These,
or portions of them, are essential to the motor road around
the north end of the mountain. To acquire these two tracts
I would be willing to make any reasonable contribution. For
many years I have worked closely with Mr. Dorr, done
everything I could to further his projects, and at times found
him difficult and not as cooperative as I have tried to be. I
love him dearly, as you do, and have the greatest admiration
for and appreciation of what he has done for the Park. I would
not be interested to consider paying off the mortgage. I would
be interested to finance the purchase of the two tracts so
immediately necessary if they could be taken out from under
the mortgage and given to the Park. Let me speak of this specific
question. Unless these two tracts were sold at auction, they
would presumably have to be sold at their present appraised
value. Since the Quarry Tract adjoins the Potter Palm Tract,
which in turns adjoins the Attwater Kent Tract, it is important
that the value put upon it should be the value at which the
two adjoining tracts could properly be acquired when available.
If, for the sake of helping Mr. Dorr, any higher price than
its present appraised value were paid for Quarry Tract, it would
obviously work against the purchase of the two adjoining,
privately held, tracts. The same considerations are true to a
degree regarding the value of the Bear Brook Pond Tract which,
while not contiguous, is in the same general area. There are
in these two tracts of Mr. Dorr's 9 and 7 acres respectively,

a total of 16 acres. I should think these lands were worth $100 an acre, that is what I thought the Potter Palmer Tract was worth. One might justify $200 an acre, but that would double the price of the Potter Palmer Tract, unless because it lies on a steep mountain side, it might be thought less valuable. But even at $200 an acre for these 16 acres, the total price would be $3200. It is possible one could add something as the value of the Quarry, but again the whole question is whether anyone wants to develop a quarry. Even if one were to say arbitrarily that the quarry added $2000 to the value of the acreage, that would bring the total price only to $5200. Frankly, this would seem to me a very full price for the property today. However, I would be willing to pay this much for it if the bank would sell on that basis and would release the property from under the mortgage, and if Mr. Dorr would agree to deed it immediately to the Park. There would certainly be no harm in taking up with the bank a proposition of this kind, not stating the value I put on the property, but seeing whether they would be willing to sell it out from under the mortgage at its present appraised value. If it would help in bringing about that result I would be willing to consider the further purchase of the 25 acres in the Gorge and the 89 acres between Echo Lake and Great Pond on some similar basis of value, with the understanding that they also would be deeded immediately to the Park. This would leave the houses, their contents and the nurseries as security for what would remain of the bank loan. If this whole situation were explained to the bank and if the bank felt that the properties left under the mortgage could ultimately be sold for enough money to liquidate the mortgage, they might be willing to go forward with the matter. But knowing Mr. Dorr's state of mind so much better than I do, you may feel that any such proposal as the above would never be considered for a moment by him. If so then, so far as I am concerned I see nothing to do but let the situation develop as it will.

Perhaps if this letter reaches you in time you will write me your views before I sail. We shall be here at the Crillon in Paris until the morning of July 20th. We sail from Gherbourg on the Europa. In any event, unless you write me to the contrary

177

WORTHWHILE PLACES

I will talk over the situation with Mr. Rodick when I reach Maine early in August and have before me the map of Mr. Dorr's properties, a copy of which you say he and Mr. Hadley are sending me.

As to the other matters which you mention, all so interesting, let me comment briefly. I am delighted that the Kebo Valley motor road is so well received and that the survey for its continuation to the Quarry meets so fully with your approval.

As to the proposed horse road in the Kebo Valley section, I shall have to refresh my memory by referring to my agreement with the Government. I had hardly supposed that the Government would want to build horse roads. Under present financial conditions I doubt if I should want myself to spend the money involved in their construction. If the under-passes could be constructed at this time without great cost, my disposition would be to do nothing now about the construction of the horse roads themselves. I will go into this subject further when I get home and write you again.

I note with interest what you say about the Jordan Pond road outlet to the motor road through Mr. Dane's property. This sounds good. I will take up at once the question of the early construction of the new entrance to Mr. Dane's place, in line with your suggestion.

What you tell me about Mrs. Rinehart is interesting and significant. Mrs. Rockefeller and I will make it our business to meet her at the earliest opportunity.

I am immensely pleased that the Colonial Historical Park bill has not only been passed by both Houses, but signed by the President. I suppose this means that construction of the road will be promptly entered upon. When do you expect to get back home? I hope your stay on this side will be pleasant and restful.

My cordial remembrances to Mrs. Albright and yourself, and hoping for some word from you before I leave Paris,
I am,

Very sincerely
JOHN D. ROCKEFELLER, JR.

178

My dear Mr. Rockefeller:

Although I have thought a great deal about the Acadia land problem for a month, - I still have formed no suggestions for you to consider. Unless the situation is changing this summer I see no early solution along any line that does not recognize for the present at least some kind of Dorr Fund which will give some promise, however vague, that his personal property-homes, books, etc will not be dissipated or rather sold and dispersed.

I wish that in 1934 I had pressed him for details of his financial situation. I naturally felt that with the receipts of the sales to you he had cleared up his indebtedness to the banks.

I can make no further comment on your review of the general Dorr plan. Your arguments are unanswerable. Just the same I can not convince myself that we could accomplish anything by proceeding in the way you have outlined. I am afraid the old gentleman wild just decide to wait.

I realize I am not being helpful in the least degree. As soon as I return, I will find out what has been done or can be done in Washington, and if you approve perhaps write Mr. Dorr that in my opinion his program will have to be modified rather drastically.

With every best wish,

Faithfully yours,
HORACE M. ALBRIGHT

September 16, 1938

Dear Mr. Albright:

I have at length secured from Mr. Rodick and Mr. Hale a plan showing the ownerships of property involved at the north end in connection with the around the mountain road. From

179

this plan it becomes clear that if it were possible to secure the Dorr quarry lot which, bounded on the west by Y-Z, the purple line, contains under four acres and to get from Mr. Dorr a right of way over the red line from C to D, also over the purple line from D, to F, not only would the construction of the road around the north end be possible but the road leading to it and the temporary purple road D-F would also be made available, the former permanently, the latter temporarily.

In discussing this plan Mr. Hadley points out that the entire Tract B, which contains 26 acres, really ought to go to the park ultimately. With this I agree although the small piece to the west of the red line C-D would not be necessary except a margin along the red line for protection. Aside from the quarry lot no further portion of the second Dorr lot, marked Q and containing 22 acres, would be required for the around the mountain road. Mr. Hadley feels strongly, however, that the whole area should go to the park.

A compromise measure would be that all of the Dorr owned property east of the dotted line H-F might be acquired by the park the balance to the west not being included. At the moment, however, whichever one of these alternates might finally be best is more or less of an academic question. The question is, will Mr. Dorr, on the basis of such a letter as I suggested your writing him when I wrote you on August 31st, be willing to even consider the proposal therein outlined? If so, we could then take up the question of how much land he would be willing to part with and how much at its to be appraised value I would be willing to provide the money for in order that the property might be purchased from under the mortgage if the bank could be induced to cooperate in such a plan. Mr. Rodick knows of no reason from his point of view why such a letter from you to Mr. Dorr as I outlined might not be sent. He frankly feels, however, that there is little probability of Mr. Dorr being willing to even consider any proposal at this time. If that were the outcome, it would be the worst that could happen. You will know whether in view of your relation with Mr. Dorr it would be unwise for you to make him any such proposal. This is my best thought on the subject and in presenting it, I urge nothing although, naturally, I find it difficult not to be a bit irritated to think that with all Mr. Dorr's assurances about this property, now that we really want it, he, the superintendent of the park, is holding up the project.

We are staying on here for two weeks and shall be in New York a few days thereafter.

Very sincerely,
JOHN D. ROCKEFELLER, JR.

P. S. Since dictating the above I have received your letter of September 14th and note that after seeing Mr. Cammerer you have in mind to write Mr. Dorr perhaps sometime next week.

I am interested in what you say about the Jackson Hole situation, also in your friendly comment about David.

Benjamin Hadley. Superintendent of Acadia National Park.

September 21, 1938

Dear Mr. Rockefeller:

I have received and carefully read your letter of September 16th in reference to the Dorr quarry lot and other lands. I am not at all surprised by what Mr. Rodick says about Mr. Dorr's probable attitude to any suggestions that are made that do not provide for one hundred per cent compliance with his plan. This is exactly the view that I have held all along, and which I endeavored to convey to you in my letters to you from London and Nuremberg.

I have received letter from Mr. Hadley, which reads as follows:

"Mr. Dorr is beginning to look forward to your return from Europe, and hopes that you

181

will find it possible to come to Bar Harbor around the first of October. The matters which we discussed during your June visit have lain dormant during the summer. Mr. Dorr, being aware of the uncertainty of human life, is most anxious to get as much as he can into such a state that there will be no likelihood of complications in the future. He has asked me to write with a view to learning from you when you may be expected.

"I shall be out of town from the 17th to the 24th of September; hence the October 1st suggestion."

I have had to answer this letter by saying that it looks quite impossible for me to go up to Maine this autumn. I have an accumulation of business to occupy my time for several weeks, and there is the annual meeting of my company to arrange for. Late in October I must make an inspection of our properties in New Mexico. There a law suit will be tried in which we are deeply interested, and it may be after the middle of December before I return to New York. In other words, I will be here until perhaps October 25th, then away most of the time until December 15th or 20th.

I have been endeavoring to get the latest views of the National Park Service on the Acadia land situation; then I will write to Mr. Dorr. I still hope to get the letter off this week. I am awfully sorry that this matter cannot be moved faster. However, my experience over a period of twenty-five years has been that Mr. Dorr is one man that cannot be moved very fast under any circumstances.

Sincerely yours,
HORACE M. ALBRIGHT

November 12, 1938

My dear Mr. Rockefeller:

Upon my arrival here at Carlsbad after a trip to California I find a letter of November 1 from Mr. Dorr, which I am quoting:

"Thank you for your letter and the kind thought that you have given to working out our problems here. I am anxious to get all the immediate problems that I can worked out while I am here to cooperate. I am entirely in sympathy with the plan you propose, which I think can be worked out to the benefit of the public and the Park. The long-continued depression has placed me in a position of commitment to the bank which does not leave me free to do what otherwise I would wish and dedicate the lands I have held so long to the execution of the Government's plans.

"The study of such a solution as you suggest may clear the way and would be, I think, highly desirable. I am working over this with those who are interested in it with me and with whom I have planned to leave the disposal of my property, which I may say in passing I plan to leave - such as it may ultimately prove to be - to the benefit of the public. By the time you return from your western trip I trust to know more fully what can be done."

It seems to me that I have made some progress, and I shall get in touch with Mr. Dorr again as soon as I return to New York November 21.

I received a copy of Mr. Chorley's memorandum of October 31 to you referring to the language covering acquisition of the right of way for Colonial Parkway which is proposed to be included in the next Interior Department appropriation bill, which will soon be discussed with the Director of the Budget. I fully concur with Mr. Chorley in his observations. I hope every effort is going to be made to secure the desired authority. If it is secured there will certainly be no grounds left on which to object to immediate resumption of work on the Parkway, including the tunnel.

I hope you and Mrs. Rockefeller are having a delightful vacation in Old Williamsburg.

Faithfully yours,
HORACE M. ALBRIGHT

November 18, 1938

Dear Mr. Albright:

Your letter of November 12th from Carlsbad, New Mexico, was received with much satisfaction. Mr. Dorr could not have taken more charmingly your suggestion. The fact that he is already at work on it indicates that he sees in it the next best possible approach to a solution of his problems. Assuming that he means from what he says to you that he is discussing this matter with Mr. Rodick, I have taken the liberty of writing Mr. Rodick a letter of which I enclose a copy.

Without his revealing any confidences to me, Mr. Rodick and I did discuss this whole situation last summer when I was trying to make up my mind to suggest to you writing Mr. Dorr along the lines you finally wrote him. Mr. Rodick, therefore, is familiar with the details of the program that I had in mind and, if he has the blue print of which I speak, will be in a position, without reference to you or me, to make helpful and specific suggestions to Mr. Dorr about ways and means of carrying out your proposal so that some definite program may have been outlined by the time you get into touch with Mr. Dorr again.

I shall be in New York Monday morning and right along thereafter and shall be glad to discuss this matter with you any time at your convenience.

In connection with the latter part of your letter referring to monies for the completion of the Williamsburg-Jamestown Parkway, you will be interested to know that Secretary Ickes and his wife spent last weekend with Mrs. Rockefeller and me here in Williamsburg. Mr. Chorley and I had an opportunity to go over with him not only the existing parkway but the plan for its extension through Williamsburg, pointing out in detail the course it would take, where it connects with the present parkway after emerging from under the railroad and where it would come out from the tunnel alongside of the court house and how it would go on through the valley below the new Lodge. The Secretary seemed to get a new understanding of the situation, to realize its importance, and raised no questions or objections to the tunnel route.

After the route had been thoroughly discussed and understood, the Secretary said to me, "How are you going to finance it?" - which seemed rather naive in view of all that has been said to him on that subject. My reply, of course, was that that was a matter for the government and that I had greatly hoped he could secure funds from the large allotments for public works. We then discussed that situation in some detail. I will not take your time to repeat the conversation now. The outcome was that the Secretary gave both Mr. Chorley and me the very definite impression that he would go at the matter vigorously and that he intended to put it through. I mentioned the danger of its never being completed if he should go out of office without having so arranged. He spoke strongly on that subject, and said he definitely felt it should be completed, that he wanted to have it completed and seemed to be thoroughly committed to its completion. Mr. Chorley is to send the Secretary a final estimate of the cost of the completed project and the Secretary has asked him to stop in and see him when he is next in Washington, which Mr. Chorely will make it his business to do in the near future. I think the situation is in better shape than it ever has been before.

Very sincerely,
JOHN D. ROCKEFELLER, JR.

The Williamsburg-Jamestown Parkway is now part of the Colonial National Historic Park, including Jamestown, York-

town, and Cape Henry Memorial, which marks the site of the first landing of the Jamestown colonists. The parkway is 23 miles long and connects the historic sites. A section of the parkway travels through a tunnel in the historic section of Williamsburg.

May 3, 1939

Dear Mr. Rockefeller:

I am terribly sorry to tell you that Mr. Cammerer suffered a very severe heart attack at 4 a.m. Sunday. The diagnosis of the heart specialist I understand was that it was coronary thrombosis, and our friend is in a dangerous if not critical condition.

The doctors said yesterday morning that if he could get through another 24 hours they had hopes he would recover to the extent where he could resume his work although at not quite so active a pace. That 24 hours has passed, and there is no bad news. He is at his home at 4664 -25th Street North, Arlington, Virginia.

Of course, the thing that is worrying us is that there might be some action taken by his superior Secretary Ickes in reference to filling his place or refusing him leave of absence, etc., which might have a serious nervous reaction endangering his recovery. I wish there were some way of assuring that such moves will not be made.

The gossip in Washington is that the Secretary's home is about to receive a "bundle from heaven" to use the expression of one of the newspaper commentators on Hollywood affairs. Perhaps this happy event may inspire the Secretary to generous treatment of Mr. Cammerer, whose unfortunate situation must certainly be due in part to the strain he has been under.

Sincerely yours,
HORACE M. ALBRIGHT

July 19, 1939

Dear Mr. Albright:

Since you felt it would be all right for me to send Mr. Cammerer $1,000 in view of the expense of his illness, which must be very heavy, I did so before leaving New York. In a charming letter which I have just received from Mr. Cammerer he returns the check and says:

> "In ordinary circumstances I should not hesitate to accept your check for it would be silly for me to say that it would not come in very handily in times like these, but I am constantly reminded of so many incredibly queer and unprecedented occurrences that have come to my attention in recent years, of which you can have no conception, that have been involved in investigations and what not, and in some of which I myself have been involved, that I deem it wisest for me to ask you to let me return the check to you. Perhaps I am too cautious about this, my dear friend, but I value your friendship so much that I would not want the slightest thing to arise where I am involved that might result at any time in casting the slightest shadow on it."

While it had not occurred to me before that the acceptance of this check by Mr. Cammerer, if known, might be used against him, I am not surprised at his thinking it wise to err on the side of safety and return it. I might better have sent the check to Mrs. Cammerer. Thus Mr. Cammerer would not have been involved and the same end would have been accomplished. Perhaps I can still do this although it may be better to let the matter rest for the present and not suggest so doing until we see how things develop.

I am wondering whether you have heard anything from Mr. Demaray about the letters to Messrs. Kent and Palmer. Mr. Kent, at least, ought to have replied before this. I shall

187

be interested to get any news if you have any. It is beautiful on Mount Desert Island and we are very happy, as always, to get back here.

Very sincerely,
JOHN D. ROCKEFELLER, JR.

Mr. Arthur E. Demaray. Associate Director of the Park Service, 1933 to 1951. Demaray served as Director for eight months in 1951 before retiring. He was succeeded as Director by Conrad Wirth, who held the post until 1964.

July 22, 1939

Dear Mr. Rockefeller:

Your letter of July 19th was on my desk this morning when I returned from Washington.

I had dinner with Mr. Cammerer last night and had a very interesting hour with him. He is making good progress, although he looks pretty badly. His wife told me that the doctors say he is too energetic and has to be held down. They are going to try to get him away where the Park Service people cannot bother him. Mrs. Cammerer herself has been quite ill in bed for over a week. He showed me his correspondence with you, and with tears in his eyes expressed his gratitude for your effort to help him. The fact of the matter is that like everyone else in the Interior Department, he is desperately afraid of misdirected action by the Secretary. Had your message been sent to Mrs. Cammerer the gift would have been gratefully accepted, I am sure.

With Mr. Demaray I went over all of our problems— Acadia, Williamsburg, Jackson Hole. I advised Mr. Demaray to write Mr. Palmer a letter urging him to walk over the route with an engineer, and arguing that the cliffs would not be scarred and that there is a good view from the point where the road would turn around the mountain, and that there would be no dust and noise from traffic up theré. I do not expect that another letter would accomplish much, but I think it is worth trying.

I advised that nothing be done in answer to Mr. Kent. The Secretary apparently is not going up to Acadia. The news that he was planning to go there escaped from the Acadia office and when invitations began to come in he changed his plans because he wanted to be absolutely isolated in order to rest and because of Mrs. Ickes' condition.

Faithfully yours,
HORACE M. ALBRIGHT

July 28, 1939

Dear Mr. Albright:

Your letter of July 25th in reply to mine regarding the Day Mountain project is received. Last night there came to me the following telegram from Mr. Demaray:

"Day Mountain project will be advertised July 28th."

to which I this morning replied as follows:

"Telegram received. Delighted early action Day Mountain project. Hope other road project may also go forward shortly."

The other project referred to is, of course, the around Newport Mountain project. I am delighted that, as a result of your personal interest in the Day Mountain project and your having telephoned Mr. Demaray, such prompt action has been secured. I hope before Mr. Demaray goes to Hawaii some decision in the around Newport Mountain project may have been reached so that that can go forward. I myself took the liberty of suggesting to Mr. Grossman that he go right ahead with the two or three weeks of work which he said would be required to get this project, in line with my suggestion to Mr. Demaray, in shape for advertising. Since this work would have to be done even if condemnation were adopted, Mr. Grossman saw no reason why he should not proceed at once with it. This, of course, is between him and me.

I have also received your letter of July 24th in which you say that you agree fully with my recommendation to Mr. Demaray about the Kent-Potter Palmer situation. Thank you for forewarning me in regard to Mr. Demaray's possible request that I join with the government in supplying the funds necessary for a purchase under condemnation. Your view of my relation to the situation is the only view which I could possibly take and I will follow the program you suggest should such a request come.

You will be interested to hear that the rebuilding of the Icy Hill Road here at Seal Harbor, which you were helpful with Mr. Downer in getting P.W.A. funds for last year, has just been completed and the new road opened. It is a vast improvement and I am delighted that it has at length been put through. Again my thanks to you.

I received favorable news from Mr. Downer the other day in regard to the progress of the Williamsburg-Jamestown parkway project. He says an agreement as to price has been reached with the State Hospital people and that the government representatives have decided to acquire by filing declarations of taking practically the entire route of the parkway to Jamestown and including the tunnel. This will greatly expedite the matter. Thus it would appear that real progress is being made along various fronts in connection with these several matters in which you and I have both so deeply interested.

I hope your western trip may be at least partly a pleasure and note that you expect to be back in your office the middle of August.

Very sincerely,
JOHN D. ROCKEFELLER, JR.

Day Mountain and Newport Mountain projects. These were the names given to the contracts to build sections of the roads in the areas of these mountains.

Jay Downer. Road planner. Worked with Rockefeller in Westchester County and Virginia.

August 28, 1939

Dear Mr. Albright:

Your letter of August 25th with its enclosures I have read with interest and telegraphed you last night as follows:

> "Letter 25th with enclosures received. Am told Black Woods contractor worked 'til Nov. 15 last year. Stop. Ralston always continues my road building advantageously at least that late stop. Should regard it nothing short of a calamity not to have around the mountain contract let this fall."

I agree with every word you say about the unwisdom of waiting until spring to let the contract for the around the mountain road. There may not be money available or other park needs may be regarded as more urgent and it is just taking another unnecessary chance to wait. Moreover, I think it would be entirely possible for the piece of road on the south and east, going from the Ocean Drive at the sand beach to the Homans property, to be practically built this fall. You will see from my telegram that it is easy for a contractor to work at least until the middle of November here and, if the season is at all favorable, he could go on considerably beyond that.

I do hope you will be able to overcome the growing lethargy of the park and roads people and get them to put this last road under contract this fall. Please let me know if there is anything more I can do to be helpful.

I have been waiting to hear from the park office of the arrival of Mr. Tillotson but, not receiving any word, called up this morning and learned from Mr. Hadley that he had been and gone and that Mr. Hadley telephoned my house Saturday but, not being able to get either Miss Warfield or me, left no message nor made any further effort to advise me. I am greatly disappointed.

Very sincerely,
JOHN D. ROCKEFELLER, JR.

Minor Tillotson. Park Service regional director.

Janet M. Warfield. Rockefeller's personal secretary.

———

August 31, 1939

Dear Mr. Albright:

The copies of your two letters to Mr. White and his letter to you were duly received. Thank you for them.

I fear Mr. White is getting a little peeved at my insistent interest in these Acadia Park road problems. If he only knew how many years I had spent in acquiring the lands necessary for these roads and what an infinite amount of painstaking negotiation I have gone through to make them possible, he would perhaps better understand my profound, although wholly disinterested, solicitude in their construction and not feel that the burden they are putting on his shoulders is really very heavy after all in comparison with the burden I have carried in making them possible. Perhaps you have gone as far in this matter as it is wise to go and that it is not best to push Mr. White any further.

For your information I am enclosing a copy of Secretary

Icke's last letter to me which obviously Mr. White dictated. You will see from the last paragraph that the letting of the contract next spring is recognized by the Secretary as a possibility. On the other hand, since undoubtedly this thought has been put in his mouth by Mr. White, it is presumable that the Secretary will not be opposed to letting the contract this fall if it can be done. In any event I am taking that for granted in my reply, of which I am enclosing a copy.

Very sincerely,
JOHN D. ROCKEFELLER, JR.

Mr. John R. White. Acting National Park Director, 1939.

August 12, 1940

Dear Mr. Rockefeller:

I am deeply grateful for your thoughtful letter of August 10th in which you tell me about your plans for returning to New York about September 1st and asking whether it would be possible for us to be your guests Friday night, August 30th. I believe this can be arranged. I will have to look over my schedule, which is at home. I will do this tonight or tomorrow and will write you before I leave here on Friday.

Mrs. Albright and our son Robert I know appeciate as much as I do your invitation for us to spend the night of the 30th with you. We are traveling in our own car, and will be coming into Maine from Quebec. I sincerely hope it will be possible to reach Seal Harbor before you leave because it would be interesting and valuable to make a survey even though a brief one of all the projects in which we have been interested.

Mr. Cammerer's last day of service was August 10th, and he is now in his new position as Regional Director of Region I, which includes all of the national parks east of the Mississippi River. This means that he will be directly responsible for the administration of all of the parks where you have given us such great assistance and in which you personally have been so much interested except Grand Teton project, Yellowstone and Yosemite. Mr. Cammerer's jurisdiction will extend over Acadia, Great Smoky Mountains, Shenandoah, and the Colonial Historical National Park. While his headquarters will be nominally at Richmond he will be in Washington most of the time at least for a year or two. Personally I doubt very much whether you and I will miss Mr. Cammerer in his position as Director because of the very great influence that he will wield in the affairs of these eastern parks.

Of course, we want to assist in acquainting Director Drury with the problems of these parks as opportunities present themselves. I suspect, however, that Mr. Drury will devote himself to the larger western parks for some months to come since so many of them will be closed for the winter. Mr. Cammerer may still be acting as Director even though his resignation took effect Saturday, the 10th.

With another expression of gratitude for your invitation and all good wishes, I am

Faithfully yours,
HORACE M. ALBRIGHT

Newton B. Drury. Former secretary of the Save-the-Redwoods League. Director of the National Park Service, 1940-1951.

October 17, 1940

Dear Mr. Rockefeller:

For your records I quote Section 8 of the new Federal Aid Road Act approved by the President September 5, 1940, which provides for continuation of construction, reconstruction and improvement of roads in national parks during the fiscal years ending June 30, 1942 and June 30, 1943:

> "For the construction, reconstruction, and improvement of roads and trails, inclusive of necessary bridges, in the national parks, monuments, and other areas administered by the National Park Service, including areas authorized to be established as national parks and monuments, and national park and monument approach roads authorized by the Act of January 31, 1931 (46 Stat. 1053), as amended, there is hereby authorized to be appropriated the sum of $4,000,000 for the fiscal year ending June 30, 1942, and the sum of $4,000,000 for the fiscal year ending June 30, 1943. Provided, That hereafter appropriations for the construction, reconstruction, and improvement of such park and monument roads shall be administered in conformity with regulations jointly approved by the Secretary of the Interior and the Federal Works Administrator."

With this basic legislative authority on the statute books it would be extremely unlikely that appropriations to meet obligations incurred under this Act will be withheld. It would seem that we can now look forward confidently to the completion of the projects in which we have been especially interested.

Director Newton B. Drury of the National Park Service was here this week and both Mr. Downer and I had an opportunity to review a good many matters with him.

I expect to be in Washington on October 29th and 30th. I hope, however, that before that time the new road project in Acadia will have been placed under contract.

Faithfully yours,
HORACE M. ALBRIGHT

P.S. Please do not take the trouble to acknowledge this - HMA

WORTHWHILE PLACES

March 26, 1941

Mrs. John D. Rockefeller, Jr.
740 Park Avenue
New York, New York

Dear Mrs. Rockefeller:

I have personally acknowledged receipt of your check for $4,000 for the American Planning and Civic Association, representing the last installment on the pledge of $9,000 which you were kind enough to make last year for the roadside improvement work. I would like to make another and more official acknowledgment of your gift, and I take this means of doing so, at the same time expressing our deep appreciation of your further support.

Perhaps this is a good time to summarize the work of the Association for roadside improvement since July, 1935 - less than six years. You will remember that when you made the initial grant to the Association in the Spring of 1935, you suggested that we employ someone versed in the law, who would explore the legal possibilities for extending the outposts of roadside control through planning, zoning and other similar methods.

In July, 1935, Mr. Flavel Shurtleff, as counsel, began his study of existing laws, and his search for possible legal proposals to establish public control over the strips of land lying adjacent to the highways of the country.

The Association was able to stretch the $10,000 donated by you for each of the years 1935, 1936 and 1937 to cover its work from July, 1935 to the autumn of 1939, when you made an additional gift of $2,000 to complete the work for that year. For the years 1940 and 1941 we were given $5,000 and $4,000 respectively. In addition to the $41,000 which you have made available during these years, the American Telephone and Telegraph Company has given $1,000.

Of course there have been many organizations and persons working for roadside improvement in the United States, and the American Planning and Civic Association cannot claim full credit for all that has happened since 1935. On the other hand, it seems that we have played an active part in molding public opinion along new lines, in bringing about actual legislation and in aiding in the drafting of bills now pending in a dozen legislatures.

In the first place, in 1935 all of the bills which had passed or were proposed in the various States were what we term permit and license bills, or bills establishing specific setbacks from corners, curves and other dangerous places or setbacks from the right-of-way. It had become apparent to all that this type of legislation, while it contributed to the safety and orderly procedure, did not in fact reduce the number of billboards or free scenic areas from desecration.

By 1935, in the cities, great progress had been made in zoning ordinances under which billboards were prohibited in residence districts, though non-conforming billboards in these neighborhoods at the time of the passage of the ordinances were permitted to remain. (In passing I may say our Association and others are now working on ways and means to bring an end these and other non-conforming uses under zoning ordinances.)

In 1935 practically all of the planners thought that we should depend on county zoning to free our roadsides from billboards and other objectionable intrusions.

In April 1936, in Planning and Civic Comment, we published an account by Mr. Thomas Adams of the Ribbon Development Act of 1935, which was administered in England by the Ministry of Transport. In November 1936, the American Planning and Civic Association published in Planning Broadcasts its first legislative suggestions, as a result of Mr. Shurtleff's studies. Recognizing that county zoning was making such slow progress that we could not depend on it to establish responsible control of the roadsides of the enormous mileage of highways in the United States, Mr. Shurtleff proposed that the States themselves act, not as in Massachusetts, to delegate authority to control billboards to cities and towns, but directly to set up control of the roadsides by the State itself. From that time Mr. Shurtleff has issued several revisions of his proposals. Mr. Alfred Bettman has prepared a more elaborate

197

bill along similar lines, and the American Automobile Association, through a committee on which both Mr. Shurtleff and Miss James served, has issued still another draft prepared by Mr. Hugh Pomeroy, embodying similar principles. While none of these measures has yet passed any legislature, bills to establish highway restrictive areas, to be administered by a state highway commission or a similar agency, have been pending in the legislatures of or are to be introduced in Maine, Rhode Island, Connecticut, New York, Pennsylvania, Maryland and Washington, and probably in New Hampshire, Ohio, Indiana and Colorado. In Maryland Mr. Shurtleff has cooperated closely and appeared before the Legislative Council in the autumn. Also we have sent copies of the summary of the 1940 Roadside Improvement Conference to the members of the Senate Committee considering the bill. Whether one or more bills of this type will pass in the 1941 Legislatures we cannot say, but we can say that public opinion has rolled up to include organizations of business men as well as professional groups and we think it is safe to predict that either in 1941 or 1943 this entirely new type of legislation will be passed, and when some State does adopt it, there will be established the first state-wide public agency to control uses of roadsides. This is a contribution of no little importance.

In the first Planning Broadcast on this subject issued by the American Planning and Civic Association in 1936, we called attention to the promise of freeways and parkways. The parkways of Westchester County had already become popular, but since that date three national parkways have been planned and built or are in process of building. The parkway plan has spread rapidly. The freeway proposal is now more commonly called "limited access", and six States have passed legislation authorizing this type of highways — New York and Rhode Island in 1937 and Maine, Connecticut, California and West Virginia in 1939. Here is definite progress - progress that can be extended to other States and that will show results in these six States as limited access highways are built.

The billboard industry itself recognized these accomplishments, and in its different organizations is spending considerable money to oppose all proposed legislation, not only so-called anti-billboard legislation but also all proposals to zone or limit access to highways.

When the highway funds of the American Planning and Civic Association are exhausted, in 1941, we shall be able to take stock of the legislation passed in the two legislative sessions since we were able to mobilize our forces for the 1939 legislative session. We have encountered more stubborn resistance than we expected. On the other hand, we have found many new allies, and can say with impunity that public opinion has marched along very rapidly, as evidenced in the two Joint Roadside Conferences which we organized and held in New York, the first in November of 1938, the second in December, 1940. Proposals for establishing highway protective areas or State zoning of roadside strips, which at first were scouted by many planners and laymen, were accepted in the 1940 Conference without question or opposition from anyone.

We cannot say that our work is done; but we know we have made new proposals of real importance which sooner or later will be adopted in most States of the Union. We believe that the time of such adoption will be considerably shortened if we can continue Mr. Shurtleff's services and the New York office, (part of which is supported by a grant from the Russell Sage Foundation.)

I hope that you will feel that you have made a good investment in the work carried on by Mr. Shurtleff and the American Planning and Civic Association. I am sending you a package of literature of the Association since your first grant, arranged chronologically. I know you have received these publications with your membership, but I believe that if you will look over this package of literature and note the special bulletins and marked articles in the quarterly, you will observe the cumulative effect of what we have accomplished since July, 1935, when we started our work under the inspiration of your suggestion that we explore the legal possibilities for setting up new controls.

I hope Mr. Laurance Rockefeller whom you have asked to confer with some of the Oil Company executives, on the roadside protection program, will be able to spare the time to read this review of our activities, and at his convenience peruse the publications referred to.

Very sincerely yours,
HORACE M. ALBRIGHT

American Planning and Civic Association. Albright was president of this organization. It was influential in conservation and civic affairs. Rockefeller made small annual contributions to its budget in addition to the one-time large gift made by Mrs. Rockefeller for roadside improvement work.

April 21, 1941

Dear Mr. Rockefeller:

I was in Washington last week and had some talks about the Acadia bridges, and I have on my desk some blue prints of the bridges as they stand at present. I like the designs very much.

I am sorry to say, however, that the Duck Brook Bridge plans have not been completed, and seem to have been interrupted by one or more defense projects. Also there have been some expressions of doubt as to whether there will be enough cash and authority to contract to permit the placing of the bridges under contract this summer. I have strongly protested to the Director that this outlook is discouraging and depressing, and hard to believe in view of the appropriations that are being made for construction of all kinds.

I have asked Mr. Drury to look into the matter personally and review it with Mr. T. H. McDonald, Director of the Bureau of Public Roads. Mr. Drury writes that he will be here Wednesday, and is going to Acadia Thursday for a couple of days. I had previously asked him to make the Acadia trip at a time when I could join him so that I could personally discuss with him on the ground the history of the projects in which you and I have been interested; in fact, give him there in Acadia the whole history of the park, and the development of its land, road, horse road, and trail programs. I do not know why he suddenly planned to go up this week. I cannot go to Maine now.

I will be with him Wednesday at luncheon and perhaps later in the day. So if you want me to give him any special suggestions you can catch me here by telephone or telegraph.

I hope Mrs. Rockefeller and you are enjoying the spring weather in Williamsburg, and finding the stay restful and beneficial in every way.

With best regards, I am

Sincerely yours,
HORACE M. ALBRIGHT

July 9th 1941

Dear Mr. Rockefeller:

Your radio address last night was perfect. I hope that it was recorded and will be rebroadcast all over the country.

I have sent newspaper reports of it to my wife and children in the West. Unfortunately, all of them were traveling on a train last night and I am afraid they did not hear you speak.

As a citizen and as a father I am deeply grateful that you made this moving address.

Faithfully yours,
HORACE M. ALBRIGHT

Rockefeller radio address. An appeal for support of the United Service Organization. He was honorary chairman of the board of directors, but also served as a member of the general policy and executive committees.

WORTHWHILE PLACES

This speech contained a statement of Rockefeller's personal Credo which has been engraved in stone at Rockefeller Center.

November 27, 1942

My dear Mr. Secretary:

Nearly fifteen years ago I purchased some thirty thousand acres in the Jackson Hole country on the earnest recommendation of the then Director of National Parks. This I did for two reasons: first, having in mind the winter feeding of great quantities of game which was being gradually exterminated by starvation; and, secondly, never for a moment doubting that the Federal Government would gladly accept the land as a gift for addition to its national park system and would forthwith take whatever steps were necessary to that end. During the years that have intervened there have been, as you know, numerous negotiations with Government representatives in regard to the matter. As you also know, all of these negotiations have come to naught. Over this period I hve expended in connection with the property, which cost me $1,000,000, half as much again for taxes, maintenance, handling, etc. Today it stands me in at a total cost of roughly $1,500,000.

In view of the uncertainty of the times, like everybody else I am and have been for some time reducing my obligations and burdens in so far as I wisely can. In line with that policy I have definitely reached the conclusion, although most reluctantly, that I should make permanent disposition of this property before another year has passed. If the Federal Government is not interested in its acquisition, or, being interested, is still unable to arrange to accept it on the general terms long discussed and with which you are familiar, it will be my thought to make some other disposition of it or, failing in that, to sell it in the market to any satisfactory buyers.

Because you have been desirous of having this property added to the national park system and have given so generously

202

of your time and thought in the effort to bring that result about, I would not for a moment think of proceeding to carry out the program above outlined without having first advised you of my decision. Having done that, I am confident that, being so familiar with the situation as you are, you will be the first to say that I have shown every consideration in the matter. Moreover, because you know so well how eager I have been to have this great area preserved for the benefit and enjoyment of the people of the nation under the wise control and operation of the National Park Service, with which it has been my pleasure to cooperate so closely in many of its national parks and for which I have long had such high admiration, you will realize better than most people with what regret I now face the possible abandonment of that dream.

Very sincerely,
JOHN D. ROCKEFELLER, JR.

The Honorable Harold L. Ickes
Secretary of the Interior
Washington, D.C.

Harold L. Ickes responded to Mr. Rockefeller's letter on December 4, 1942. He said, "This great conservation project which you have made possible would have been accepted long ago if it had been within my power to do so. You know the selfish local interests that have prevented the final consummation of your praise worthy plan. . . . as a public official intimately concerned, I appreciate your further generous attitude and within the year allowed, I will do everything within my power to bring about the acceptance of your gift as an addition to the national park system."

Rockefeller went to Washington to visit his sons, John 3rd, Nelson A., and Laurance S., for the Christmas holidays. While there he met with Ickes about the project.

WORTHWHILE PLACES

January 5, 1943

My dear Mr. Secretary:

It was most gracious of you to receive me almost on the eve of Christmas and I thoroughly enjoyed my visit with you.

During the course of our talk you made it clear that it is your intention at an early date to bring to the President for his signature the order for the incorporation as a National Monument of both public and private property within the Jackson Hole area, thus rounding out the Grand Teton Park project. While we were in agreement that such action on the President's part may call forth some criticism, both political and local, we were fully in accord in believing that because this proposition is so eminently sound and so wholly in the interest of the American people, such criticism would quickly die down and would be followed shortly, even on the part of the objectors, by general approval of the President's action.

There are few men in public office today who, like yourself, have the courage to incur even temporary criticism in order to do what they are convinced is in the public interest and will ultimately be generally approved. I rejoice, therefore, at your determination to bring this matter to an issue forthwith at the earliest favorable opportunity and feel confident that your efforts will be crowned with success.

Since this is your determination, I will, of course, be glad to delay for a few weeks the action which I had in mind to take for the disposal of my Jackson Hole property. While I definitely hope and expect that within the next month your efforts will have met with success, if I hear nothing from you by the end of February, I will take it for granted that you will not expect me to delay further putting into effect the program of which I wrote you in my letter of December 15th.

With New Year's Greetings to you and Mrs. Ickes and with sentiments of high regard, I am,

Very sincerely,
JOHN D. ROCKEFELLER, JR.

The Honorable Harold L. Ickes
Secretary of the Interior
Washington, D. C.

February 10, 1943

My dear Mr. Secretary:

I was distressed to learn from your letter of January 28th that you had been ill and sincerely hope you have stayed in bed long enough to insure your complete recovery. My experience is that giving up to a cold in its early stages usually greatly shortens the total period of inactivity.

Your references to the Jackson Hole project, which lies so close to your heart, have led me to wonder whether a personal letter to the President from me might be helpful to you in forwarding the matter. Merely for your consideration I have written and am enclosing such a letter, which please feel wholly at liberty to change in any way that seems to you best or to reject and destroy unless you think it will be definitely helpful. Should you adopt the former course, upon receiving the letter with your suggested changes, I will rewrite it and forward it to you at once.

In making this proposal I recognize there are several dangers. One is that if the letter falls in the hands of a White House secretary, it might as a matter of routine and with the best of motives, be taken to some Senator, Congressman or other official, the result of which might be to impede rather than expedite matters. Another possibility is that if the letter should reach the President personally, he might reply expressing his interest in the project but indicating that while the war is on, he could do nothing and wanted me to let the matter lie another year or two. This would be embarrassing for, as you have yourself agreed, I have already waited far longer than any citizen could be expected to wait, under similar circumstances.

Before closing, let me mention another aspect of the question. When the matter of the acceptance by the Government of the Jackson Hole lands for a national park was first brought up, the chief objection raised then and for some years thereafter was the fact that when the local taxes on the property ceased to be paid, there would be no funds from which to meet the annual school tax in the community of some $8,000 or $10,000. This was always regarded locally as a very significant and insurmountable obstacle. In the meantime, however, the various laws that have been passed have completely changed the picture. The figures as I have them are that in 1941 tax collections in Yellowstone Park by the State of Wyoming under permission given in a law enacted only a few years ago amounted to:

State gas tax	$88,915.61
State sales tax	35,958.92
State liquor tax	5,636.76
Other taxes	21,152.84
	$151,664.13

Moreover, I am informed that agreement has about been reached on a general bill in which counties would share in revenue from concessions, automobiles, entrance fees, utility charges, etc. in the park. That income would, of course, be on top of such taxes as are set forth above. In the light of these huge revenues, the loss of $8,000 or $10,000 of school tax is as but a drop in the bucket.

Awaiting your reply, I am,

Very sincerely,
JOHN D. ROCKEFELLER, JR.

The Honorable Harold L. Ickes
Secretary of the Interior
Washington, D. C.

February 10, 1943

My dear Mr. President:

Many years ago I purchased some thirty thousand acres of land in Jackson Hole, Wyoming, on the earnest recommendation of the then Director of National Parks. This I did in order to provide winter feeding for the great quantities of game which were being gradually exterminated by starvation, and to preserve the superlative scenery of the Grand Teton approaches, confidently expecting that the Federal Government would gladly accept the land as a gift to be added to its National Park System. Fifteen years have passed. The government has not accepted the property. I am still its owner. It cost me a million dollars. Taxes, maintenance and other costs have increased that figure roughly by half a million dollars. I have now determined to dispose of the property, selling it, if necessary, in the market to any satisfactory buyer.

Because of your interest in the National Parks and in the conservation of great areas for public use, I have preferred to advise you in advance of my intention, rather than to have you hear of it first as an accomplished fact. As you know the Jackson Hole valley lies at the foot of the Teton Mountains, than which there is no more majestic range of mountains in this country. Because it is so uniquely beautiful an area, you will understand with what deep regret I am at length abandoning the effort to make it a place of permanent enjoyment for all the people, to which I have devoted myself so assiduously during these many years.

This letter is written for your information only and, of course, calls for no reply.

With sentiments of high regard, I am,

Very sincerely,
JOHN D. ROCKEFELLER, JR.

The President
The White House
Washington, D. C.

WORTHWHILE PLACES

After further discussion, Rockefeller sent his proposed letter to President Franklin D. Roosevelt about the Jackson Hole project to Ickes for handling. Ickes presented the letter to the President.

March 9, 1943

My dear Mr. Secretary:

I appreciated greatly your courtesy in seeing me when I was in Washington the other day and thoroughly enjoyed my visit with you.

From what you have told me, it would appear that there now remains only the actual signing of the order to consummate this important public development to which you have been devoting yourself. All of the steps leading up to that last one you have taken with consummate wisdom and tact.

Because he is so greatly burdened with countless matters, it is apparent from what you said that it is exceedingly difficult to get an appointment with the President. You told me that Colonel Watson had explained the matter to him subsequent to your visit and had returned your memorandum approved by the President. If an interview is not possible without undue delay, I am wondering whether if you were to send the order to Colonel Watson, having attached thereto your memorandum which the President had approved, the Colonel could at some convenient moment bring it the President for his signature. This may be very irregular and not at all feasible. It is merely a thought which came into my mind and which I am passing on for what, if any, consideration it may be worth.

Again my congratulations on what has been accomplished and my best wishes for your early success in carrying through the final step.

Very sincerely,
JOHN D. ROCKEFELLER, JR.

The Honorable Harold L. Ickes
Secretary of the Interior
Washington, D. C.

Colonel Edwin Martin Watson. Military aide to President Roosevelt, 1933-1939; personal secretary, 1939-1945.

March 17, 1943

My dear Mr. Secretary:

Although you and I cannot get together to satisfactorily celebrate the news which you gave me over the telephone yesterday, I am sure we are both of us singing in our hearts "Praise God from Whom all blessings flow".

Except for your vision, your courage, your determination, there was every prospect that this uniquely beautiful area, now in a way to be preserved for all time as a national park for the enjoyment of all the people, would have been permanently lost. I take off my hat to you. Please know what a pleasure it has been to me to have a part in this matter which has lain close to my heart for so many years.

Since you thought some word from me would be appreciated, I have written the President a letter of which I enclose a copy.

Knowing how overburdened you were with many important matters, I counted it only the more gracious of you to have received me in your office the other day and purposely made my visit as short as possible although I would have liked to have inquired about Mrs. Ickes and sent my compliments to her. I appreciate greatly your reference to Mrs. Rockefeller, who, when opportunity offers, will, I know, enjoy seeing you and Mrs. Ickes as you have so kindly suggested. We come to Washington very rarely and then chiefly to see our children and grandchildren who are living there. But the time will come again when life will not be so hectic. Then we shall look forward to a repetition of the delightful visit with you and Mrs. Ickes which we had in London when you were on your honeymoon. Mrs. Rockefeller joins me in cordial greetings to you both.

Very sincerely,
JOHN D. ROCKEFELLER, JR.

The Honorable Harold L. Ickes
Secretary of the Interior
Washington, D. C.

In a characteristic action, Rockefeller gave credit to Ickes for the success in gaining National Monument status for the Jackson Hole land. But his satisfaction was to be cut short when Congress refused to provide funds for the Monument. After this setback, Rockefeller gave most of the land he owned in Jackson Hole to the private foundation, Jackson Hole Preserve, Inc. The transfer was completed in October 1945, when Rockefeller transferred 28,937 acres in addition to 2,727 acres he had given the Preserve earlier making the total holdings 31,664 acres. The foundation held the lands until 1949, when the impasse was finally broken, and the Rockefeller land was transferred to the Federal Government as part of the Monument. In 1950, Congress added the National Monument to Grand Teton National Park. Between 1949 and 1952, the Preserve gave additional land to the Park Service for Grand Teton National Park and after 1954 made matching fund cash contributions of $1 million to the Park Service for the purchase of additional lands in the park. In 1945,

210

1934 – 1943

Rockefeller retained ownership of approximately 3,188 acres comprising the JY Ranch and two other smaller properties. In the 1980's, Laurance S. Rockefeller gave most of this land to Dartmouth College, Princeton University, Vermont Law School, and Memorial Sloan-Kettering Cancer Center. The recipients have sold the land to the Park Service.

In 1943, three of Rockefeller's sons, John 3rd, Laurance, and Nelson worked in and out of Washington. John was a lieutenant in the Naval Bureau of Personnel. Laurance was a lieutenant in the Naval Bureau of Aeronautics. Nelson was Coordinator of Inter-American Affairs and later Assistant Secretary of State. The two younger sons, Winthrop and David, enlisted as privates in the army. Winthrop became a major and fought in the South Pacific until he was wounded in 1945. David became a captain in the Army Intelligence and served in North Africa, Italy, and France.

March 23, 1943

Dear Mr. Rockefeller:

I was not very well satisfied with the information I got in Washington the other day about the proposed dams on the upper Rio Grande that might affect the Indian pueblos, so I wrote to our General Counsel in New Mexico who is an extremely able and well-informed man, and I am enclosing a copy of a letter that I have just received from him. This shows that there is some very real danger to some of the pueblos, but not until the war is over I would prefer that this letter not be used other than to inform Mrs. Rockefeller of the situation.

I have noticed the friends of the Indian pueblos have apparently "smoked out" the Congressman from New Mexico, Clinton P. Anderson, who introduced H. R. 323 and he has gone so far as to defend his position by his remarks in the Congressional Record of March 18th, pages A1350, A1353

211

and A1354. It seems that the bill merely authorizes exploration for proposed dams on the upper Rio Grande. Secretary Ickes has approved the bill but has asserted in his report to the Committee that protection would be given the pueblos and that he will see that this is done.

The Commissioner of Indian Affairs has written a letter to the Governors of all the New Mexico pueblos whom he has tried to pacify, telling them that the bill H. R. 323 is only to authorize engineering explorations and that the bill ought not to be defeated. He goes on to say that damage could come to some of the pueblos if dams are built, but he promises that the Indians will have every opportunity to protect their property and their rights.

My advice to Mrs. Rockefeller still is that she keep posted on this legislation, but that there is no present danger to the Indian pueblos. The bill would only provide for explorations; there would have to be another one later to authorize construction, and there would be no money appropriated for construction until after the war is over. Of course, in the National Park Service, we always resisted bills authorizing explorations in national parks or monuments for the reason that the surveys and studies provided convincing data with which to take the next step, namely, procure appropriations and authority for structures that would mean invasion of virgin park territory and exploitation of the park resources. Generally speaking, the Indian pueblos will be safer if no bill is passed not even the pending one authorizing exploration.

Sincerely yours,
HORACE M. ALBRIGHT

April 8, 1943

Dear Mr. Rockefeller:

You will be interested in the following quotation from the Congressional Record of April 6th, page 3067:

"Re-reference of H. R. 323

"Mr. Anderson of New Mexico. Mr. Speaker, I ask unanimous consent that H. R. 323, which was heretofore considered by the Committee on Irrigation and Reclamation of the House, and unanimously reported favorably by that committee, and is now on the Consent Calendar, be taken from that calendar and re-referred to the Committee on Indian Affairs.

"The Speaker. Without objection, it is so ordered.

"There was no objection."

This indicates that friends of the Indians have made enough complaints to force the Congressman to have his bill reconsidered, and this time in the Committee on Indian Affairs. My opinion is that the situation in which we are interested is much improved.

Sincerely yours,
HORACE M. ALBRIGHT

June 23, 1943

Dear Mr. Rockefeller:

I am enclosing a clippings from The Santa Fe New Mexican of June 16th which will give you some late information regarding the status of the pending bill which provides for exploratory work on pueblo lands along the Rio Grande.

It looks as though the pending bill is going to be seriously changed by amendments which will give a great deal of protection to the Indians, including their right to appeal to the courts in case any damage is done to their pueblos as a result of the exploration work.

Also, provision is to be made for studying the upper watersheds of the Rio Grande from which most of the silt comes. Dams on the tributaries of the river I am sure are what should be installed rather than such structures on the Rio Grande on or near pueblo lands.

I still feel that the right kind of an amendment would prohibit any exploration of Indian lands. Then, of course, such an amendment is just a possibility.

Sincerely yours,
HORACE M. ALBRIGHT

June 29, 1943

Dear Mr. Albright:

Many thanks for your note of June 23rd and the enclosed clipping regarding the Indian reservations near Santa Fe.

Things seem to be well in hand. The people interested are certainly doing a good job. Perhaps we should get the Indians to come and testify at the Jackson Hole hearing.

Very sincerely,
JOHN D. ROCKEFELLER, JR.

July 22, 1943

Messrs. John D. Rockefeller, Jr.
Kenneth Chorley
Vanderbilt Webb
Harold Fabian

Gentlemen:

In Washington on July 20th I was at the Capitol and interviewed the Chairmen of the Public Lands Committees of the Senate and House of Representatives -Senator Carl A. Hatch and Congressman J. Hardin Peterson respectively. From them I learned the plans for subcommittee investigations and inspections this summer. Senator Hatch is not very well, and cannot go West. This is the doctor's orders.

He has appointed a subcommittee under the O'Mahoney resolution to investigate national monuments composed of the following: Senator O'Mahoney, Chairman, and Senators McCarran of Nevada, Murdock of Utah, Hatch of New Mexico, Gurney of South Dakota and Nye of North Dakota. As stated above Senator Hatch cannot go West.

Chairman Peterson of the House Committee has appointed the following subcommittee: Chairman Peterson of Florida, and Representatives Murdock of Arizona, Robinson of Utah, White of Idaho, O'Connor of Montana, Hugh Peterson of Georgia, and Barrett of Wyoming. It is possible that Mr. Fernandez of New Mexico will be appointed. Chairman Peterson does not expect all of these members to attend all of his meetings in the West.

Mr. Peterson and Senator O'Mahoney have had a conference, and they have decided to join forces in the Jackson Hole on August 16th. Mr. Peterson proposed that there be no hearings at all for the reason that he thought the same people would speak who have spoken in past hearings, and there would be no point in listening to a lot of discussions which would cover old ground.

He proposed that there be a very careful inspection of the monument, so that the Senators and Congressmen may understand the land status, wildlife problems, the questions of drift of cattle, etc. Senator O'Mahoney agreed to these proposals.

I had a half hour's talk with Chairman Peterson, and he plainly showed his interest in and enthusiasm for the monument. He spoke of Congressmen Murdock and Robinson as being on our side.

Senator Hatch very patiently listened to my review of the whole project from its beginning to the present time. He as well as Chairman Peterson promised that I would be given further opportunities to appear before their committees in Washington. Senator Hatch was particularly pleased that Senator Nye is going to be with the Senate Committee because he was Chairman of the subcommittee in 1928 in the Jackson Hole and again in the big hearings of 1933. No Senator is as well acquainted with the Jackson Hole project as Senator Nye. I understand that Senator Nye will be in Yellowstone for some time previous to the inspection in the Jackson Hole.

The Senate subcommittee is going to consider in the West matters other than national monuments. Most of its time will be put on study of the western coal fields and hydrogenation of coal properties. The committee will be on the coal studies at Pittsburgh on August 6th, Salt Lake City the 9th, and Sheridan, Wyoming the 11th. The House committee will study the Elk Hills oil problem as well as inspection of the Jackson Hole.

Another committee that will visit the West and the Jackson Hole particularly is a subcommittee of the House Appropriations Committee composed of Congressmen Norrell of Arkansas, Kirwan of Ohio and Jensen of Iowa. The first two are Democrats; the last a Republican. This subcommittee will go into the Jackson Hole from Yellowstone, and will be under the guidance of national park officials. It will not conduct any hearings.

Personally I am very greatly pleased with the composition of these committees and the constructive policy of arranging for a thorough inspection rather than hearings. I feel confident that the results of the committees' work will be favorable to our project.

As for myself I will be in Massachusetts from July 23rd to August 9th, in New York August 10th, and in New Mexico August 12th to about the 23rd. I shall be back here about the 25th or 26th of August. I expect to remain here thereafter.

Sincerely yours,
HORACE M. ALBRIGHT

216

September 1, 1943

Dear Mr. Rockefeller:

I returned from New Mexico on Thursday, the 26th. I have not had an opportunity to talk with anybody but Director Drury about the Jackson Hole situation, but from him and from letters I find on my desk, I am able to form a tentative opinion that the Jackson Hole National Monument is perfectly safe and the worst of our troubles are well behind us. This view may be revised as I get into things a little deeper, but I do not think that this will be the case.

I enclose a clipping from the Santa Fe New Mexican of August 18th, giving you further information regarding the efforts of the Pueblo Indians to protect their lands from the reclamation schemes that are under consideration. The people I talked with in Albuquerque seem to think that the Indians and their friends have made very strong cases for non-interference with their rights and that the reclamation enthusiasts would have to look for the control of silt upstream where the Indian pueblos and lands would not be imperiled. I might say that this particular Congressional Committee was largely under the guidance of the National Park Service.

I hope that Mrs. Rockefeller and you have had a pleasant, restful summer. You must miss the gardens, roads and trails and other cherished things of Acadia.

Sincerely yours,
HORACE M. ALBRIGHT

November 12, 1943

Dear Mr. Albright:

I am enclosing a letter I wrote to Mr. Hadley on October 20th regarding the deer situation in Acadia National Park together with his reply of November 3rd, both of which please return ultimately and wholly at your convenience.

You will note that Mr. Hadley seems to devote more thought and attention to the question of an adequate census of the deer than to the real question which is their destructiveness to vegetation. Whether there are ten deer or ten thousand, it seems to me is of little interest so long as the forest undergrowth in many places is being disfigured or destroyed and various types of growing things are being exterminated or badly mutilated. It is these visible evidences of serious inroads on the beauty of the vegetation of the Island which have disturbed me in the park for some years past.

Mr. Hadley, with the best of intentions, is not a big enough or strong enough man to get anything done by the state legislature. Mr. Drury has too much else on his hands to concern himself about this problem nor would he, I fear, bring to it the necessary decision and force even were he to interest himself in it.

The only practical and adequate solution seems to me that the park rangers should, in this park as in other national parks, destroy the surplus deer; but apparently this cannot be done in a national park in the state of Maine without some legislative action. Undoubtedly, such action would not be popular among the voters, who would much prefer to see the park open to hunters. But the feasibility of that solution has been fully considered and, as Mr. Hadley indicates, the people on the Island recognize how dangerous such action would be.

The result seems to be a stalemate and a vicious circle. I presume it is not worth while to give the matter any further consideration until after the war when things become more normal, but it does seem to me as though some workable solution ought to be found and, as always in such matters, I am turning to you for counsel and advice. There is no slightest haste about considering this question. You may prefer to let the whole matter lie until I am in the office again in early December when we can discuss it.

Very sincerely,
JOHN D. ROCKEFELLER, JR.

November 17, 1943

Dear Mr. Rockefeller:

I have just received and read your letter of November 12th with its enclosures regarding the overabundance of deer in Acadia National Park. I recall some years ago we discussed this problem, and I had assumed that by this time it had been possible to work out with the state some practical means of control of the deer population so that serious destruction of vegetation could be stopped.

Of course, there are two problems to be solved. One is the fixing of responsibility for the control of the herd and with it an agreed method of effecting control, and the other is the reaching of a decision as to how many deer should be retained in the area, what the optimum size of the herd should be let us say, and of course this would require collaboration between the National Park Service and the state authorities.

In many of the national parks the states have ceded exclusive jurisdiction over national park lands, and in such cases the National Park Service has ample authority to control animal populations in order to protect other park values. For instance, in Yellowstone, which has always been under complete Federal jurisdiction, elk killing has been done by rangers in places and at times fixed by the Director. The size of the buffalo herd has been controlled by the Director, and for years a number of buffalo have been removed from the herd each autumn or early winter.

In Acadia, however, the state has exclusive jurisdiction, and under the famous Supreme Court case involving the Indian Race Horse it was decided that even on Federal lands the state owns the game. Therefore, in Maine the state must pass appropriate legislation to control the deer in Acadia Park or it should cede exclusive jurisdiction over all national park lands to the Federal Government in which case Congress would have to accept the cession before complete control of the animals would pass to the National Park Service.

In view of the fact that there are a number of isolated park areas on Mount Desert Island, and also in view of the fact that the park is not an area of great size, it would probably be best to try to work out the control problem with the state authorities.

I will look into the matter further, and by the time we get a chance to talk things over together perhaps I will have more information and advice to impart. I realize that what I have said above is not very helpful.

It so happens that Senator McCarran of Nevada has introduced a bill in Congress that is now the subject of hearings in the West. It provides that the Federal Government may control wildlife populations on all public lands. The bill is very broad and is meeting lots of opposition. However, there may be some compromise worked out that would be applicable to a condition such as exists in Acadia National Park, but I really doubt this.

I sincerely hope that the weather in Williamsburg is good, and that Mrs. Rockefeller and you are enjoying a pleasant restful visit.

Sincerely yours,
HORACE M. ALBRIGHT

PART III
1944 – 1960

Acadia National Park, Bull Creek Grove, Carter's Grove, Colonial Historical National Park, Colonial Williamsburg, Dunderberg Mountain, Grandfather Mountain, Great Smoky Mountains National Park, Grand Teton National Park, Jackson Hole National Monument, Linville Falls, National Park Service Personnel, Palisades Interstate Park, Park Museums, Rockefeller Forest, South Calaveras Grove, Virgin Islands National Park.

August 24, 1944

Dear Mr. Albright:

Mr. Dorr's going brings sorrow to all his friends but is for him a happy and well earned release.

When in Seal Harbor lately I saw Mr. Serenus Rodick, who gave me, in confidence, the enclosed copy of Mr. Dorr's latest will. This I thought you might be interested to look at. We can speak of it when we meet. Please return it to me ultimately.

Very sincerely,
JOHN D. ROCKEFELLER, JR.

April 27, 1945

Dear Mr. Albright:

Mr. Wirth of the Park Office spent yesterday here with Mr. Chorley and me considering the possible future use of the present Camp Peary area. We had a delightful day together.

Mr. Wirth gave me a copy of Mr. Demaray's letter to you of April 23rd with its enclosure from Assistant Superintendent Thompson in connection with the bridge designs in Acadia National Park.

It is gratifying that the old Eagle Lake Bridge is completed and that only one architectural plan is still to be finished for the new Eagle Lake Bridge. It is less gratifying that the Duck Brook Bridge, on which the architects have been working off and on for the past four or five years, still lacks 25% of being complete so far as design is concerned and 75% so far as engineering details are concerned. Mr. Spelman estimates two months' full time of the bridge engineers to complete the engineering details. Mr. Demaray feels that all of the work on the Duck Brook Bridge will be ready before funds are available. I hope his feeling is justified. In the light of past experience, my guess is that when money is available and a contract for these bridges could be let, we will still find that the work on the Duck Brook Bridge is unfinished.

These are just passing reflections. No reply to this note is expected.

Very sincerely,
JOHN D. ROCKEFELLER, JR.

May 3, 1945

Dear Mr. Rockefeller:

I received your letter of April 27th from Bassett Hall and was pleased that you had such an interesting day with Messrs. Chorley and Wirth in considering the potentialities of the Camp Peary Area.

This seems to be an appropriate time to review some of our problems:

1) Acadia Park. I have been pressing the National Park Service for completion of the plans for the Acadia Park Road and while I was glad to see that considerable progress has been made as set forth in Mr. Demarary's letter of April 23rd, like you, I was disappointed that the Duck Brook Bridge is still so far from being completely designed and made ready for contract. I expect to see Mr. Demaray either this week or next and I shall emphasize again the advisability of getting all of these bridges ready for advertising the moment new road work can be undertaken. I shall also get in touch with Tom Macdonald, the Public Roads Administrator, formerly known as Director of the Bureau of Public Roads.

2) Acadia Park. I have had some recent correspondence with Superintendent Hadley which indicates that he is very much interested in carrying out items of improvement that have been discussed for years without results. He, and I might say I, too,

223

are hoping that Mrs. Rockefeller and you will be at Seal Harbor for a while this summer so that there will be an opportunity to review matters in the light of Mr. Hadley's thinking on his own responsibility and his ambition to get results of a thoroughly satisfactory nature.

3) Williamsburg. Camp Peary. Naturally I will be greatly interested in hearing whether any satisfactory program is worked out for the acquisition and future management of Camp Peary with or without the cooperation of the National Park Service. I sent Mr. Chorley a note regarding the policy recently adopted to the effect that the Interior Department is likely to have control of lands now used by the Army and Navy which will be valuable for grazing or mineral development in the future; whereas lands that may be valuable for forests and cropping will be disposed of under the Department of Agriculture. I was hoping that there might be enough forests on the Camp Peary land to justify its being turned over to the Department of the Interior. It is my recollection that we found out after we bought a good deal of land in the Yorktown battlefield that there was timber on many acres worth as much as $100 per acre.

4) Jackson Hole. In my judgment this project is in very good shape as far as Congress is concerned. I saw the chairmen of the Public Lands Committees of the House and Senate a few weeks ago and both assured me that there was no pressure at the time for the consideration of legislation to abolish the monument or the Monument Act under which President Roosevelt issued his proclamation. On the other hand I am very apprehensive that we are about to lose a year in completing the plans for the future management and administration and protection and development of the Jackson Hole area.

I have given a great deal of thought to this subject recently and I wish with all my heart that some way could be found to have Harold Fabian put in the summer reviewing all of the plans that have been under consideration in the past, correlating new ideas as to public relations work and directing new planning to the end that by Autumn we would have a complete program available for discussion. My hope is that it might be possible to let Mr. Kendrew go out there for a while. There is a real need for work to be done on the ground on the important project which Laurance has been discussing with Fairfield Osborn. Not only should this be laid out on the ground very carefully, but in as much as the execution of it will involve both Government lands and those owned by you, there is a job of correlation of ideas and plans between Government naturalists and our own group.

Perhaps I am unduly disturbed about this matter, but I feel that this is a critical year, considering the progress being made in bringing the wars to an end and also because Mr. Fabian is at a point where he is not likely to be available unless we can utilize his services now. He has an extraordinary grasp of all phases of the Jackson Hole project, is widely and favorably know in Wyoming and the adjacent states and I feel is quite as capable of dealing with the National Park Service as any of the rest of us. I would like to see Mr. Fabian put in several months in the Jackson Hole this year if there is any way to bring that about. I have no idea how much time he could give to the project.

I have recently had some correspondence with Mr. Murie which clearly indicates that he and some of the other naturalists are coming back to some of the fundamentals of the project. I mean by this that they recognize the vital importance of the Monument in controlling the migration trails of the elk and the utilizing of lands you have acquired in protecting the elk herds. It looked for a while as if the Government naturalists had gone over to the side of those who wanted lands now in the Monument made available for killing with a view to cutting the herd down to a relatively small proportion. Now I am convinced that there is a change back to the well grounded program of 1927 and the years following.

5) Palisades Interstate Park Commission. It looks as though the work of this Commission is going to be very interesting. I assume that Laurance is keeping closely in touch with affairs and knows about the projects that have been programmed for construction as soon as men and materials are available. It is possible, however, that he has not had an opportunity to tell you that top priorities in the budget of the Commission are plans and preparations for construction of the New Jersey section of the Parkway, $180,000 being

available for this and $535,000 for the acquisition of land needed for the entire New York section of the Parkway. Construction plans for the entire New York section are well under way.

I realize that this is a long letter, but I thought that at Williamsburg it might not be too much of a burden on you to read it and also in view of the fact that I soon have to go to New Mexico for several weeks, I thought this might be my only chance to get some of my thoughts before you. I expect to be in Washington May 8th and 9th and again from the 14th to the 17th after which I shall be going directly to New Mexico. I will be in New York May 10th, 11th and 12th.

I was sorry to read that Winthrop had been hurt in the Okinawa area. I remember that the last time we were together I was worried about him, feeling that he might have been sent into the Okinawa invasion. I hope the news you are getting from him now is all good.

I hope Mrs. Rockefeller and you have been having a happy and restful visit at Bassett Hall.

Sincerely yours,
HORACE M. ALBRIGHT

Camp Peary. A wartime military installation northeast of Colonial Williamsburg. It was not given to the Department of the Interior after the war.

Laurance/Osborn project. An effort to create a wildlife park in Jackson Hole.

July 30, 1945

Dear Mr. Rockefeller:

This is a report to you on my interview with George W. Nolte, who wrote you on July 24th about the Bliss Tract. By

226

appointment Mr. Nolte came to the office this morning. He proved to be a Commander in the Navy, but from his conversation I gathered that he is connected with one of the Atwater Kent companies or perhaps is a member of the family. He seemed to be very familiar with Mr. Kent's private affairs.

He began his talk by stating that Mr. Kent is no longer interested in Mount Desert Island in general or Bar Harbor in particular. He has moved to California and expects to spend practically all of his time there. Commander Nolte said that Mr. Kent is glad to make it possible for the Bliss Tract to pass to the National Park Service and hopes that all features of the transfer can be worked out in a period of four months, after formal tender of funds. Commander Nolte said that there would be no restrictions put on the management of the land and he did not see any reason why, if by any chance the National Park Service did not want to keep the entire acreage, some of it could not be disposed of if that should be the policy of the Service.

On the other hand, he was very enthusiastic over the beauty of the unimproved water front part of the Bliss Tract and said that the cliffs were precipitous and the tree growth together with the rocks made a very pleasing composition that he regarded as superb scenery. He even went so far as to say that he personally thought the Park ultimately should own the land between the Bliss Tract and the Satterlee property including Schooner Head, which he thought was one of the prettiest on the Island.

He mentioned the fact that Mr. Kent had ten acres north of the Park known as the Gurnee property and said Mr. Kent had torn down the house and he thought he might be interested in giving this property to the Park. I told him I would mention the Gurnee property to you. I assume that while you are up there, you will have an opportunity to look over these Bliss and Gurnee properties and that you will have suggestions to make as to what course the National Park Service should pursue with respect to them.

When we got into discussing ways and means of carrying out Mr. Kent's desires, I called attention to the National Park Trust Fund Act of July 10, 1935 and gave Commander Nolte a copy to take away with him. Under this act Mr. Kent through

227

his Atwater Kent Foundation, Incorporated, a Delaware Corporation, can make available to the National Park Service $21,000 and can state in the letter tendering these funds just what he wants done with them and the time in which the proposals can be carried out. If his wishes are not fulfilled within the time limits he would have the right to take back the money.

The Commander said he thought Mr. Kent would only wish to tender the money and ask that it be devoted to the purchase of the Bliss Tract, comprising approximately 69 acres, to be made a part of Acadia National Park, and that an appropriate plaque in line with the suggestion of the late Director Cammerer be erected on a boulder near the Park road recording Mr. Kent's generosity.

I told the Commander that I thought the procedure would be for the National Park Service to prepare a draft of the offer with the conditions Mr. Kent suggested and send this to the Atwater Kent Foundation, Incorporated, together with a draft of a reply to the offer agreeing to use the fund of $21,000 as stipulated, in the purchase of the Bliss Tract from the Atwater Kent Properties Corporation, a Florida Corporation, which now owns both the Bliss Tract and the Gurnee Tract, according to my understanding of the Commander's explanation.

I pointed out that there might be costs of title search and other miscellaneous items which the National Park Service probably could not bear and the Commander said he was sure an additional gift could be counted on to cover such costs or that perhaps the Properties Corporation might be willing to take a little less of the $21,000 fund in order to leave a balance to meet title and other expenses.

In other words, if the National Park Service wants this property, it can be obtained, the money being deposited in a trust fund by one Kent Corporation and the land being acquired from another, the National Park Service to prepare drafts of all necessary papers.

Commander Nolte thought Mr. Kent would want the matter closed up in a period of four months after the formal offer is made. I told him I thought this could be done providing there were no great difficulties affecting the titles.

It was quite evident to me that Commander Nolte speaks with authority. He knows Mr. Kent's attitude toward Mount Desert Island properties and that this attitude is best expressed by saying that Mr. Kent no longer has any interests up there. He may not ever go back, although Commander Nolte states that he is in good health.

I can see no reason why the National Park Service should not take advantage of the opportunity to acquire all of the property which composes the Bliss Tract. If Mr. Kent is making a gift and disposing of his property to benefit himself from the standpoint of taxation, that is really Mr. Kent's business and it is not the affair of the National Park Service to explore any personal legal problems that might arise out of the proposed Kent transfers. To me, these transfers present no difficulties and it ought to be easy to complete them in a period of four months.

I make no observation regarding the Gurnee property but I think Commander Nolte would like to hear from you or from the Director of the Park Service about this property if it seems to have value to the National Park Service.

I am rushing this letter up to you with the thought that if you want me to do anything more before I leave here next Sunday, you can send me a wire expressing your wishes. The next step, I suppose, is to fully advise the National Park Service of the opportunity it has to acquire the Bliss Tract. I have had an extra copy of this letter made, which I thought I could send to Mr. Drury if it should be your desire that I should use it in this way. The alternative would be to write Mr. Drury the substance of my interview with Commander Nolte and add your recommendations as to what course he should follow. Or, in the thought that you might want to write Mr. Drury yourself, I am sending to you an extra copy of this letter.

The address of the Atwater Kent Properties Corporation and the Atwater Kent Foundation, Incorporated, is 1105 A Market Street, Wilmington, Delaware.

Sincerely yours,
HORACE M. ALBRIGHT

WORTHWHILE PLACES

August 31, 1945

Dear Mr. Rockefeller:

Following up my telephone conversation with you the other day, I had a talk with Mr. Demaray in Washington yesterday and he said that so far as he could see, negotiations with Commander Nolte for the Atwater Kent property are proceeding satisfactorily. All of the necessary papers in the case were originally drafted by the Park Service lawyers and were sent to the Commander for comment and criticism. He made some changes and returned the papers. The revisions were satisfactory to the Park Service and the final papers are now or should be in the hands of Commander Nolte.

I also asked about the status of the bridges because it seems to be certain that there will be early appropriations for road construction. Mr. Demaray said that he had just been in touch with the Public Roads Administration and had learned that all plans for the Acadia road structures are finished except the Duck Brook bridge and its plans are 60% finished. Inability to get bridge engineers has prevented completion of the plans for the Duck Brook structure. It is at the top of the list for completion and the Roads Administration officer assured Mr. Demaray that by the time the appropriations are available the plans will be completed so that the Acadia road structures can be included in one of the first contracts to be let.

I have received informal advice which I did not seek to check with the Interior Department to the effect that Assistant Director Conrad L. Wirth of the National Park Service has been appointed a Colonel on the staff of General Lucius Clay and is being sent to Germany to advise on the preservation of scenic and historic areas as a part of the planning for the rehabilitation of Germany. I thought you might like to know this in the event that you thought we ought to have any further talks with Mr. Wirth about any of the problems around Williamsburg. Mr. Wirth himself has not told me about this appointment.

Sincerely yours,
HORACE M. ALBRIGHT

March 25, 1946

Dear Mr. Rockefeller:

Knowing that you will be going to Williamsburg soon, I thought you might be interested in reading the attached report from the Colonial National Historical Park, in which references are made to several items that we have had under consideration in the past.

I was talking with Senator Brewster, of Maine, while in Washington last week. He told me that Secretary Ickes is very anxious to again spend his summer vacation at the Homans House. Afterwards, in talking with some Park Service people, it seemed to be their view that there were not necessarily any objections to his doing this; unless, of course, the new Secretary should want to stay there. People who know the new Secretary think he will want to spend the summer getting acquainted with all of the various activities under his jurisdiction.

The Navy is insistent on keeping and making permanent the temporary radio station on Mount Desert Island near the site of the one we got moved. Should we not exert some pressure to make the Navy comply with its promises? Maybe your naval officer sons can give us some advice on this subject.

I find the new Secretary and I have many friends in common. I am hoping to meet him when I am in Washington April 9th and 10th.

Faithfully yours,
HORACE M. ALBRIGHT

New Secretary of the Interior. Julius Krug.

Naval officer sons. John 3rd and Laurance.

March 29, 1946

Dear Mr. Albright:

Thank you for your note of March 25th and the interesting enclosure. Your letter contains several items of more than passing interest.

I know that the ex-Secretary and his family greatly like the Homans House and am not surprised at their wanting to return there. Just how a park house could be thus used, you would know better than I.

The Radio Station to which you refer I presume is the one beyond Sea Wall where the large motor camp is. It would, indeed, be a calamity to have that area permanently shut off as a naval station. I doubt if my Navy officer sons can be of any help in the matter. A letter to Secretary Forrestal would seem to me the wisest approach. This I could write if you thought it wise and would draft the letter.

I am interested in what you say about the new Secretary and shall be glad to have your reactions after you have met him. Like yourself I never have met him. What one hears about him is gratifying and reassuring.

Very sincerely,
JOHN D. ROCKEFELLER, JR.

Secretary of the Navy. James B. Forrestal.

April 26, 1946

Dear Mr. Rockefeller:

I am sending you a letter dated April 4th which I received from Ben Hadley regarding affairs in Acadia National Park. Of course, the outlook for the road and bridge building program is immensely complicated by the inflationary labor situation and the scarcity of materials.

I have noted that the general policy has been adopted of accepting bids if they are on the 1940 basis of construction costs plus 35 per cent.

This would mean that everything planned for Acadia Park might be undertaken if contractors can be found who will build under this policy.

Mr. Drury has sent me copies of his correspondence with you about his interview with Mrs. Potter Palmer. I certainly agree with you that he has a great opportunity to convince her that the motor road project ought to be completed and that she has everything to gain by cooperating.

Faithfully yours,
HORACE M. ALBRIGHT

April 29, 1946

Dear Mr. Albright:

Thank you for Mr. Hadley's letter, which I am returning herewith.

In view of the general strike condition throughout the country and the reluctance of people to leave the $25 a week dole and get back to work, also in view of the sky-rocketing of costs of all kinds of work and material, the prospects of early resumption in the National Parks of road completion do not seem very good.

Very sincerely,
JOHN D. ROCKEFELLER, JR.

WORTHWHILE PLACES

July 15, 1946

Dear Mr. Rockefeller:

This is just a note to say that I have had an opportunity to do considerable thinking about the various matters discussed in your office the other morning and I find myself in heartiest agreement with the program. I can readily appreciate the fact that one's perspective of the Tetons would be improved by getting up on the bench which Mr. Kendrew's route would follow to the south end of Black Tail Butte. Of equal importance is the fact that dropping down from this bench around the southwestern end of the Butte one would get an extremely impressive view of the Grand Teton which would be immediately in front of one as he moves northward. However it would be a simple matter to move the road up on the bench at some later date.

The basic feature of the program which is so thoroughly sound is that it can be moved forward at once leaving out so many things that might be controversial and which probably would be easy to solve in the future; and, on the other hand, that it does not finally preclude certain other phases of the problem such, for instance, as a possible future parkway along the line of Mr. Kendrew's suggestion back of Black Tail Butte.

I want to say again how exceedingly happy I am that you had an opportunity to visit the Jackson Hole again and had a chance to see for yourself that the fundamentals of the project have been carried out by letting nature take back the country. Your acquisitions, of course, saved the region and I still think it is the loveliest mountain country in America if not the world.

Hoping that your summer in Maine will be extremely pleasant in every respect, I am,

Faithfully yours,
HORACE M. ALBRIGHT

August 20, 1946

Dear Mr. Rockefeller:

This is a letter about a number of things, and certainly requires no reply.

I have a letter from Under Secretary of the Interior, Oscar L. Chapman, who says he has had the best vacation of his life in Maine. I wonder if he was at the Homans House, and if so, he saw you. I think he has a very great deal of influence with the new Secretary, and I know he has always been welcome at the White House, both in the times of Roosevelt and Truman. Mr. Chapman did not mention the location of his holiday in Maine.

Mrs. Albright and I are again at this old Dwight L. Moody hotel for a three weeks vacation. It is a lovely spot and the folks here are as fine as we have been with at a summer resort.

Among the splendid people we have met, are Dr. and Mrs. Stuart Nye Hutchinson. Dr. Hutchinson is pastor of the Liberty Presbyterian Church of Pittsburgh, a man of exceptional personality and talents. He is deeply interested in Williamsburg. As far back as 1910, he was pastor of a church in Norfolk, and came to know the mouldering city of Williamsburg. He was wont to taking friends over to see the old places. Once he was stopped by a pleasant man who offered to show him the college and other points of interest. Dr. Hutchinson had some friends with him. They had a wonderful walk with the kindly fellow, and when they parted, they whispered about tipping him, but decided not to do it. The man was Dr. Chandler, they learned a little later. Dr. Hutchinson said that at the time, many people in Norfolk had a low opinion of the populace of Williamsburg. They said it was where "the lazies sat and watched the crazies".

WORTHWHILE PLACES

The Isle Royale National Park will be dedicated on August 27th. This park is in Lake Superior, north of Duluth. Mr. Drury will preside. I am hoping he will visit Acadia before the summer is over, and go over the motor road route with Mrs. Potter Palmer.

Your Tarrytown municipal survey and study interests and excites me. Arthur Packard sent me some clippings from the local paper about it. The Reeds, who will make the study and report to you, are old friends of ours. Grace and I were in Dr. Reed's classes at the University of California as early as 1909, when he first went west. We see this able couple from time to time, and are very fond of them. We had not known of their selection by you for this study. I can testify that a more competent pair could hardly have been found in the entire country.

The main thing that interests me about the study, is that it is a sound planning step, and whether it results in reorganization of corporate affairs in the cities affected or not, physical planning of improvements, preparation of long term capital budgets, etc., are certain to be expedited and placed on a firmer foundation than could otherwise have been possible.

So, the survey is bound to be a great public benefit to that lovely Tarrytown region.

Incidentally, Arthur Packard's Planning Commission in Rye has done a superb job of city planning, and it is already receiving highly merited acclaim.

The Palisades Parkway fight is on again as you know. Already the issues are being clearly and openly defined and the enemy is being exposed more completely than was the case last winter. This is a little premature, but we had no choice in the time of discussion. Anyway, anytime after Labor Day when people are home again, will be appropriate to join issues and see the thing through. I have no doubt about the outcome.

Enclosed is a clipping from an Englewood paper, the first in a series. Perhaps your own office has already sent this to you. It indicates the agressiveness of the opposition.

I am still happily contemplating your recent trip to Jackson Hole. I have wanted so much for you to see what a tremendous conservation job you did when you stopped the ruthless exploitation of that lovely land, protected the game driftways, and restored the landscape in the foreground of the Tetons, not to mention safeguarding the values inherent in the historical associations of the region.

I'll be back in New York on August 26th; in Washington September 4th and 5th; in Denver the week of September 9th; and in New York again until late October.

Grace joins me in all good wishes to Mrs. Rockefeller and you, and any of the young folks who are with you.

Faithfully yours,
HORACE M. ALBRIGHT

Tarrytown municipal survey. Rockefeller financed a study of municipal government by Dr. Thomas H. Reed and his wife Doris. They recommended that the towns of Tarrytown, North Tarrytown, and Irvington-on-Hudson be combined into one city. They proposed a charter commission and a referendum. The proposal was not adopted.

January 20, 1947

Dear Mr. Albright:

When John visited the Big Smoky National Park within the past year, he was distressed to find the bronze tablet on top of the mountain so corroded and weather stained that it was practically illegible.

Whether it is possible to prevent that condition or correct it I do not know. If correction or prevention of this condition is reasonably possible it would seem worth while to apply the necessary remedies, which I would, of course, be glad to pay for. Perhaps through some of the park superintendents you can get a report, wholly at your convenience, on the situation, as the result of which some recommendation for its correction may develop.

Very sincerely,
JOHN D. ROCKEFELLER, JR.

January 23, 1947

Dear Mr. Rockefeller:

I have your note of January 20th about the bronze plaque on the memorial in the Great Smoky Mountains National Park. The situation you describe has occurred since 1944 when I saw the tablet. Of course in the meantime there has been a change of superintendents, Mr. Ross Eakin, the man who was in charge from 1931 to 1945, having died after a long illness. I do not know the present Superintendent. You can be sure that I will find out about the situation and have it remedied.

I am going to be in Washington from next Monday, the 27th, to February 9th and expect to interview National Park Service officials on a number of matters. I shall also see the Regional Director of the National Park Service who has general supervision over Great Smoky Mountains National Park.

Are there any other matters bearing on the various park projects in which we are interested that I ought to inquire into while I am down there? I thought I would check up on the road and bridge plans and of course I particularly want to do anything I can to oppose the proposal to build a bridge over the York River at Yorktown.

I am sure you must be gratified by the news that is coming to you about the very much brighter prospects for early commencement of work on the Palisades Parkway.

Faithfully yours,
HORACE ALBRIGHT

April 9, 1947

Dear Mr. Rockefeller:

In January we had a conversation over the telephone about the condition of the bronze plaque at the memorial at New

Found Gap in the Great Smoky Mountains National Park. I discussed the matter with Associate Director A. E. Demaray of the National Park Service who got some preliminary information, I think, from the Regional Office to the effect that the patina of the plaque probably was such that in certain lights the wording was not easily read.

It now appears upon further investigation, which was conducted by Mr. R. A. Wilhelm, one of the landscape architects of the National Park Service, that the plaque did need some special treatment and that it is now getting this treatment and will continue to get it so that the situation John discovered will not occur again.

I thought you might be interested in a memorandum dated March 18th which with its enclosures was loaned to me. The enclosures have more of a bearing on criticisms I have made of conditions I observed at New Found Gap in 1944.

That was in the midst of the war and not having funds the revision of planting and certain needed stone work had to be postponed. Apparently all of the needed work is likely to be done soon so that we can assume that the memorial will be satisfactory to all of us—or at least more nearly satisfactory before long.

If you have any comments on the enclosures, I would appreciate your letting me have them with the return of these papers.

Faithfully yours,
HORACE M. ALBRIGHT

July 14, 1947

Dear Mr. Albright:

Yesterday Mrs. Rockefeller and I drove over the two first sections of the Acadia Park Motor Road which are awaiting bridges. The first section is the one on the north side of the old Eagle Lake road and the first link needed to connect the present motor road. The second section is the section from the new Eagle Lake road to the Duck Brook Bridge. These two sections are in fine condition both as to road surface and surrounding area. The views from them are magnificent. Our drive made us all the keener to see at least these two bridges constructed without too long a delay. I am only confirmed, therefore, in my interest in knowing what the probable cost of the bridges would be and whether contractors could be found who would take such contracts in these times.

The mountain road never was more beautiful. The heavy rains during the spring and early summer have prevented blights and the partial dying of trees on the mountain as so often occurs in the ordinarily dry season.

The Ocean Drive and the old radio station area are also beautiful.

But the Black Woods road all the way from the Jordan Bond Road past the Dane Farm and to Otter Creek has never had the dead timber cut off of it and it is a disgrace to the park. Long stretches where the fill bank is twenty or thirty feet high have nothing growing and the blight which has attacked all birch trees this past year or two has killed or partially killed many hundreds if not thousands of trees along this entire area. I realize, of course, that the difficulty lies with the scarcity of labor and the fact that the park's funds have been so severely cut that even ordinary maintenance must suffer. What a difference from the days when you were at the head!

But the purpose of this letter is only to emphasize my interest in knowing more about the possibility of the early construction of the bridges.

Very sincerely,
JOHN D. ROCKEFELLER, JR.

July 16, 1947

Dear Mr. Rockefeller:

I have received both your letters about the Acadia Park motor roads and have read them with keenest interest.

I was delayed in answering the first letter until I could get the information about the status of the bridges, costs, estimates, and so forth. The estimates have now come in and I quote them as follows:

Duck Brook Bridge - $448,000 - estimate prepared July 12, 1946
Eagle Lake Road Overpass - $48,457 - estimate prepared September 20, 1946
New Eagle Lake Road Overpass - $76,068 - estimate prepared September 20, 1946

A letter from Associate Director A. E. Demaray, dated July 15th points out that the above estimates are the latest that the Public Roads Administration has made and that the Public Roads Administration is the agency that will be responsible for the advertisement of the projects and the construction of the bridges.

The final paragraph of Mr. Demaray's letter is also quoted:

"Because of the small appropriations for roads, trails and physical improvements contained in the pending 1948 Interior Department Appropriation Act for the National Park Service, no major projects can be undertaken at Acadia this coming year. I regret sincerely that this is the case."

It is difficult for me to understand why the Interior Department is not able to handle its budget more successfully. While the Department of Agriculture also suffered very large cuts in its estimates for road and trail building in the National Forests, in the Senate much of the House reduction was restored and it looks very much as if all of the agencies in the Department of Agriculture will have ample road and trail funds during this new fiscal year which began July 1st.

You will note that as far as the two Eagle Lake Road bridges are concerned, your own estimates were not wide of the mark, both being slightly higher than the estimates of the

Public Roads Administration; but, as to the Duck Brook Bridge, your estimate is very much lower than that given by the government agency. Of course all of the estimates quoted above were made in 1946 and do not take into consideration price rises that have occurred in the past year.

You do not ask my advice as to whether you ought to undertake the construction of these bridges but I will venture to say that in my judgment we can get this work undertaken by the government within a year or so if we can get a chance to work on the budget. For that reason I do not recommend your trying to build the structures yourself.

I wonder if you know that Governor Horace A. Hildreth of Maine, who was a ranger in my organization for two or three summers, when he was a student at Bowdoin in the 1920s, has just been in Yellowstone and Jackson Hole. Mr. Fabian had a good visit with him and found him extremely sympathetic to all we've been doing out there.

I wish I could see Acadia Park again; I love that area. I shall always be grateful for the opportunity I had to play a little part in its development.

With all good wishes to Mrs. Rockefeller and you, I am,

Faithfully yours,
HORACE M. ALBRIGHT

July 21, 1947

Dear Mr. Albright:

Thank you for your letter of July 16th about the Acadia Park bridges. Since the estimates which you quote are nearly a year old, I presume the cost today would be much higher. I did not ask your opinion in writing you for the figures because I am so eager to see this road finished and in use that I had quite made up my mind to pay for at least the first two bridges myself if they could be built shortly and the cost was not too high. In the light of the figures you submit and what they would probably be today, I am hesitant about doing anything, the more so since you feel that there is a possibility of the park's building at least the first two bridges within the year. You say this possibility is dependent upon "if we get a chance to work on the budget". Does that mean that you would be willing to so present this subject that a budget appropriation would be made therefor? If that is possible and if you are willing, it would be wonderful. Is there anything I can do to help?

I am glad you reminded me about your earlier relation to Governor Hildreth. I had not known of his former interest in national parks and am delighted to hear that he has recently visited Yellowstone and Jackson Hole. In this connection, the enclosed copies of letters that have passed between Governor Hunt and Secretary Krug are not very reassuring. I am sending copies of these letters to Mr. Chorley also.

Thank you for the material about the Great Smoky Mountains and the Colonial National Historical Park, which you have sent me. I was glad to see this material and, as you suggested, am destroying it.

How I wish you could come to Acadia again this year! If you could spend a day or two, nothing would please us better than to have you stay with us. We shall be here until toward the end of August. Should this be possible, do let me know.

Much appreciating the trouble you have taken to get this bridge information, I am,

Very sincerely,
JOHN D. ROCKEFELLER, JR.

July 30, 1947

Dear Mr. Rockefeller:

I have received your letter of July 21st and read it very carefully. Answering your question, what I have in mind is

243

that during the autumn I will get an opportunity to discuss the National Park Service budget not only with the Interior Department officers but also with some of the men rather high up in the Bureau of the Budget with a view to seeing to it that the National Park roads and trails item is on a sound basis with respect to other items. Then it may be necessary to do some work with the Appropriations Committee of the House of Representatives, and I think it is going to have a new Chairman; that is of the Interior Department subcommittee.

Very shortly a man will come to live in New York to serve here as a Judge in the United States Customs Court. He is the Honorable Jen Johnson of Oklahoma who was for many years Chairman of the Interior Department Subcommittee of the House Committee on Appropriations. He has always been interested in your projects. We can get him to help by working with his old colleagues.

I think it is safe to proceed in this way because with the summer of this year almost gone and bearing in mind the time it would take to re-estimate the cost of the bridges, have them advertised for bids, let contracts and so forth it would be almost impossible to get anything done during the fall or winter.

My thought is that we should aim to develop a financial structure for these projects with a view to having them advertised early next spring. There would still be an opportunity for you to undertake the two smaller ones if you felt that you would like to make sure that these two bridges are built next year.

If, however, you should decide to go ahead now, I will be glad to do anything I can to facilitate action.

Sunday Mrs. Albright and I are going up to the Northfield Inn at East Northfield, Massachusetts. You should have no hesitancy in writing me there if you wish to pursue this matter further.

Mrs. Albright joins me in words of gratitude for your suggestion that we spend a day or two with you at Seal Harbor. We still look back with keen pleasure to the little visit we had with Mrs. Rockefeller and you there in 1940. We would like to see you again but I am afraid that we will not get that far east. If it should prove to be possible at all to go to Maine it would have to be during the week of August 24th.

I hope you were not too much concerned about H. R. 1330, the Barrett bill affecting the Jackson Hole National Monument. It was objected to on the Unanimous Consent Calendar. I am still confident that we have that Jackson Hole National Monument secure and that this pending legislation can be defeated if it comes up in the next session.

With best wishes to Mrs. Rockefeller and yourself, I am,

Faithfully yours,
HORACE M. ALBRIGHT

The Barrett Bill. In 1944, the Barrett Bill to abolish the Jackson Hole National Monument passed both houses of Congress. President Roosevelt killed the bill with a pocket veto. In 1947, Congressman Barrett of Wyoming reintroduced his bill, but, by then, strong support for the monument had developed among conservationists and their friends in Congress. The 1947 bill died in the Rules Committee.

August 1, 1947

Dear Mr. Albright:

Your letter of July 30th interests me greatly. If you feel there is any reasonable possibility of successfully carrying through the program you outline and securing the allocation of the necessary funds for the construction of the three Acadia Park bridges next summer, it would be wonderful. Clearly, this is the wise program if you are willing to assume the burden of carrying it out. It has my hearty approval and you have my sincere gratitude. The inauguration of this program would not prevent my aiding the construction of say, the first bridge over the Old Eagle Lake Road by a contribution to the park to help carry through its program for the three bridges. That we could take up later if it seemed wise. So far as I am concerned then, I shall be delighted to see this program undertaken and will do anything I can to help you in carrying it through. This automatically cuts out any thought of my trying to go ahead with even one of the bridges this fall or winter.

Mrs. Rockefeller and I are sorry that there seems to be so little chance of our seeing you and Mrs. Albright on Mt. Desert Island this summer. You mention the possibility of being able to come up the week of August 24th but, unfortunately, we are going back to New York that week to get ready for our trip to Jackson Hole the following week. Our early departure from Seal Harbor we the more regret if, as a result, we are deprived of seeing you and Mrs. Albright here.

What you say about the Barrett Bill is most reassuring. That wonderful vision of yours which we discussed in Jackson Hole so many years ago and have been both working on ever since, must be realized some day. We will neither of us stop hoping or working for that end.

Mrs. Rockefeller appreciates your kind remembrances and sends her greetings to you and Mrs. Albright.

Very sincerely,
JOHN D. ROCKEFELLER, JR.

August 20, 1947

Dear Mr. Albright:

The visit to Acadia National Park of Messrs. Drury, Allen and Vint, which lasted from Friday afternoon to Monday noon, was, for me, very pleasant and I think from every point of view worthwhile. The three problems which I discussed primarily with these gentlemen having to do with Acadia Park were the three links required to complete the present motor road system:

1. The three bridges.
2. The connection through the Potter Palmer property or the by-pass around it.
3. The permanent connection at the Jordan Pond Road of the Stanley Brook Road with the motor road through the Dane property that was temporarily put along their boundary line at the Jordan Pond end because they were unwilling to make available sufficient land at the time to make an appropriate, permanent connection with the Stanley Brook Road.

As to No. 3, there has still been no further word from the Danes about the completion of the gift of the Wildwood Farm property. I have written their lawyer and also young Mr. Dane, to whom I was referred by the lawyer and from whom I have not heard. These park gentlemen understand the problem, which is easy of solution and will not take much time or cost a great deal when the title to the property has passed. I am hoping to hear from the Danes any day.

As to No. 2, Mr. Drury and the other gentlemen viewed with Mrs. Potter Palmer from the Pike property the flags in the trees along the proposed line of the road above Mr. Dorr's quarry that had been put there so that Mrs. Potter Palmer would see just where the road would go and get some idea of how much it would show. There were several interviews but apparently no change of heart on the part of Mrs. Potter Palmer. My guess is that she does not believe the park can go ahead with the bypass now because of lack of money even if it desired to do so and she is, therefore, gambling that the by-pass may not be built. Mr. Drury, however, seemed firm in his determination to build the by-pass as soon as funds were available therefor.

No. 1 - the three bridges - I took the gentlemen over the fragments of this road and they were greatly impressed with the importance of building the bridges. I suggested building one bridge first, following it with the second and third as rapidly as possible; or building the two less expensive ones first, leaving the third if that was necessary. This was considered and thought desirable. But apparently the cost of the bridges has gone up since the estimates submitted to you -Mr. Vint thought possibly as much as 100%.

On the question of money for the bridges, I talked with Mr. Drury along the lines of the suggestions made in your letter, asking him, first, whether he would not now agree to include the three Acadia Motor Road bridges in the 1949 fiscal year budget with enough cash to begin construction in 1948. Mr. Drury's reply was that he seriously doubted the possibility of his being able to do so. I asked him whether I was right in assuming that he had power to allocate under the 1948 fiscal year appropriation funds to be made available in the following fiscal year, that is, the year beginning July 1, 1948, and thus be in a position to let one or two contracts during the coming winter. To this his reply was, "no", that he had no such power. Mr. Rodick had told me that he was under the impression that $500,000 had been set aside for these bridges and could be drawn upon. Without revealing the source of my information, I asked Mr. Drury if this were not true. His reply was that there had been an appropriation made but that with all other appropriations it had been frozen and could not be drawn upon under present congressional or administrative rulings.

I expressed a great desire to see at least one or two bridges built at an early date and am of the impression that Mr. Drury would like to try to satisfy that desire. He gave me the impression, however, that he was bound hand and foot and that there was little, if anything, he could do. I, of course, made no suggestion that I might be willing to contribute toward the cost of the bridges.

As you will see, these three links are all important. The two bridges would probably today cost something like $250,000, the third bridge possibly $750,000 or $1,000,000. The by-pass around the Potter Palmer property means perhaps a mile and a half of road construction. If this cost $100,000 a mile, that would be $150,000. The Dane connection, if and when possible, might cost from $25,000 to $50,000. Taking the higher figures throughout and leaving out the third most costly bridge, we have, say, $250,000 for two bridges, $150,000 for the Potter Palmer by-pass - which, of course, means a connection through the Atwater Kent western property with the present motor road opposite the Homans place and the temporary by-pass coming down to the Schooner Head Road opposite the Potter Palmer gate - and $50,000 for the Dane connection, total $450,000 - let us say, in round numbers, $500,000.

This is what has been running through my head. Instead of my offering to pay for any one of these three pieces of work, would it be anything of a leverage for me to offer to the government $1 for every $1 it agreed to expend forthwith for these three undertakings up to $250,000 from me and the same amount from the government? This, of course, is assuming that the Dane connection will shortly be possible; if not, it could be eliminated and Nos. 1 and 2 undertaken.

With the foregoing as a background, I shall be glad to have your reaction to my suggestion and your views as to what other course might give greater promise of early results.

I talked with Mr. Drury about Jackson Hole. He told me that the data for the road survey was all in hand and that the survey ought to be on paper within another month or so.

We also discussed the Otter Creek swimming pool project and made some progress toward its further study and development.

The gentlemen likewise agreed to a location on the top of Cadillac Mountain for a rebuilt tavern to take the place of the one on the Summit that is so badly located from a business point of view and that would cost so much to put in order as a result of its occupation by the Army during the war.

This is a long letter but I wanted to give you the facts about the problems here and what I had sought to do about these problems in the light of your two-page letter to me from Northfield Inn outlining what you hoped Drury would do and also what you were prepared yourself to do. I should add that Drury seemed to be conscious of the agreement made by Secretary Ickes on behalf of the Department of the Interior with me about the completion of the motor road system and did not question its validity nor the Department's intention to carry it out. The only question was when monies could be secured therefor.

You will be interested in the following facts which my office has just sent at my request. I have contributed to date to Acadia National Park 6900 acres of land, the gift value of which is $900,000; and have built roads, the gift value of which is some $2,00,000. I have still some land which I have agreed to give to the park and which I am proceeding to transfer currently. This will probably make the total land gift figure something like $1,000,000.

Very sincerely,
JOHN D. ROCKEFELLER, JR.

Thomas C. Vint. Chief of Design and Construction for the National Park Service.

August 21, 1947

Dear Mr. Albright:

I am enclosing herewith a letter which Mr. Hadley wrote me under date of July 22nd and my reply of the 28th, also a letter from Mr. Drury dated January 24, 1947, in which he says - referring to browsing of the deer - "the trend of affairs is significant and indicates that our problem on Mt. Desert Island is abating"; and, finally, a memorandum of May 26, 1947 signed by the Director in which I call your special attention to the marked paragraph on the first page, suggesting the desirability of preparing the people of the Island for the need of "instituting public hunting in the early stage of a deer irruption".

As you will see in my letter to Mr. Hadley, I take the position that, in so far as I have been informed, the park, whatever its authority, has never been prepared to take any action itself in the control of the deer and until it was ready to do so should occasion arise, it seemed to me a waste of time and money to pursue this meticulous study of the rise and fall of the deer herd and the amount of browsing. Mr.

Hadley's letter to me and my reply, I showed Mr. Drury and reiterated the point just made. Mr. Drury seemed to feel that the park had power to act, even destroying deer by the rangers if it seemed wise, but that the park would so act or think it wise to take such action seemed in his mind quite another question. I expressed my lack of sympathy with this study of the deer over the years and its futility so far as protecting vegetation is concerned or reducing the number of deer, but Mr. Drury still seemed to think it was a desirable thing to go ahead with. We did not discuss the matter to a conclusion.

The folly of the expenditure of money for this purpose over the years in this so purely academic manner and in the light of the absolute lack of monies for even reasonable park upkeep seems to me so patent that I dislike to be a party to encouraging it. On the other hand, it is a small thing and perhaps I am being small about it in not wanting to consent to the use of the horse roads by rangers for the pursuit of the study. I shall greatly appreciate your frank opinion in the matter. Please return the enclosures with your reply.

Very sincerely,
JOHN D. ROCKEFELLER, JR.

September 3, 1947

Dear Mr. Rockefeller:

I want you to know that I have received and carefully read your letters of August 20th and 28th relating to your interviews with Messrs. Drury, Allen and Vint and Acadia Park officials when they were in the park the middle of the month; and as to your letter of August 28th, it quoted from a communication you had from Mr. Drury about his talk with Secretary Krug regarding next year's estimates for road building in the national parks.

WORTHWHILE PLACES

Let me say first that I am surprised and discouraged about the fact that Mrs. Potter Palmer has seen fit to remain adamant in her refusal to permit the extension of the motor road across her property. This is one of the most shortsighted, selfish decisions strictly adhered to that I have ever encountered. I have almost reached the conclusion that it would have been better if her husband had lived for further discussions on the subject because Mrs. Palmer may be holding her position partly out of respect for her husband's judgment on this project. If that is so, I can see that it may never be possible to budge her.

As to the connection from the Homans House to the Potter Palmer property going through the land given to the park by Atwater Kent and the road through the Dane property to a connection with the Jordan Pond road, I think your suggestion about including these items in next year's budget a good one even if one of the bridges has to be postponed.

I still have the feeling that all of this work can be put on the road program and contracts let for most, if not all, of it including the three bridges knowing that it will probably take at least two seasons to bring all the projects to completion. This would require the use of a certain amount of cash perhaps somewhat over half of the cost of the projects for one year and the use of so-called authority to contract to be met by appropriations the following year. This may seem complicated but as you know for a long time it has been the practice of the Congress to appropriate a certain amount of money for construction work in the national parks and authorize the obligation of future appropriations to be met by subsequently enacted laws.

President Truman discussed this point at some length in his comments on the performance of the first session of the 80th Congress in trying to explain why it is difficult to estimate how much money would be spent in a fiscal year. On the one hand the Congress finds itself confronted with estimates for deficiency appropriations to meet obligations authorized in previous sessions of Congress and on the other hand it is engaged in authorizing future commitments for which it does not appropriate money. Both Republicans and

Democrats have always resorted to the practice of confusing the public on appropriations. The minority party usually adds the commitments as to future appropriations to the amounts actually appropriated while the majority and responsible party tries to tell a different story by merely mentioning the money actually appropriated for a fiscal year often leaving out on the one hand appropriations made to fulfill commitments of the past and ommitting on the other authority for new commitments to be met by appropriations in the future.

Secretary Krug has gone West again but will be back before the end of the month. I shall be in Washington either late in September or very early in October but in plenty of time to discuss all of the Acadia projects both with the Secretary and with the officers of the Bureau of the Budget as well as with the officers of the Park Service.

In the meantime you will have returned and we can review the various projects again if that seems to be feasible.

I have the feeling that you have pretty strongly impressed Messrs. Drury, Allen and Vint with the necessity of completing the Acadia projects and that they are going to really put their hearts into doing something about these unfinished public works.

Sincerely yours,
HORACE M. ALBRIGHT

September 3, 1947

Dear Mr. Rockefeller:

I have taken time enough since I returned to really study the background of the deer problem at Acadia National Park, the legal situation and so forth. My conclusions are:

1. You should grant permission for the naturalists to use the horse roads, and in granting that permission, if I were you, I would take occasion to make a brief comment on the expense and futility of investigating the perfectly obvious—the over-

abundance of deer and the damage that is being wrought by these animals.

2. We should try to convince the National Park Service that they should take action this winter to reduce the deer population or, if it is necessary, secure adequate authority from the State of Maine to remove deer from the park.

The National Park Service does not own the deer in Acadia National Park. It is in the position of a proprietor of land just as you are the proprietor of the property on which you live in Maine and other property which you own there. You have the right to fence this property and post it against hunting or permit hunting within the hunting seasons prescribed by the laws of Maine. Just so the National Park Service cannot kill deer except in the season because the animals belong to the State of Maine. It can fence the park and post it against hunting on the one hand and on the other, after the Secretary of the Interior has declared that there is an excess population of deer and that they are detrimental to the natural features of the park, the area can be opened to hunting or the animals can otherwise be taken but only as prescribed by the laws of the State of Maine. In other words Uncle Sam has no more rights so far as managing his land in Maine than have private owners of land.

This is not so in parks like Yosemite, Sequoia and so forth. In those parks the states have ceded exclusive jurisdiction to the federal government and the Congress has accepted the tendered jurisdiction thus giving the federal government not only ownership of the land but control of everything on the land including wild life. It is the federal government therefore that has the right to prescribe when wild animals may be captured or killed and in what numbers.

It is possible, of course, that the State of Maine has enacted laws under which the deer problem of Acadia Park can be solved. This had not been done when I was last concerned with this deer problem. Mr. Hadley would know what the situation is.

The point of this dissertation is that even if the National Park Service is disposed to reduce the deer population there is no way to do it lacking exclusive jurisdiction over the park wild life, short of permitting hunting in the authorized season. It would seem to me that now is the right time to proceed to do something about the Acadia deer. The present Governor of Maine is a pretty good wild life expert himself. He has been a National Park officer. I am sure he could be counted on to be sympathetic to the present needs of Acadia Park for a solution of its deer problem. I think he could be counted upon to sponsor the right kind of legislation and I should think that an early conference with him by officials of the National Park Service is in order.

I am returning herewith the papers you sent me with your letter of August 21st on this subject. I want to say that I am in complete accord with everything you said in that letter with reference to the proceedings of the National Park Service in its consideration of the deer problem and its depredations.

Sincerely yours,
HORACE M. ALBRIGHT

October 26, 1947

My dear Mr. Rockefeller:

This is just a note to tell you what I am sure you already feel, that I am deeply distressed and worried about the holocaust that has overtaken Acadia Park. The night in Sante Fe that word came that the fire had surrounded Bar Harbor I could not sleep, for I knew the hopes, sacrifices and endless effort that had gone into establishing and developing that lovely park. Tonight secretary Krug arrived here and told me that he thought one-third of the park is already devastated with fires still spreading in places. One of his young aides told me that he thought the fires had taken all the north and east sides of the park and up to the Bubbles. He thought Cadillac had not been swept by the fire.

I anxiously await word of the end of the fires and a map showing what was saved. I hope with all my heart that the Seal Harbor region was spared.

255

WORTHWHILE PLACES

It is an appalling thought that only last Monday we were talking about the beautiful Acadia Park with only its future improvement and now that whole section is destroyed.

Krug is here for two or three days at a mining Congress and I shall see him again.

With best wishes,

Faithfully.
HORACE M. ALBRIGHT

On October 23, 1947, a widespread fire damaged almost 18,000 acres of forest land in the town of Bar Harbor, Maine. In addition to the damage in the forests, over 170 homes of year-round residents, sixty-seven summer cottages and four hotels in the town were destroyed. A total of 29 square miles of land was burned over, 16 square miles in the park. Most of the burned-over park land was land donated by John D. Rockefeller, Jr. The rest of the Mount Desert Island, including the village of Seal Harbor, was largely untouched. The fire smouldered in the ground in much of the burned area until January, 1948, when sufficient rain fell to dampen it.

WESTERN UNION TELEGRAM

OCTOBER 30, 1947

HORACE M. ALBRIGHT, UNITED STATES POTASH CO., CARLSBAD, NEW MEXICO

DEEPLY APPRECIATE SUNDAY'S LETTER. NO ONE UNDERSTANDS BETTER THAN YOU WHAT THIS CONFLAGRATION HAS MEANT TO ME. THERE IS STILL THE FUTURE. AM WRITING.

JOHN D. ROCKEFELLER, JR.

November 14, 1947

Dear Mr. Albright:

May I supplement my telegram of October 30th with further thanks for your beautiful letter of October 26th about the fire on Mount Desert Island. No one understands quite as you do how much the destruction of this fire in Acadia Park and on the Island means to me. Thank you also for your letters of November 4th and 5th.

For your information I am enclosing a copy of a letter I wrote to Mr. and Mrs. Noyes, two Seal Harbor residents, which gives you a good idea of what has been going on on Mount Desert Island. I am also enclosing a map sent me by Mr. Simpson which shows roughly the area burned over.

Mr. Bartholomew has been in Williamsburg for a day since his first visit to Bar Harbor and lunched with Mrs. Rockefeller and me. We thus could discuss together various of the Mount Desert Island problems. Mr. Allen, the Regional Director of Richmond, has also lunched with us, having himself been to Acadia Park for a week during the fire. Thus, you will see we are pretty well informed as to the situation on the Island.

When are you returning to New York?

Very sincerely,
JOHN D. ROCKEFELLER, JR.

Mr. Harland Bartholomew. Bar Harbor town planner. Discussed cleanup with Rockefeller after 1947 fire.

March 5, 1948

Dear Mr. Rockefeller:

I have just a little item of good news to report to you with reference to the Grandfather Mountain project in North

Carolina. The option has not been renewed but interest in the project has developed to such an extent in the state that it has become the number one item on the program of the newly established North Carolina National Park, Parkway and Forest Development Commission which has just been set up by the State.

The National Park Service has also made some suggestions with reference to the highway up Grandfather Mountain which was built by the owners of the area to the effect that if they will sell this very scenic region at a reasonable price, a twenty year contract to operate the highway as a toll road might be granted. Thus the company would not only get a reasonable price for its land but would have an operating property tax free. It is too early to see how this will work out.

Of course your name has never been brought into any of the transactions. The new Commission knows that if a reasonable price for the property can be obtained, there is a probability that some outside money can be found to match funds that might be raised down there.

Mrs. Albright and I thoroughly enjoyed the week at Williamsburg. The program of Trustee sessions and inspections and committee meetings was so interesting that none of us wanted to get away from the work at any time although, of course, we did enjoy social affairs at the noon hour and in the evening.

Mrs. Albright, Gus Eyssell and I visited Carter's Grove. Mrs. McRae is much worried about what will happen to this place should she pass away or have to leave it on account of disability. She is coming to New York soon and said she wanted to talk with me very seriously about it. Once she suddenly turned to me and said, "I may give this place to you." Of course, she was speaking to me as a Williamsburg Trustee or as a former Director of the National Park Service. I passed on this information to our Board Chairman—John.

The Jackson Hole project remains in *statu quo* . We are watching it closely as Mr. Chorley has undoubtedly advised you.

You are fortunate to be out of this bad weather. It does not get better as time goes on. We hope that Mrs. Rockefeller

and you are thoroughly enjoying your stay in Arizona.
    With all good wishes, I am,

                              Faithfully yours,
                         HORACE M. ALBRIGHT

The Grandfather Mountain project in North Carolina never became part of the national park system. It eventually became part of the North Carolina state park system.

Carter's Grove. A 600-acre plantation, overlooking the James River and seven miles from Colonial Williamsburg, was purchased in 1963 by the Sealantic Fund founded by John D. Rockefeller, Jr. The plantation was given to Colonial Williamsburg in 1963, and since then, the mansion has been open to the public. Since 1984, it has reflected the life style of its occupants in the 20th century as a Colonial Revival showplace. The plantation includes the recently uncovered remains of an early 17th-century townsite, Wolstenholm Towne.

                                        March 11, 1948

Dear Mr. Albright:

    What you write me under date of March 5th about the Grandfather Mountain project is both interesting and gratifying. The situation is apparently developing, although slowly.
    I am glad Mrs. Albright could have shared with you the week in Williamsburg and that the meetings were so interesting and worth while. Mrs. McCrea has for years talked with us about the disposal of her place. At one time she was anxious to sell it forthwith, later she was unwilling to sell it. She has talked with Mr. Ickes and with others about giving it to the National Park system. What either the National Parks or the Williamsburg Restoration could do with the place, I do not know. It would seem to me a great burden to either organization,

and a very considerable expense to maintain and operate. Then too, while very beautiful, in fact outstandingly beautiful, it is not an authentic restoration by any means, and to make it one would rob it of much if its present charm and beauty.

All goes well with us here. I had the pleasure of meeting your Mr. Bicknell the other day and liked him very much. He gave no information about the various points of interest in the surrounding country. We are looking forward to getting home the first week in April.

Very sincerely,
JOHN D. ROCKEFELLER, JR.

April 6, 1948

Dear Mr. Rockefeller:

Grace and I were deeply shocked and grieved by Mrs. Rockefeller's death. We extend to you heartfelt sympathy in your overwhelming loss.

To know her was to love her, and the ennobling experience of knowing and loving her for well over twenty years has been some thing that we have cherished dearly.

We hope that the beautiful memories of your long and supremely happy life together, and your firm and abiding faith will comfort and sustain you.

Ever faithfully yours,
HORACE M. ALBRIGHT

Abby Aldrich Rockefeller, John D. Rockefeller, Jr.'s wife, was born on October 26, 1874 and died April 5, 1948. She was a patron of the arts and an active philanthropist. The Museum of Modern Art in New York and much of the folk art in the Abby Aldrich Folk Art Collection in Colonial Williamsburg are examples of her lasting contributions.

December 13, 1948

Dear Mr. Rockefeller:

This letter relates to the matter we discussed with map before us regarding the new approach road to the town of Bar Harbor. The problem is whether a move should be made at this time that would foreclose the extension of the horse road system to a site for adequate stables near the town through the construction of a fill rather than a bridge.

I feel that I am probably not qualified to give sound advice on this subject. I have given it much thought, however, and give you my reasoning and conclusions for what they are worth.

Naturally I go back in my thinking to the beginnings of the Park and the long-range plans that were made in the first years after it was established and on through my administration. One of the principal features of the program was the horse road system and the trail system for the people who like horseback riding. Since these horse road and trail systems were basic features of the master plans for the park it would seem that they must be given the same consideration, unless the program is to be seriously modified, that the motor road system receives.

If this assumption is correct, then I do not see how the road we are discussing to a possible stable set-up where saddle horses and carriage outfits could be procured can be abandoned. On the other hand, if there is a lessening interest in horses and the prospects for eventual establishment of stables and accompanying equipment are not good, then it might be difficult to argue against a proposal of the Park Service to abandon this one bridge and by so doing cut off the opportunity to extend the horse road to the stable site. Here is where my lack of information regarding the present habits and requirements of the tourists and summer visitors makes me doubtful of my judgment on a problem of this kind.

Summing up, I would say that if my assumption of the horse roads and trails being a basic and thoroughly sound feature of the plans for Acadia Park is true and if, on the other hand, the visitors to the Park, including the summer residents, are interested in horses and horse-drawn carriages, then by all means this horse road we are discussing should be kept on the plan and should be built, and this means that the bridge should be built.

It does not seem to me that I have been helpful to you in this case. Personally, being an enthusiast about horses, I would like to see the horse road and trail program kept intact.

Sincerely yours,
HORACE M. ALBRIGHT

June 16, 1949

Dear Mr. Albright:

The enclosed statement with reference to the desperate condition of the National Parks is most disquieting. I suppose there is nothing that anyone can do about the matter nor any way in which the financing of the reasonable preservation of the parks can be brought to the serious consideration of the Congress.

I pass this statement on with no suggestion and realizing that it refers to a situation which you know only too well.

Please do not trouble to acknowledge this note.

Very sincerely,
JOHN D. ROCKEFELLER, JR.

Rockefeller was referring to remarks made in Congress by Representative Louis P. Heller on March 29, 1949.

June 22, 1949

Dear Mr. Rockefeller:

While you told me not to acknowledge your letter of June 16th, I thought I would like to do it simply to assure you that the National Park Service, while in every bit as bad condition as Bernard De Voto's article in *Harper's* says it is, has prospects of a substantial improvement in its financial situation for the fiscal year which begins July 1st.

Its appropriations for the new fiscal year as authorized in the Interior Department Appropriation Bill which has passed the House of Representatives and which is pending in the Senate amount to $28,056,000. This is to be compared with $13,110,304 available in the current year which ends June 30th, an increase of $14,945,696. Among the increases going to make up this total are: an increase of $85,000 for the regional offices; $775,000 for maintenance and protection of national parks; $525,000 for maintenance and protection of national monuments and historical areas; $50,000 for the acquisition of lands (the new appropriation is $250,000 as compared with $200,000 last year); $6,600,000 for parkways; and $7,500,000 for roads and trails. Also there is an increase of $3,500,000 for miscellaneous construction items—buildings, sewage and water systems, and so forth.

Considering the general status of Federal finances, I think we can be fairly well satisfied with what has been done for the National Park Service this year, but, of course, when you consider the enormous waste that goes on in every branch of the military services we could wish that more efficiency could be put into the Department of Defense thus making more funds available for some of these conservation agencies. Of course, I am delighted that Bernard De Voto wrote as he did and undoubtedly he influenced Congress. I do not think the Senate will make any cut in what the House has appropriated and it might even increase it to some extent; it usually does add items recommended by the Budget but eliminated or reduced in the House.

You will be going west before I return from a trip I am just leaving on to New England and Canada, but I will be here in New York again from July 4th to the 12th before starting for California.

I do not know whether you are giving any consideration in these times to new conservation projects which you might want to participate in carrying out. If you do feel in a position to discuss any new ones, I would like to mention the Calaveras South Grove of Big Trees which is in the gravest danger of destruction. This project has been confused a good deal by demands for saving in connection with it a very large area of sugar pine. I visited the area last September. I suppose I am the last conservationist to have been there. Tremendous efforts are being made to save the Big Tree grove itself and some progress is being made. The State legislature also has the project under consideration. There is nothing definite to consider at the moment. There are ample state funds to match private subscriptions, and payments can be made over a number of years.

I am not attempting in this letter, of course, to make any presentation but simply to again call to your attention what I regard as the only great natural feature conservation job to be done. I am holding myself available to discuss it should you be interested in talking about it at a later date. I have tried all these years not to bring new projects to your attention and I am not doing that now in the sense that I am suggesting that you take action one way or another.

I sincerely hope that you will have a restful, delightful, and altogether interesting visit in the Jackson Hole. The wildflowers ought to be springing up and everything should be fresh and lovely after the long winter of deep snows.

With best wishes, I am

Faithfully yours,
HORACE M. ALBRIGHT

Albright was referring to a Bernard DeVoto "Easy Chair" column in Harper's Magazine of March, 1949. DeVoto devoted two pages to a litany of what was wrong in the parks - from worn out telephone lines, unworkable toilets, crowded camp grounds, decaying roads, mutilated scenic wonders such as Morning Glory Pool in Yellowstone, and real estate developments encroaching on the parks - to the lack of rangers and graffiti on monuments and natural features such as Old Faithful. He ended his column saying, "The Park Service must have a lot more money than it has been getting. And it must begin to get it at once."

Calaveras South Grove. A stand of Giant Sequoia trees west of Yosemite National Park.

June 28, 1949

Dear Mr. Albright:

Thank you for your letter of June 22nd. I am gratified to learn that there is so good a prospect of a larger appropriation for national parks this year.

You will not misunderstand my saying to you that the high regard in which I held the National Parks when you were its head has undergone a marked change with the passing years and my enthusiasm for cooperating with the Service is considerably dampened. It is not probable that I would be interested to contribute to any further park projects, however, if you care to tell me more about the Calaveras South Grove, its location and the reasons why you regard it as important, I will at least review the situation.

I wish you were going to Jackson Hole with Mr. Chorley and me tomorrow. We shall be thinking of you while there. We will be back in New York in about ten days.

Very sincerely,
JOHN D. ROCKEFELLER, JR.

February 2, 1950

Dear Mr. Albright:

How kind of you to remember my birthday and send me so friendly a message of greeting, many thanks! It was a happy day for me when our paths crossed. How much of interest and enrichment you have brought into my life.

With warm regards, I am,

Very sincerely,
JOHN D. ROCKEFELLER, JR.

August 18, 1950

Dear Mr. Rockefeller:

Mrs. Albright and I are leaving for a two-months trip in Europe and will be away from New York from August 19th to about November 1st. Had it not been for this trip I would have sought an opportunity a little later on after you have returned from Maine to discuss with you the South Calaveras Grove of Giant Sequoia trees in California. It is not my wish that this letter be forwarded to you while you are away on vacation at Seal Harbor. Perhaps when you return to New York there will be time for you to read it and give it such consideration as it merits.

So far as I can recall, since I left the directorship of the National Park Service, I have not made any proposals to you regarding important conservation projects. I have taken the position that you have done more than your share in saving great scenic areas, forests, wildlife, and historic sites and structures. For nearly twenty years I have been extremely reluctant to even think of presenting a new project to you and I still feel that way. However, the South Calaveras Grove presents a situation that deserves the review of all of us who are interested in the conservation of very great natural features of our American landscape.

This Grove, which I think must be regarded as holding the same position among groves of Giant Sequoia trees that the Bull Creek Grove holds among the Coast Redwoods, has been isolated from the currents of traffic and communication

266

since its discovery. Its sister grove, the North Calaveras Grove of Big Trees, was one of the first to be discovered and opened to travel. Even a camel train was taken into the North Grove in the 1850s. The South Grove, which lies in the midst of a vast forest in the Stanislaus River basin, has been almost inaccessible. Today it cannot be visited by automobile except by the roughest travel over roads built to take out logs. The isolated valley in which it lies has no roads in it. To be enjoyed today it must be traversed on foot.

Mr. Mather and I visited this area in 1924 going from the North Grove by horseback to the western entrance of the South Grove valley and walking all the way through this great timbered area. We were tremendously impressed by the South Grove but felt that its acquisition and protection as a public reserve might be a matter that would be postponed anywhere from 30 to 50 years. The Stanislaus watershed was one vast, untouched forest and at that time it seemed, considering all the other timber resources of California, that it would require many years of cutting on the fringes, so to speak, to make any serious dent in the Stanislaus forests. World War II tremendously speeded up the cutting of timber all over California. I was shocked when I returned to the Calaveras Grove country late in 1948 to find railroads built all through the Stanislaus region and the great South Grove itself threatened.

State Park authorities became alarmed as early as 1944 and 1945. Frederick Law Olmsted was engaged to make studies of the region and work out feasible park projects. This he did and submitted some very interesting and valuable reports. In 1947 while you were at Tucson your attention was directed to some newspaper reports on the necessity for saving other sugar pine forests in California and you asked your office to obtain information about these forests. I was asked for data and upon looking into the matter found that the sugar pine areas were in the region of the South Calaveras Grove and constituted one of the units in Mr. Olmsted's state-park plan. The only data I had or could get at the time was contained in Mr. Olmsted's report which I forwarded to your office, and it was sent to you. You later advised us in sending the report back that you felt that this was too large a project for you to consider.

267

Meantime, the logging railroads have penetrated the forest more deeply and cutting of timber has gone on at a terrific rate. The South Calaveras Grove now is in grave danger. On the other hand, strong agencies have joined in attempting to work out a program for preserving the area. I call attention to a press release dated March 31, 1950 issued by Warren T. Hannum, Director of Natural Resources of the State of California. I have obtained additional information and find that the State of California has allocated one million dollars toward the acquisition of the South Grove and this will be used to match a million dollars that the Forest Service is ready to contribute on road construction. I neglected to say that the state-park plan contemplates a parkway through beautiful and untouched forests connecting the North and South Groves. There is also Forest Service timber in and adjacent to the Big Trees valued at $250,000 which will be contributed but the value of which must be matched. The difficulty still to be met is to get a firm price on the land and timber needed to carry out the project. It appears that there is $2,250,000 in state cash, federal timber values and road construction available, so that if the total cost of the project should be $2,500,000, as may be the case, there would be $250,000 "matching" money still needed. On the other hand, if the cost should be higher than $2,500,000, naturally there would be more "matching" money needed. It seems to me that the total "matching" funds that must be raised might be as high as $500,000, perhaps somewhat higher. Efforts are now being directed toward obtaining a firm price. There may be something definite known by the time I return from Europe.

I know the South Calaveras Grove very well from my two visits there. Two things impressed me aside from the magnificence of the mixed forests. One is the great variety of trees and the unusual size of almost all varieties, and the second is the fact that the Giant Sequoia Trees have grown like columns appearing to be the same diameter almost all the way to the top. Timber cruisers have told me that these trees do not follow the tapering rules and contain very much more timber than would be measured by following the standard formulae in computing their contents.

I wish it could be possible for you to see the South Calaveras Grove. One can get there, as I have indicated above, by station wagon over roads built by bulldozers to bring out logs but it is not a difficult horseback ride from good roads easily reached by automobile.

I have maps and Mr. Olmsted's report available in the event that you should want to look them over in advance of my return. Mainly, my present objective is to bring the matter to your attention in the thought that you might be willing to review it. With kindest regards, I am

Faithfully yours,
HORACE M. ALBRIGHT

November 16, 1950

Dear Mr. Albright:

Your letter of August 18th regarding the South Calaveras Grove has remained unanswered but not unconsidered. Since I shall be returning to New York within the next ten days, suppose we talk the matter over the latter part of the month at some mutually convenient time.

As you know, I have gotten increasingly out of conceit with the National Park situation these past years and have not the enthusiasm for backing up its plans that I once had. This I say although it appears that the proposition of which you write is not as yet in park hands. However, I presume it will ultimately find its way into that department of the government.

With this brief statement, let us leave the matter until we can talk it over. I will telephone you shortly.

Very sincerely,
JOHN D. ROCKEFELLER, JR.

November 22, 1950

Dear Mr. Rockefeller:

Your letter of November 16th regarding my communication to you about the South Calaveras Grove reached me today just as I am on the point of leaving for a brief visit to New Mexico. I will be back here December 1st. Of course, I shall be very happy to talk with you about this conservation project at your convenience. In the meantime, before we meet I shall take pains to obtain from California sources the very latest information about the project.

While at this time I cannot say positively what agency would have jurisdiction over the South Calaveras Grove if it should pass into public ownership, in my judgement it would become part of the State system and would be joined by a parkway, which incidentally would be a most spectacular highway, to the North Calaveras Grove, the older and smaller grove that was acquired some years ago.

Of course, there is no question but that the South Calaveras Grove is of National Park stature. We always point out that this is true of Bull Creek in the coast redwood area but it remains under state control and I must admit that when I saw it in the summer of 1949, it was receiving excellent care and was in superb condition.

Hoping this finds you thoroughly enjoying the autumn weather in Williamsburg and getting a good rest and with very warmest regards, I am

Faithfully yours,
HORACE M. ALBRIGHT

Mr. Albright regretted that he had to leave for New Mexico before this letter was ready for his signature.

January 27, 1951

Dear Mr. Rockefeller:

Monday is your 77th birthday and this is just a little note to express the hope that it will be a day filled with happiness with all your young folks and old friends with you or in touch with you. I was happy to see you in the Rainbow Room a few days ago and to note that you looked strong and well as ever. This is a condition that must continue for many years to come because more than ever our country needs your spiritual, moral, and business guidance in the trying times we are facing and those that lie ahead.

Please don't take time to acknowledge this note, but be assured that Mrs. Albright and I will be thinking of you on Monday and renewing in our hearts the good wishes that I have tried to express here.

Sincerely yours,
HORACE M. ALBRIGHT

March 30, 1951

Personal and Confidential

Dear Mr. Rockefeller:

I have just returned from two days in Washington and I thought you would be interested in a few of my observations based on interviews and experiences down there.

Director Drury is ending his service tomorrow and will leave on Sunday for the West. The tension has eased a good deal and he is going away relaxed and, I think, really happy that he is getting back to California. He has been appointed Director of the Division of Parks and Beaches of the State and will be in a position to resume his excellent work in building up the state-park system, already one of the best in the nation. There was a party for him at the Cosmos Club Thursday night. Representatives of 21 organizations interested in conservation from one standpoint or another were present at this farewell gathering for him and a scroll, the text for which had been written by Dr. Waldo Leland, was available for signature by the representatives of all these organizations. It was a delightful affair and gave Mr. and Mrs. Drury much pleasure.

Yesterday I had some very interesting talks with Mr. Arthur Demaray who will assume the duties of Director on Monday, April 2nd. He confirmed the report that he would be Director for a period of a few months. He expects to retire, but not before the end of the tourist season. He is much devoted to Conrad L. Wirth who becomes Associate Director and who is scheduled to be Director on Mr. Drury's retirement. Mr. Demaray takes a very unselfish attitude toward his new position. He wants to carry on the work of the previous Directors and I was pleased to find that he is tremendously interested in some of the things that you and I were talking about the other day. He seems deeply devoted to Acadia National Park and wants to do everything in his power to advance restoration there. I found him to be completely in accord with our ideas about roadsides and he can be depended upon to reinforce and strengthen that program you began so many years ago. He is also much interested in the completion of the motor road and was full of praise for Mr. Drury's accomplishment in getting Mrs. Potter Palmer to yield in the matter of a right-of-way. He has the same feeling I have that a three-hundred foot right-of-way in that terrain is sufficient because no commercial use can be made of the land above and below the road and, in any event, planting can protect the road, located as it is in a side-hill cut.

I talked with Mr. Wirth and he made a statement that was naturally pleasing. He said that he had no other ambition than to manage the national park system according to principles laid down long ago, and I am sure he was not trying to be flattering when he said that he wanted to adhere at all times to policies that I followed when I was Director and that he hoped to be in constant consultation with me.

I am in hopes that both of these men may be in Williamsburg while you are there and that you may have an opportunity yourself to talk with them. There has been some doubt expressed among conservationists that either or both of these men are strong enough to withstand the pressures from public irrigation and power proponents and the Reclamation Service and the Corps of Engineers, etc. I find, however, that a number of people have been quite as frank as I have been in telling them of these doubts that have been expressed and they in turn have made the strongest kind of assurances that they will not yield to any pressure. Should they come to Williamsburg, I hope it may be at a time when you will be free to see them. They would be pleased and honored by an opportunity to talk with you.

I am certainly pleased and relieved by my discussions with the two men. On the other hand, I talked with fifteen or twenty men and women very active in conservation work in associations and government bureaus and no one seemed to be able to think of anyone who could be considered in lieu of Mr. Wirth for the Directorship.

As to the projects we discussed at the luncheon the other day, I will be in touch with you a little later about them after I have procured additional information.

With best wishes, I am

Sincerely yours,
HORACE M. ALBRIGHT

Dr. Waldo Leland. President of the American Council of Learned Societies.

April 2, 1951

Dear Mr. Albright:

Thank you for your interesting and informing letter of March 30th. The result of these different interviews about which

273

you write only goes to confirm your hope and belief as to what the attitude of these new officials would be. It is all very reassuring.

I am glad for Mr. Drury's sake that he was given such a fine testimonial dinner upon the completion of his work. It will mean much to him.

As to the two matters we spoke of the other day, my recollection is as follows: The western forest, which you feel is so important to preserve, would require some four or five hundred thousand dollars to make available Governmental matching money, and other funds on hand to insure its purchase. The Linville Falls area, if my memory serves me, would require something like seventy-five thousand dollars. You say in your letter that you will shortly have additional information about these two matters which you will send me.

Since you think both projects so important from a conservation point of view and so outstanding, if one half of the monies required in each case were secured from other interested individuals, my present disposition would be to provide the other half. I state the proposition in these terms preferring to be in the position of matching money which other people have agreed to give rather than of having them asked to match money which I had agreed to give.

I thoroughly enjoyed our luncheon together and was glad to find you so well. I shall be here in Williamsburg until the end of the month.

Very sincerely,
JOHN D. ROCKEFELLER, JR.

Linville Falls area. A scenic gorge and falls adjacent to the Blue Ridge Parkway, northeast of Asheville, North Carolina.

June 5, 1951

Dear Mr. Rockefeller:

I had the good fortune to be invited to attend the meetings celebrating the 25th anniversary of the establishment of the Industrial Relations Counselors. It was an exceedingly inspiring, interesting, and valuable series of experiences that I shall long remember. As far back as 1942 we had had the Industrial Relations Counselors study our personnel and labor relations problems and there has been submitted to us a very valuable report which has been a useful guide for us now for nearly ten years.

(My reason for writing this letter and I hope you will not take the time to acknowledge it) is that I wanted to tell you that Winthrop made a tremendous impression on everybody present at these 25th anniversary meetings. In the afternoon he gave a talk full of interesting facts after an introduction by Mr. Fosdick. In the evening he was toastmaster at the dinner, taking Mr. Fosdick's place. He made an excellent toastmaster.

He was never at a loss for a word. In fact at every turn he was perfectly at ease in his introductions and he was really eloquent in both the afternoon and evening. So far as I know, he had no notes whatever, and I have the greatest admiration for his magnificent performance. He met every requirement of public speaking, using the right words and perfect sentence structure and at the same time putting into the talk high spirit and good will, and I think all who heard Winthrop went away regarding him as an accomplished public speaker.

I thought you would like to have these views on this fine son of yours.

Faithfully,
HORACE M. ALBRIGHT

Industrial Relations Counselors. A labor relations consulting firm which grew out of Rockefeller's interest in economic problems. Originally a non-profit operation, Rockefeller *contributed over $1 million to it. In later years, it became profit making and self-sustaining. The firm offered assistance to industry in the field of labor relations. John D. Rockefeller, 3rd and Winthrop Rockefeller served on its board of directors.*

June 6, 1951

Dear Mr. Albright:

How could I fail to thank you for your letter of June 5th, speaking in such unqualified terms of Winthrop's conduct of certain of the Industrial Relations Counselors anniversary meetings and expressing in such generous language your admiration of the ease and forcefulness with which he spoke. Such expressions as your letter contains are most welcome to a father. I deeply appreciate them and thank you for them.

Lest my letter to you of April 2nd failed to reach you, I am enclosing a copy herewith. This I do, not because I am anxious to make further gifts to the National Parks at this time, but simply because I always want, if possible, to support you in any movement in connection with the parks which you think particularly significant and important. Unless and until such time as other monies are found to be available for the two projects of which you spoke, the enclosed letter calls for no attention on your part.

Very sincerely,
JOHN D. ROCKEFELLER, JR.

October 9, 1951

Dear Mr. Rockefeller:

I have been hoping for some time that I might have some worthwhile information to give you about the two projects we discussed last spring and on which you made a tentative commitment with the understanding that your name was not to be used in whatever I might say about the two projects. Your authority merely extending to my informing interested parties that I could assure them that if half of the funds needed to carry out each project up to certain top limits could be secured, then the other half would be forthcoming from another source.

Here is the present status of both projects:

1.   In the case of the North Carolina project involving the Blue Ridge Parkway in the neighborhood of Linville Falls not far from Grandfather Mountain, there is a notable scenic composition of bold mountain, waterfalls, river and forest. The figure I discussed with you is $75,000. Superintendent Sam Weems of the Blue Ridge Parkway now writes me that the best figure he can get in the way of an option is for $100,000 good for 90 days and he tells me also that he does not know where he can obtain half of this amount even if my friend would be willing to raise his matching contribution by as much as $12,500. I have written Mr. Weems that it is my feeling that my friend would not want to undertake the entire project but I said I would advise him of the situation. Hence this letter.

2.   The South Calaveras Grove in California is still in dire danger of destruction. I am more than ever convinced that this is the greatest remaining conservation project to be undertaken in America. It does not seem to me that there can ever be another one like it or equal to it in importance. Of course, I am not referring to conservation projects such as the building of great structures for control of rivers, floods, and so forth. I am referring to scenic and historic conservation projects. Here again we have not been able to get definite figures of what remains to be raised by subscription after all federal and state sources of funds have been exhausted. Governor Warren told me when he was here the other day that certain agreements regarding exchanges of timber have been executed between the federal government and the State of California covering the corridor between the North Calaveras Grove and the South Grove, that there have been more careful appraisals made of the timber to be protected forever

and that negotiations are under way to endeavor to get a price from the owners of these lands for their virgin forests. The figure I used in talking with you was $500,000 but that has not become a certainty by any means.

I am leaving for New Mexico and California tomorrow and will be gone until about December 1st. While I am in the West I hope to obtain additional information regarding the South Calaveras Grove Project and perhaps even take a hand myself in the negotiations to arrive at just what will be needed to complete the project and assure the permanent protection of this great South Calaveras Grove and its adjacent protective areas.

I sincerely hope your interest in both these projects may be continued pending our arrival at something more definite to submit to you. Of course, the North Carolina project is in rather definite form at the present time. It is possible, of course, that the owners of the Linville Falls area may proceed to sell the forest cover, which would be a very deplorable act. On the other hand, they may find that there is more to be gained by letting the country stay in its present condition and as time goes on may develop less lofty ideas as to the values of their lands and timber.

I assume you will be in Williamsburg in November. I hope with all my heart it will be a beautiful month and that Mrs. Rockefeller and you will have a most enjoyable visit there amid the beautiful buildings and grounds you have restored.

Faithfully yours,
HORACE M. ALBRIGHT

On August 15, 1951, Rockefeller married Martha Baird Allen, the widow of a fellow Brown University alumnus.

WESTERN UNION TELEGRAM

NIGHT LETTER OCTOBER 19, 1951

HORACE M. ALBRIGHT, 920 HIGHLINE ROAD, GLEN-
DALE, CALIFORNIA

LETTER OCTOBER NINTH CAREFULLY NOTED IF YOU
ARE IN AGREEMENT APPROVE AND AUTHORIZE
CLOSING OPTION OF ONE HUNDRED THOUSAND
DOLLARS ON BLUE RIDGE PROJECT EVEN IF I PAY
ENTIRE AMOUNT.

JOHN D. ROCKEFELLER, JR.

October 25, 1951

My dear Miss Warfield:

I want Mr. Rockefeller and you to know that the telegram
of October 19th reached me promptly, and that I got things
moving in North Carolina at once. This morning I received
a telegram from Superintendent Weems that the project is well
in hand, although the new efforts to get a lower price do not
seem to be bearing fruit. There is no question of anymore option
troubles, so the figure of $100,000 is bound to be the highest
we shall hear about. I insisted on one more serious effort to
scale this down, and it may yet happen.

I have also received Mr. Rockefeller's observations on my
letter of October 9th through your letter of the 22nd which
just came this morning. I have not had an opportunity to dig
into the Calaveras project, but am going to Sacramento on
Sunday night and then to San Francisco for a few days. At
these places, I will get accurate, up-to-date information on the
project, and as I said in my letter of the 9th, I may take a
hand in the negotiations myself, that is, if an opportunity to
accomplish something worthwhile presents itself.

There should be further advice regarding the North
Carolina project coming to me in a few days, and I will promptly
relay this to you.

Clippings from New York papers reaching me this morning tell of the acquisition of the Dunderberg for the Palisades Interstate Park and is a gift to the State by Laurance Rockefeller. Of course, I knew this purchase was being made. It is a fine tract, and the gift a very important one that will be greatly appreciated in the years to come.

With all good wishes, I am

Sincerely yours,
HORACE M. ALBRIGHT

P.S. Please pardon the terrible typing. It's my own. HMA

Dunderberg Mountain. Located in Bear Mountain State Park, New York, part of the Palisades Interstate Park.

November 5, 1951

My dear Mr. Rockefeller:

This is just a brief note to advise you that the North Carolina project is securely held by an option for 90 days at $95,000.00, and that the work of title searching and preparation of warranty deed is proceeding. I assume that we can report further to you when I return to New York on December 1st. By that time, the title work and all documents should have been prepared, and the project ready for completion.

We realize that you may have special reasons for wanting all details of the project completed and even payment made before December 31st, and these objectives can be attained I am sure.

We will want to know what your wishes are with regard to public information regarding this very important project. Naturally, we want to get up and broadcast a suitable statement regarding this acquisition for the Blue Ridge Parkway, but there is no reason for not taking a long time in which to prepare such a statement. I suggest that we prepare something for your perusal, and that you decide what you want said and when it shall be said if you authorize anything at all.

I have been in Sacramento and San Francisco, and have talked with interested people regarding the South Caleveras Grove of Big Trees. The Governor took me to the Sutter Club in Sacramento and talked about the project for almost an hour. Of course, he has no intimation of your interest, but I can say that his interest is very great. He spoke most appreciatively of your courtesy to him at the Rockefeller Center Club and of Nelson's hospitality at his home in the country. I also talked with some of the men who have been advisers to the Pickering Company which owns the Grove. They realize that the Grove is a national monument and that it will not be cut without a national struggle if not a battle in halls of Congress and State Legislature. However, they are out to get as much as they can for their stockholders.

With another expression of thanks for undertaking the North Carolina project, I am

Faithfully yours,
HORACE M. ALBRIGHT

December 6, 1951

Dear Mr. Rockefeller:

As you know, I have been in the West for almost two months. While in California I was at luncheon with the Governor and also had several talks with Newton B. Drury, now Chief of the Division of Beaches and Parks. They told me of the revival of the proposal that has been made from time to time over a period of many years that the magnificent Bull Creek Grove which was saved through your generous contribution of funds for its purchase be renamed in tribute to you and

281

that Mr. T. S. Peterson, President of the Standard Oil of California, had brought back from New York the information that you had acquiesced this time in the plan to rename the grove in tribute to your great conservation act in assuring its preservation. I, of course, was very happy that you are going to permit this renaming proposal to be carried out.

I seem to have been drawn into the project still further by receiving at this time from Sacramento a portfolio showing how it is proposed to mark the grove, what wording shall be put on the plaque, etc. Apparently it was the feeling of the authorities in California that inasmuch as I am here in the building and inasmuch as I had had experience in a number of other grove markings I could perhaps answer questions that you would want to ask and that, therefore, I should be the one to present this portfolio to you. It seems to me, however, that there is little to add to what is contained in the portfolio and I therefore send it to you herewith with the single observation that should you think I can be of any assistance in the giving of information or in carrying out any special thoughts you may have about the plaque, its location, or the dedicatory ceremonies, I can communicate them to the authorities in California. I expect to be here most of the time for the next two months and shall be at your disposal.

It seems to me that the principal point to be decided now is what wording you prefer for the plaque. There are several suggestions offered. The proposal has also been made that instead of calling this park the "Rockefeller Grove" it be called the "Rockefeller Redwood Forest". As I understand it, you have made the stipulation that you are not expected to attend dedicatory ceremonies. It is not likely that any date has been set for these ceremonies, but I should think it would be some time in the spring or early summer after the rainy season is over. I assume that the dedicatory ceremonies will be under the direction of the Save-the-Redwoods League and the California State Park Commission which at the present time is headed by the Honorable Joseph R. Knowland, publisher of the Oakland *Tribune*, one of the largest newspapers in California, and father of United States Senator William F. Knowland.

With all good wishes, I am

Sincerely yours,
HORACE M. ALBRIGHT

Rockefeller's $2,000,000 contribution to the Save-the-Redwoods League, made between 1927 and 1931, along with gifts from others such as the California Federation of Women's Clubs and the Garden Club of America, enabled the League to buy 19,562 acres of virgin redwood in 1931. The lands became part of the Humboldt Redwoods State Park. There are many groves in the Park dedicated to the memory of generous donors. The Rockefeller Forest is one of these areas.

December 17, 1951

Dear Mr. Albright:

Your letter of December 6th with the accompanying booklet was duly received. From my brother-in-law, Mr. Winthrop Aldrich, I had already heard of the proposal of which you write.

I have carefully considered the various inscriptions that have been suggested for the tablet. The enclosed seems to me adequate; moreover, because of its brevity and simplicity, much more appropriate than anything more extended or elaborate. If the grove must be named for the convenience of travelers in finding it and in referring to it, I shall not object to its being called the Rockefeller Grove although I would be quite as happy were that not thought to be desirable.

As to the dedicatory reference and date which appear in the proposed tablet, both can be worked into the simple phrase I have suggested should that seem to be desirable.

Should you care to discuss this matter with me, I shall be glad to see you when next I am in the office.

WORTHWHILE PLACES

Greatly appreciating your kindly interest and with cordial holiday greetings, I am,

Very sincerely,
JOHN D. ROCKEFELLER, JR.

The wording for the plaque which Rockefeller approved reads:

The preservation of this grove was made possible by a gift from John D. Rockefeller, Jr. May those who come here find inspiration and peace in the enduring splendor of these magnificent trees.

December 21, 1951

Dear Mr. Rockefeller:

The purchase of the Linville Falls and Gorge property on Blue Ridge Parkway has now reached the point where payment of $95,000 in cash is indicated. Do you prefer to transmit the sum of $95,000 to the Treasurer of the United States for disbursement in the purchase of this land, or would you prefer to take title to the property yourself and then deed it to the United States of America?

My own recommendation would be that the fund be made available to the National Park Service and that the Service be authorized to make the purchase, clear title, accept the deed, and so forth.

We are arranging a press release which will be accompanied for the larger papers with pictures. As soon as a draft is available, I will send it to you for your perusal should you wish to see it.

The purchase of the Linville Falls area is one of the highlights of the National Park Service in the year of 1951 and of course everyone inside and outside of the Service, including old-timers like myself, appreciates your contribution more than we can tell you.

Sincerely yours,
HORACE M. ALBRIGHT

P.S. Of course, I would be happy to handle all the details of closing this transaction, including the forwarding of the funds should you wish me to do so.

February 18, 1952

Dear Mr. Albright:

Your letter of February 6th was most welcome. I shall take it for granted that the Little River Country of North Carolina is not an area that needs national consideration unless I hear from you to the contrary.

How much you enjoyed your three day stay in Williamsburg, I can well imagine. The Brush-Evarad House is wholly charming, is it not? Mrs. Rockefeller and I visited it with Mr. Graham last fall and felt that he had done an extraordinary piece of work in its restoration and furnishing. To walk up and down the streets, as you say you did on various occasions, is one of my greatest delights. I always see something that interests me particularly and thoroughly enjoy the atmosphere of the old town. It is extraordinary how quickly a newly constructed building melts into the landscape and takes its place as one of the old buildings. I think this must be true partly because the buildings as reconstructed are so accurate in their detail and so just what that particular building was or might have been when it was first built, that it seems from the outset to be a part of the original picture. Our architects and all of the people who have worked on the restoration have brought to the undertaking outstanding ability and a meticulous devotion to detail that has meant everything in the result of their work.

WORTHWHILE PLACES

What a fine man Mr. Kendrew is - cultivated, intelligent, delightful, thoroughly trained in his profession and utterly devoted to the restoration.

If you had not been to an evening candlelight party at the Palace before, I can well imagine how impressed you were with the beauty of the scene with which you were confronted at the time of the concert which you attended. The success of the Antiques Forums is extraordinary and most gratifying. From the educational point of view, these forums are also highly valuable.

We made no mistake in the investment we have made in Williamsburg. No one has gotten more pleasure from what has been done there than I have. Your cooperation in maintaining and operating the restoration and in its further development is deeply appreciated.

We have been here in Tuscon now for ten days, as comfortable as ever in our cottage just across the street from the hotel. We have already taken a number of delightful drives in the surrounding country.

It is kind of you to suggest sending us information about places which we might be interested to visit. This we shall be glad to have available should we find it conveniently possible to take the longer trips which you doubtless have in mind. Arizona is a wonderful state and this a peculiarly beautiful part of the state.

When I think back to the summer we took the house owned by Mr. Hamilton and others adjacent to Yellowstone Park, at which time you were superintendent of the park, and remember the buffalo stampede you staged for us at that time and then review in memory the many interesting and delightful associations I have had with you since, I am grateful indeed that our paths crossed so many years ago. But we have so many interests in common that it is not strange that a warm friendship soon developed between us.

With cordial remembrances to you and again with thanks for your letter, I am,

Very sincerely,
JOHN D. ROCKEFELLER, JR.

March 3, 1952

Dear Mr. Rockefeller:

In 1947, when you were in Tucson, you wrote John asking him to obtain information for you about certain sugar pine areas in California. The plight of these stands of sugar pine had been called to your attention by a newspaper article you had read. I found that the article referred to the sugar pine forest adjacent to the South Calaveras Grove in California which lies in a great watershed for many years untouched by lumbering operations. At John's request I sent you Mr. Olmsted's report on the South Calaveras Grove and later, on your return to New York, you sent it back to me with the statement that you thought that the project was a little too large for your consideration at that time. Of course, I made no proposals or recommendations to you about either the sugar pine or the sequoia grove project. However, I did bring it to your attention nearly four years later, in the fall of 1950. Subsequently, you permitted me to discuss it with you at luncheon and then I was able to explain that while definite figures on the cost of this project were not available, partly owing to the rapidly rising values of timber but also due to status of state funds, we could not give a definite estimate of private contributions needed to match available state and private funds already in hand. You told me that I could say to Governor Warren and other appropriate officials that I had a friend who would consider matching public funds up to the amount of $250,000. This according to my records was early in 1951. My last report to you was on October 9th, 1951 and even then I was unable to give definite information regarding the cost of this project.

My object in writing this letter is to ask whether, while you are in the West on your present trip, you would like to review some of the reports and maps relating to this South Calaveras Grove project. It is in better shape than it was but the danger to the great grove daily grows more serious. I would like to say again that I think this is the one large project involving the conservation of a great natural resource that remains to be completed but which unfortunately requires not only State but private funds in view of the way the State laws on the purchase of land for park purposes stand.

I do not want to burden you in any way with any of these matters unless it is entirely in accord with your own wishes as to what you want to see or hear and when. With another expression of my appreciation for the consideration you have already given this project, I am

Faithfully yours,
HORACE M. ALBRIGHT

March 7, 1952

Dear Mr. Albright:

Thank you for your letters of March 3rd. I greatly appreciate your writing to the various superintendents of nearby parks.

As to the South Calaveras Grove, you say: "You told me that I could say to Governor Warren and other appropriate officials that I had a friend who would consider matching public funds up to the amount of $250,000. This according to my records was early in 1951. My last report to you was on October 9th, 1951 and even then I was unable to give definite information regarding the cost of this project." You go on to ask whether I would like to review the maps and other data referring to this South Calaveras Grove while in the West. I do not need to see this data but I am still interested in the project of saving the grove and am still ready to participate to that end as set forth in the above quoted passage from your letter of March 3rd.

Is this proposal of mine still one that will be interesting to the state? If so, you are at liberty to renew it in any way you see fit. The proposal will be good for the balance of this calendar year. If the State of California is not able to accomplish anything on this basis, what basis of cooperation on my part do you suggest?

Very sincerely,
JOHN D. ROCKEFELLER, JR.

Letters to various superintendents. Albright had informed the superintendents of Rockefeller's intention to visit some park areas while he spent time at the JY ranch in Jackson Hole.

May 12, 1952

Dear Mr. Rockefeller:

When we were talking on the telephone this morning I asked if I might bring to your attention more data regarding the South Calaveras Grove in California.

As I mentioned in my letter to you of March 3rd addressed to you at the Arizona Inn this project was first brought to your attention in 1947 when there were a good many communications about the sugar pines in the vicinity of the South Calaveras Grove which were in danger of being cut as logging operations advanced in that great wilderness region of the Stanislaus River. Several years later, in the fall of 1950, while I was your guest at luncheon one day and we were talking about conservation projects, I spoke about the peril of the South Calaveras Grove and the project which had been developed in California for saving the grove but which was languishing because of the inability to raise private funds which would make available equal contributions from the State of California. At that time you authorized me to say that I had a friend who would consider matching private funds up to the amount of $250,000, a total of $500,000 which in turn would call for an expenditure of another $500,000 by the State of California. On March 7th, writing me from Tucson, you again confirmed this commitment as follows:

WORTHWHILE PLACES

> I am still interested in the project of saving the grove and am still ready to participate to that end as set forth in the above quoted passage from your letter of March 3rd.

As I explained both in my personal conversation with you and in my letter of March 3rd, it has been very difficult to define this project because of an unwillingness of the Pickering Lumber Company to quote a price that could be relied upon for any length of time. Sugar pine timber is very scarce and the price mounts by leaps and bounds. Even today it is not known whether the value is $45 per thousand for sugar pine or whether it is as high as $55 or even $60. The demand for timber has become so great that Giant Redwoods are again being cut and one grove south of Sequoia Park has been destroyed in the past year, something that has not happened in 30 years, to my knowledge.

In many respects the South Calaveras Grove is the finest of all the groves of Giant Sequoia Trees. As I understand it, the trees in this grove, not only the Redwoods, but some of the other species, do not follow the normal principles of tapering as the trees grow taller. These trees, therefore, have more bulk and give more the appearance of columns even than those in others of the great forests of California.

At any rate it appears that this project cannot be consummated for less than three million dollars. It has seemed to me that probably the best way for you to visualize the size of the project is to suggest that you read the attached letter from Governor Warren of California dated April 28th to which are attached memoranda regarding the timber and land values and the funds, both public and private that are available or are needed. Referring to the map, the North Calaveras Grove is already a state park. This was the first of the great groves of Big Trees that was made accessible to the public. It was opened nearly 100 years ago. There are pictures extant showing a camel train going into this grove. It was acquired by the State some years ago. Lying between the North Grove and the South Grove is a tract of land that has just been acquired from the Federal Government under an old land exchange law. Then comes the South Calaveras Grove area with several units. Those lying within the red boundaries are the ones that ought to be acquired in order to conserve this grove. The units north labeled "Forest Service Exchange" are sugar pine areas which can and will be acquired by the exchange of government timber for the timber in these parcels. Also, the government is going to build a parkway connecting the two groves of trees and the money that the Federal Government will spend for this parkway can be matched with state money. At any rate the relationship of the various federal and state funds to the various holdings are shown in the memorandum attached to Governor Warren's letter. The need for private matching funds is also clear. It will be noted that there are two tables covering probable maximum valuation, one based on sugar pine at $55 per thousand and one at $60 per thousand.

There is another way of getting at the project and that is to acquire only a part of the grove at this time by making a very substantial payment and then getting an option under which the remainder of the grove can be acquired over the next few years. I have asked Mr. Drury, the Chief of the California parks, to give me data on this alternative project which would require a private gift of at least $500,000 at this time. This is more in line with what I have been discussing with you as the whole project but which now turns out to be only somewhat more than half of it — about $1,825,000 as compared with $2,928,640 -$3,193,925 as referred to in the data attached to Governor Warren's letter.

As I explained in our telephone conversation this morning, I expect to go into this matter rather deeply in California while I am out there on the trip I am beginning tonight. I am therefore suggesting at this time only that you review the project as time permits and that when I return late in June you give me an opportunity to discuss the matter with you further if you feel that you would like to know more about it.

Sincerely yours,
HORACE M. ALBRIGHT

WESTERN UNION TELEGRAM

MAY 19, 1952

HORACE M. ALBRIGHT, UNITED STATES POTASH CO., CARLSBAD, NEW MEXICO

YOUR LETTER MAY 12TH WITH ITS ACCOMPANYING DATA AND MAP HAS RECEIVED FULLEST CONSIDERATION. IF ENTIRE PROJECT AS THEREIN SET FORTH CAN BE CARRIED OUT AND YOU SO RECOMMEND WILL GIVE TOTAL OF WHATEVER IS NECESSARY IN SECURITIES OF THE APPROXIMATE VALUE OF ONE MILLION TO MAKE PROJECT POSSIBLE. ON THE BASIS OF THIS PLEDGE A FIRM OFFER CAN BE MADE.

JOHN D. ROCKEFELLER, JR.

June 27, 1952

Dear Mr. Rockefeller:

Mr. Chorley has told me that you are going west tomorrow to Jackson Hole and that Mrs. Rockefeller is accompanying you. I sincerely hope you will have a very comfortable and pleasant and beneficial trip. From all I can learn, the weather conditions have been such as to make this an especially fine time to visit the Grand Teton Park country. The snows were heavy and they melted slowly. The wildflowers should be exceptionally beautiful.

When you return I would appreciate an opportunity to talk with you briefly about the South Calaveras Grove. Your generous offer has certainly made possible the carrying through of this great project. However, we are proceeding very slowly. I was able to take part in conferences regarding values while in San Francisco and Sacramento. I am confident that in a few weeks there will be something definite to report. Governor Warren was tremendously pleased with the news I was able to bring him about your interest in the project and asked me to express to you his deep gratitude. No state matter at the present time seems to be interesting the Governor more than this great conservation project.

I had the good fortune to get into Yosemite and Sequoia national parks for a few days. With the Superintendent of Yosemite I inspected the forests that were included in the purchase project of 1931. They are in wonderful condition and another thing that gave me great satisfaction and pleasure was to note the recovery of the areas which were cut over and which lie immediately adjacent to the forests you saved.

I hope that in planning for possible trips during the remainder of the year Mrs. Rockefeller and you may be able to give consideration to a California visit with ample time to see these great forests the preservation of which you have made possible. With the rapid disappearance of most of our remaining forests of large trees each day these primitive forests in the national parks become more valuable. Of course, the tremendous rise in the value of timber everywhere enables us to say, if we wish to do so, that the forests that have been preserved through your help are now worth ten to twenty times what their value was when their preservation was effected.

With more thanks and more good wishes for your Jackson Hole trip, I am

Sincerely yours,
HORACE M. ALBRIGHT

July 15, 1952

Dear Mr. Albright:

Your letter of June 27th reached me before Mrs. Rockefeller and I went to Jackson Hole and was read with interest and care. We had a delightful time at the JY Ranch and enjoyed every moment of it. The Moran transfer and the Jackson Lake Lodge Development project received considerable of our thought and attention. Certain estimates of cost are being prepared. The beauty of the Jackson Hole valley and its surroundings was brought home to Mrs. Rockefeller and me as never before. While there we drove over all of the passes which give access to the valley and became familiar with the country which surrounds it as never before.

I am glad to know that the South Calaveras Grove project is progressing and shall be interested to hear more about it from you on my return from Maine in September. We leave tomorrow for Seal Harbor. What you say about your recent inspection of the forests in the Yosemite and Sequoia National Parks which were purchased some years ago is most interesting and gratifying.

It is kind of you to again mention the possibility of a western trip this fall. Whether it can be worked in or not, I cannot say at this time but the prospect is alluring.

Looking forward to seeing you in September, I am,

Very sincerely,
JOHN D. ROCKEFELLER, JR.

P. S. I am delighted to hear there is a chance of your coming to Maine in August. Do let me know when your plans are more definite for it would be a pleasure to see you while you were there.

———

March 3, 1953

Dear Mr. Albright:

Thank you for your letter of February 4th with the interesting article which you have written for the Saturday Evening Post, about the redwood trees. Your references to me in this connection are greatly appreciated.

One thing you said is not quite accurate. You spoke of the Great Smoky Mountains National Park as having been acquired with "a $5,000,000 contribution from John D. Rockefeller, Jr. in honor of his mother.........". This gift was not made by me but from $10,000,000 set aside by the Laura Spelman Rockefeller Memorial Fund for such objects as I thought my mother would have been interested to have it go to. This I simply mention for your information should the question come up in the future.

Your article is most informing and ought to be very helpful in centering attention on these wonderful trees.

Our stay here has been most enjoyable, although the weather has been unprecedentedly cold part of the time. We shall be getting home about the middle of March.

Again with thanks for your letter,

Very sincerely,
JOHN D. ROCKEFELLER, JR.

April 20, 1953

Dear Mr. Rockefeller:

This is a letter I have hesitated for a week to write and I am wondering now whether I should do it, first because it concerns something that is undoubtedly none of my business, and second because it may disturb you while you are resting at Williamsburg. The subject is the forestry work that is being done at Acadia National Park by a crew under the direction of your superintendent.

A man who travels a great deal among the national parks and who knows Acadia Park quite well is much disturbed about the cutting that is being done in the unburned forests and especially along the ocean front. The point he makes is that trees of considerable size are being cut and that there is a good deal of criticism among the local people. The feeling is that the taking out of large trees is going to so open the forests that there will be a good deal more timber blown down. Also the point is made that in the burning there seems to be considerable destruction of young growth, and where burning is being done in the area through which the forest fire raged in 1947 the cleanup has been too complete, not leaving enough soil-building material into which seeds may fall to bring about new growth.

Before writing this letter I took the precaution to check with the acting superintendent of the Park who, while he was very cautious in his statements, I gather feels that there is need for a review of your superintendent's program. The only suggestion I have to make is that in view of what is being said it might be advisable to have the program reviewed especially insofar as it relates to the cutting of large trees in the unspoiled forests and the burning in or near these forests and the perhaps too close cleanup and burning in the 1947 burned areas.

I know you will realize that in bringing this to your attention I am taking a step that is not based on personal knowledge but merely on an apprehension that maybe something is being done that you do not know about.

Mrs. Albright and I are leaving this Friday on a quick trip to Europe and will not be back until June 8th. I hope to have an opportunity to talk with you before you make your next trip to Jackson Hole. I regret exceedingly that I will not be at the special convocation at Williamsburg when degrees are conferred on the President and the Governor of Virginia.

With all good wishes, I am

Sincerely yours,
HORACE M. ALBRIGHT

May 8, 1953

Dear Mr. Albright:

Your letter of April 20th about the fire damage clean up work which my people are doing on Mt. Desert Island is received.

As always, I am most appreciative of your keeping me in touch with anything that you may hear of significance about matters in which I am interested.

Immediately on receipt of your letter I talked with Mr. DeRevere, my Seal Harbor superintendent, who has charge of all the fire clean up work. As regards the Ocean Drive fire clean up, that was finished a long time ago. Both Mr. DeRevere and I had been in touch with Mr. Hadley, the then Acadia Park superintendent, about the fire clean up work. He was currently aware of the kind of work we were doing, expressed his complete approval of it and said that he would greatly appreciate our carrying on similar work on park property in so far as were willing to do it.

When we first began fire clean up work, we left standing trees that had even partial life in them although they were unsightly. This we did, particularly with evergreens, that seed from them might be disseminated. After observing these remaining trees for a year or two, they impressed us as so unsightly that it seemed much better to remove them than to let them stand. Moreover, some of them, having been burned in the roots, blew over and others were gradually dying. This policy we have since followed.

As a result of my talk with Mr. DeRevere, above referred to, he got in touch immediately with the new park superintendent, went over with him fully the work we had done in fire clean up and the policy which we were following. I told Mr. DeRevere to do no further fire clean up cutting on park land except with the superintendent's authorization as to area and approval as to method.

As you know, the present trend among park men seems to be to leave nature alone. If a tree is dead, let it stand; if it blows over, let it lie -on the theory that nature should be undisturbed. While this policy is one thing if pursued in the interior of a dense forest where only the hunter goes, to pursue it in any areas of a park like Acadia, through which motorists are constantly driving, is to present a roadside aspect of standing and down dead timber wholly incongruous with the existence of a broad, paved, motor road. Therefore, to clean up the dead, standing or down timber visible from roads seems to be almost essential. With this view I think the superintendent is in agreement.

All of the fire damage in the park along the motor roads had been completed before the new superintendent arrived and, therefore, nothing can be done about the criticisms in that area which your letter relays. The new superintendent did go, however, with Mr. DeRevere over the present fire clean up work which the latter is doing in the valley north of Jordan and Sargent Mountains and toward Aunt Betty's Pond. The superintendent, as I understand it, generally approved of the method Mr. DeRevere was pursuing and its continuance.

This letter I write as a matter of record and am sending a copy of it to Mr. DeRevere that he may correct to me any incorrect statements which it contains. Failing to get any supplemental letter from me on this subject, you will know that this letter has been approved by Mr. DeRevere.

Hoping to see you here in New York on your return and again with thanks for your letter, I am,

Very sincerely,
JOHN D. ROCKEFELLER, JR.

Robert DeRevere. Superintendent of the Rockefeller home, the Eyrie, and its grounds in Maine.

August 17, 1953

Dear Mr. Albright:

It was a great pleasure to Mrs. Rockefeller and me to have you with us over the weekend, and a boundless satisfaction to me to go over with you so many matters on the Island that have been of common interest and concern to us both throughout the years. The development that has taken place here is most gratifying and from my point of view fully justified.

If the Park motor road can be completed and, at least, some of the most conspicuous remaining fire damage cleaned up, Acadia Park will be something of which you and I can well be proud and in which we can, as we have over the past several days, take increasing pleasure.

I am sending you herewith a copy of the fire cleanup report which I showed you yesterday. This information I am glad to have you have for your own personal use and guidance.

With cordial greetings, in which Mrs. Rockefeller joins, I am

Very sincerely,
JOHN D. ROCKEFELLER, JR.

August 21, 1953

Dear Mr. Rockefeller:

I appreciate very much your thoughtfulness in writing me as you did on August 17th. I am glad to have the statement of expenditures in connection with cleanup of the fire damage. I hope to make very effective use of these figures without letting the details of your statement or the statement itself get out of my hands. I am going to try to work out with officials of the National Park Service some way, if feasible, to get appropriations over a period of a few years to match this fund. I do not think it will be necessary to talk about it except in the Bureau of the Budget.

Of course, I am also going to go into the matter of completing the motor roads as soon as I can see Director Wirth and his associates.

I tried very hard when leaving you at the Eyrie last Sunday afternoon to express my heartfelt appreciation of the hospitality and kindness which Mrs. Rockefeller and you so generously bestowed on me during the two days I was with you. I cannot recall that I ever had a more pleasant weekend, and certainly I never enjoyed Acadia Park more than I did while with you.

I still marvel at the transformation you effected at the Dane home site and the lovely plaza you have built there for people to enjoy the view of the rockbound coast, islands, and water.

The pictures I took Saturday morning when we first visited the point I have received from the Eastman Kodak Company, and they are fine. However, I have not yet sent in the roll of film containing the pictures exposed on Sunday.

I am sorry to tell you that the United States Civil Service Commission has just issued an order removing the protection of the Civil Service rules from six officers of the National Park Service, including the Director and three Assistant Directors. This is the first thing of this kind that has happened since the National Park Service was created in 1916. I hope no actual changes will be made although the positions are now wide open for removal of the incumbents. This action, of course, is very serious from the standpoint of morale of the National Park Service.

Once more expressing my deep appreciation of the opportunity I had to be with Mrs. Rockefeller and you last week, and with all good wishes to both of you in which Mrs. Albright heartily joins me, I am

Faithfully yours,
HORACE M. ALBRIGHT

Rockefeller sent excerpts from Albright's letter of August 21 to his son, Nelson A., then Under-Secretary in the Department of Health, Education and Welfare. He said, "A word at your convenience would be appreciated. It would appear that Mr. Albright thinks this action that has been taken will react unfavorably on the Park Service which he has done so much to build up and which I have always regarded as one of the best manned and operated of any of the government departments of which I know."

Nelson sent a copy of his father's letter to Douglas McKay, Secretary of the Interior. On September 2, McKay wrote John D. Rockefeller, Jr., "I assure you that in the foreseeable future there is no intention of exercising the authority to remove any of

the officials in the affected positions. Should an occasion ever arise where it would be necessary to go outside of the National Park Service for a person to fill one of these positions, I am confident that the person selected would be an outstanding individual acceptable to the conservation organizations so closely associated with the purposes and objectives of our National Park system."

September 5, 1953

The Honorable Douglas McKay

My dear Mr. Secretary:

I am greatly indebted to you for your full and reassuring letter of September 2nd.

In raising with my son, Nelson, the question of Park Service appointments on the higher levels, I had no slightest thought of the matter being brought to your attention.

You make it very clear that while appointments may be made outside of the Civil Service, it is not the intention to make appointments any differently than at present unless in a specific instance it seems desirable to do so in order to get a better man for a position than could otherwise be obtained. I doubt not that your position in this matter will gradually become known throughout the Park Service. As that occurs, any such apprehension as Mr. Albright feared might arise will quickly be allayed.

May I in closing express my deep appreciation of your more than generous words in regard to my interest in the National Parks. I have always counted it a privilege to do what I could to further the wise and farseeing purposes of that Service.

With sentiments of high regard, I beg to remain, my dear Mr. Secretary,

Very sincerely,
JOHN D. ROCKEFELLER, JR.

WORTHWHILE PLACES

September 5, 1953

My dear Mr. Rockefeller:

I am sending you herewith a copy of a letter I have written to Mr. Givens about his trip with me over the Park while I was in Maine last month, and about the need for agressively seeking funds to complete two pressing projects -the motor road and fire damage clean-up.

Over the telephone, I have talked with officials of the National Park Service in Washington, and I have written a long personal letter to Director Wirth on Acadia National Park and its needs. He has only recently returned from the West.

I had expected to see him and some of his associates, but I have not been able to do so. Now I am going to the Northwest for over two weeks, leaving next Thursday by air for Cheyenne, thence to Jackson Hole by automobile and later after a day or two in the Yellowstone taking the train to Seattle. However, I am sure that I have done about all that it is possible in the way of getting my views before the executives of the Service in Washington. I am looking forward with keen delight to my first view of the inn construction on Jackson Lake.

Secretary McKay has sent me a copy of his letter to you about the removal of six high-placed officials of the National Park Service from the protection of the Civil Service rules and regulations by placing them in the Schedule C category and thus making it possible to fill them by appointing men and women outside the competitive civil service, and by the same token making it easy to remove persons now holding these positions.

His letter to you is a frank strong statement, the only kind he would be expected to write you. He has not said he would move to change the new policy, but he has given you strong assurances that he does not intend to disturb the National Park Service. These assurances are most comforting and probably give the Park Service officials the same protection actually that they enjoyed before the Schedule C order affecting them was issued. I feel that you have saved the day for this fine bureau, and that in time the *status quo ante* will be restored. I am tremendously relieved so far as the bureau is concerned.

I wish I felt as happy about Secretary McKay and the Administration as I do about the Park Service. I am afraid there will be severe criticisms from many directions once the news gets out that these old professional, technical and scientific bureaus have been made subject to political disturbance whether in fact any political appointments are made or not.

I have some very good pictures in color of the "Dane" scenic viewpoint, and I am having some enlarged for you. That is a superb development that will always give all who go to it great pleasure and inspiration.

I want to say again, Mr. Rockefeller, that I had a thoroughly enjoyable and a most restful and refreshing visit with you at your home. Mrs. Rockefeller and you were most kind and considerate. Your hospitality and generosity are more appreciated than I can ever tell you. The visit with you was a wonderful highlight of the year.

With all good wishes to Mrs. Rockefeller and yourself, I am

Faithfully yours,
HORACE M. ALBRIGHT

Mr. Frank R. Givens. Superintendent, Acadia National Park, 1953-1959.

September 8, 1953

Dear Mr. Rockefeller:

Saturday at home I wrote you a rather long letter in which I referred to your letter to Nelson about the National Park Service personnel and Secretary McKay's reply to you, a copy of which he sent to me. Now this morning when I return to my desk after the Labor Day holiday I find your letter of September 5th with its enclosures, which, of course, crossed mine to you. The papers you have sent me make my file complete.

It is certain, I think, that you have fully solved the personnel problem of the Park Service for some time to come and, therefore, it will not be necessary to make any use of the information contained in your correspondence. You can be sure that I will be extremely careful not to make any other use of your letter and its attachments than you have authorized.

The apprehensions I now have are for the conservation policies of the Administration and the Interior Department. An example of mild criticism which can grow to be severe is the article by John B. Oakes in the New York TIMES of September 6th. It is in the middle of the section relating to art, music, gardens, and so forth. It is headed, "Conservation: More Hunting". The gist of the criticism in this article is that the Secretary has badly impaired policies with respect to protection of migratory birds by extending the areas and hours for hunting and, in some cases, the bag limits, when, apparently, there will be on most of the flyways fewer birds than have been available to hunters in recent years.

A hopeful sign is the President's recent selection of men outside of Government for certain advisory committees. They can be very helpful to him, especially in these early months of his administration. The Interior Department could use such a committee on general conservation problems, especially those bearing on public lands, hydroelectric power, and wildlife.

With all good wishes, I am,

Sincerely yours,
HORACE M. ALBRIGHT

November 27, 1953

Dear Mr. Albright:

I wrote you the other day asking if you thought there was anything I could do to help save the National Parks. I have since drafted a letter on the subject to President Eisenhower, of which I enclose a copy. Will you be good enough to tell me quite frankly whether you think some such letter from me to the President would be helpful and, if so, what if any, additions, omissions or changes in the proposed draft herewith, you would suggest.

Of course, all of the above is predicated on the assumption that the HARPER'S Magazine article is essentially correct as to the facts. I have taken this for granted. The more so since there have been several editorials on the same subject in the New York TIMES recently written from a like point of view. I must not write the President unless I am sure of the facts in the matter. Can you give me that assurance?

Very sincerely,
JOHN D. ROCKEFELLER, JR.

December 9, 1953

Dear Mr. Rockefeller,

I am sorry that I was not able to make an earlier reply to your letter of November 27th. I was in Washington all week and then I went to Williamsburg for the meeting of the Trustees of Colonial Williamsburg which we held there Monday and yesterday.

I took pains in Washington to make a careful check of the situation in the Department of the Interior and I find that while the prospects at the moment are that there will be recommendations for larger appropriations for the protection and care of the national parks, they are not likely to be adequate and of course there is the danger that the Bureau of the Budget may make drastic cuts before submitting the final budget to the Congress in early January.

I therefore recommend that you send the letter that you drafted to the President. It covers the ground thoroughly and

I have no suggestions to make in the way of amendments. I believe that if your letter reaches him within the next week, it can be very effective in influencing the action on the National Park Service budget.

I thoroughly enjoyed my brief Williamsburg visit. I had not been there for a year. The weather was beautiful and it seemed to me that in every respect the ancient city was more lovely and interesting than ever before.

Winthrop presided at all our meetings. He is an exceptionally good presiding officer. When he presented the twenty-year service trophies to three employees yesterday he spoke extemporaneously and his remarks could not have been better. Furthermore, there was no repetition of language, although the sentiments in each case were in the same vein. I know you would have been very proud to have seen him in action. His wide knowledge of Williamsburg affairs and deep interest in them also made a very strong impression on me. I do not think this feeling on my part is just because I have held Winthrop in affectionate regard for so many years.

Faithfully yours,
HORACE M. ALBRIGHT

December 10, 1953

My dear Mr. President:

I have just read with deep concern the article in Harper's Magazine for October entitled, "Let's Close the National Parks". The writer of the article makes the suggestion to close the National Parks apparently as a last resort in order to prevent their further deterioration and impoverishment.

Having over the years taken a deep interest in the creation, development and improvement of the National Parks, which afford infinite enjoyment to many millions of people every year, I cannot but feel that if the gravity of the present situation were fully realized, some way would be found to stem the tide of this national tragedy.

    With sentiments of high regard, I am,

Very sincerely,
JOHN D. ROCKEFELLER, JR.

The President
The White House
Washington, D.C.

President Dwight D. Eisenhower replied to Rockefeller's letter on January 8, 1954. He wrote, "I share your concern over the need to make up for the inadequate support given the parks during the war years and the period immediately following. I know that you will be pleased to learn that the Secretary of the Interior has just completed a study of the National Park Service and is putting into effect certain changes which should permit a more effective use of existing manpower in the parks."

The President's letter was complemented by a letter from Secretary McKay dated January 11, 1954. After citing increases in the parks' budget, attendance and acreage, he concluded, "You may be assured that we are devoting our best efforts toward making our money go as far as possible and also planning for rapid expansion just as early as the financial situation will permit."

January 25, 1954

Dear Mr. Rockefeller,

    Thank you for your note of January 22nd. I am glad the Secretary wrote you the letter he was working on when I saw him.

    I wonder if you happened to note in the Budget Message of the President to Congress dated January 21 that he made special reference to his recommended increase in funds for management and protection or our national parks, monuments and historic sites.

In case you did not see it, I quote the following from the President's Message:

"Expenditures for the management and protection of our national parks, monuments, and historic sites will be somewhat above the current-year level, so as to provide for improved services to the increasing number of visitors. This increase is largely offset by a reduction in expenditures for construction."

I feel confident that this vital increase in funds that has been recommended would not have reached Congress, had it not been for Bernard DeVoto's strong article in Harper's advocating that the national parks, monuments, and historic sites be closed unless more funds are provided for their protection and upkeep, and had it not been for your direct intercession with the President.

Mrs. Albright and I are going to be in Washington the end of this week and we are going on to Williamsburg for the ceremony on Saturday, and will stay there two or three days.

I am looking forward happily to this new opportunity to be in Williamsburg.

With all good wishes, I am

Faithfully yours,
HORACE M. ALBRIGHT

January 26, 1954

My dear Mr. President:

Your personal reply of January 8th to my letter of December 10th about the National Parks was as deeply appreciated as it was unexpected. I took the liberty of writing you because of the importance of the situation but with no thought other than that you would refer the letter either to the Secretary of the Interior or Director of National Parks.

As you know, I have already heard from the Secretary of the Interior and feel confident that such consideration as is wisely possible will be given to these significant recreational areas.

With cordial thanks for the personal attention which you have given the matter and with sentiments of high regard, I am,

Very sincerely,
JOHN D. ROCKEFELLER, JR.

The President
The White House
Washington, D. C.

February 4, 1954

Dear Mr. Albright:

Your letter of January 28th is received. Please know how warmly I thank you and Mrs. Albright for the good wishes on my 80th birthday which you have so thoughtfully sent me.

Surely no one ever had more to be grateful for than I have, nor could anyone be more appreciative of his countless friends than I am. Your friendship over the years has meant much to me. Therefore, the bautiful expressions which your letter contains are only the more appreciated.

Mrs. Rockefeller and I are happily located in familiar quarters here at Tucson and are looking forward with much pleasure to our six weeks stay.

With renewed thanks for your beautiful letter, and with cordial greetings to Mrs. Albright and yourself, in which Mrs. Rockefeller joins, I am

Very sincerely,
JOHN D. ROCKEFELLER, JR.

WORTHWHILE PLACES

P. S. Thank you for writing me about Mr. Lewis, who is in charge of the Saguaro National Monument. We will be glad to bear him in mind and to see him if conveniently possible while we are here.

March 31, 1954

Dear Mr. Rockefeller:

I assume it is about time for you to make your spring visit to Williamsburg. I know you will find the beautiful old town and its gardens lovlier than ever and that Mrs. Rockefeller and you will have a very pleasant stay there.

I hope there may be an opportunity for you to see the new plans for Yorktown. I saw them when I was in Williamsburg about the first of February. It seems to me that at last a program for doing something really fine with Yorktown has been developed and that it is one that can be carried out. It will be necessary to do quite a bit of work in selling superfluous lands now owned by the National Park Service and acquiring others, but the project looks feasible and I found it most interesting. I am enclosing the superintendent's report of Februrary 12th where on the first and second pages, which I have marked, you will find a brief description of the plan. This plan was given prominence in an issue of the New York TIMES about a month ago which perhaps you saw when you were out in Arizona.

A new bill authorizing funds for the building of highways in cooperation with the states, extending the highways in national forests and national parks and continuing the building of parkways, has just been reported to Congress by the Public Works Committee. There is quite a large increase in the funds authorized for parkways and if the bill passes it would seem that we ought to be able to look forward confidently to the completion of the Colonial Parkway before the Jamestown celebration of 1957, or perhaps earlier. Last week I was in Washington for three days with the members of the National Park Service Advisory Board

310

on National Parks, Historic Sites, Buildings and Monuments, of which Alfred A. Knopf is Chairman. We had the Colonial Parkway under discussion and the feeling was expressed unanimously that this Parkway should be finished forthwith.

With all good wishes, I am

Faithfully yours,
HORACE M. ALBRIGHT

Alfred A. Knopf. Publisher.

April 26, 1954

Dear Mr. Rockefeller:

At last I have had an opportunity to study the hearings before the Interior Department Subcommittee of the House Committee on Appropriations, as well as the Interior Department bill as reported to Congress and the report on the bill. I have also received from the National Park Service some analyses of the appropriations bill as it stands at the present time.

It appears now that the slash in funds estimated for management and protection of the parks, the funds in which you and I have been chiefly interested, is not as great as I reported to you recently. There still remains in the bill some $400,000 additional for protective personnel and related requirements; in fact, the cut is remarkably small considering the slashing that was done on other estimates.

One interesting thing about the action of the House Committee was the addition to the bill of $500,000 for parkways above what was asked for by the Bureau of the Budget. This, however, was earmarked for the Natchez Trace Parkway. The estimate was $425,000 and the House allowed $925,000. This, of course, was all wrong; but if they are going to do things this way, maybe we ought to try to get Senators from Virginia to do something about increasing the parkway appropriation with some earmarking for the Colonial Parkway.

It appears that the Park Service has been hardest hit in its administrative appropriations both for the Washington office and for the regional offices, and in its estimates for funds for construction of facilities.

I am sorry to trouble you about this matter, but knowing how interested you are, I thought I could undue the earlier impression I got regarding apparent adverse action on the substantial increase in estimates which the President authorized in line with his correspondence with you.

Thank you very much for your notes from Williamsburg. I know things must be very beautiful now with the flowers and trees bursting into bloom. Mrs. Albright and I are sorry that we have to leave for New Mexico and California next Sunday just as Westchester will be its lovliest.

Faithfully yours,
HORACE M. ALBRIGHT

April 26, 1954

Dear Mr. Albright:

Your letter of April 23rd is received. The itinerary which it presents is most attractive. Our thought would be to go to Washington Sunday, May 31st, spend that night with my son, Nelson, and have our car meet us at Nelson's house Monday morning to start on the trip as you have planned it. This would bring us to Ashville Thursday.

Mrs. Peter Gerry of Providence (formerly Mrs. George Vanderbilt) is one of Mrs. Rockefeller's best friends. Young George Cecil now in charge at Biltmore is also well known to her. A very nice young man, perhaps this same one - Mrs. Gerry's grandson - took us around when we were there a few

312

years ago. I mention these connections with the Biltmore estate because they will have a bearing on what we do the day we are there. That, Mrs. Rockefeller and I will have to work out.

From your schedule, it would appear that we would get to Gatlinsburg sometime Friday. There we would remain presumably over that night and over Saturday and Sunday, visiting the Great Smoky mountains at our convenience and starting north by train perhaps from Gatlinsburg probably Sunday night, leaving our chauffeur to drive the car home.

We are making this trip primarily because Mrs. Rockefeller has never been over any of the territory that we will visit and also because it will interest me to see it again. The purpose of the trip will be our own personal enjoyment of driving together through beautiful country. It will be a pleasure, as on the former trip, to meet casually and briefly any of the Park superintendents as we touch their areas. On the other hand, we are not making a Park inspection trip nor will we want to be accompanied over any of the area except possibly in the big Smoky Park by Park officials. Naturally and properly, if these officials travel with us, we want to show them every courtesy and friendly consideration but to the extent that that becomes necessary, the purpose of our trip, namely, our own individual, personal enjoyment of it, is subordinated. I speak thus frankly because I know you will understand our feeling and so that it may be made clear in advance that any contact with the Park officials will be brief.

In your itinerary for June 4th you say: "You will remember the side-trip you took to Heintooga where development work was under way. This work has now been completed and the National Park Service people are anxious for you to see this place again." If this area is one of the interesting, developed parts of the Park which any visitor should see, we will be glad to see it, but for that reason only. As to the Cherokee Village, we have both seen Indian villages in various parts of the country and would not be interested to visit this one unless it is in a part of the Park which we want to visit because of its scenery, quite aside from the existence of the Indian Village.

As to the Park Museums, while I have enormous interest in them and a high appreciation of their value to the public, except to spend perhaps five minutes in one should we be driving by, I would not want to take the time to visit them per se.

You speak of our going to Charlottesville to see the historic sites in that area on the way to Roanoke. I have been to Charlottesville several times and I think Mrs. Rockefeller has also so that I do not believe we would care to try to take it in on this trip.

I am interested to have you tell me who are the superintendents in these different Parks and areas. It will be a pleasure to see again those whom I have met before. I am most appreciative of their kindly feeling for our family in view of our interest in National Parks, while their readiness to do what they can to make our trip pleasurable is most gratifying.

This, of course, is a very personal letter just to you. With it as background, we will be able to talk more definitely on my return to New York next week. If you are there, perhaps I can see you for a few minutes on Friday, May 7th, in the office.

With great appreciation of your helpfulness in the matter of our trip, I am

Very sincerely,
JOHN D. ROCKEFELLER, JR.

May 1, 1954

My dear Mr. Rockefeller,

Now I take the opportunity to express again my deep personal appreciation of your magnificent contribution to the saving of the Calaveras South Grove of Giant Sequoia Trees.

This was a very great natural resource conservation project that never could have been carried out, had you not made the pledge you did two years ago. Of course it gave me exceptional pleasure and satisfaction because in April 1924, just thirty years ago Director Mather and I and two or three other men rode

314

into that vast Stanislaus wilderness on horseback and then hiked on through the Calaveras South Grove.

Now all that territory except the secluded valley in which the Grove lies, has been frightfully mangled by modern lumbering operations. There is one other exception, and that is the fine body of Sugar Pine on the north slope of the ridge protecting the Grove on the north which has also been saved by an exchange of company timber for United States Government timber elsewhere in the Stanislaus watershed.

With another expression of my gratitude, I am

Faithfully yours,
HORACE M. ALBRIGHT

Rockefeller did not give the funds for the purchase of the South Calaveras Grove directly. He had given Jackson Hole Preserve, Inc. over $19 million. The Preserve made the gift for the Grove from these funds.

September 18, 1954

Dear Mr. Albright:

I am enclosing a letter to Mr. Wirth in a stamped but unsealed envelope. Please read this letter and if you think there is anything in it that would be better not said or what it contains is expressed in a way that might be better expressed, I shall greatly appreciate your suggesting the changes that occur to you and returning the letter to me at my New York office since we reach New York this coming Tuesday. On the other hand, if you feel the letter is all right to send as it is, kindly mail it.

I shall hope to see you, perhaps for lunch, some day during the next month for there are many things about which I would enjoy talking with you.

Very sincerely,
JOHN D. ROCKEFELLER, JR.

WORTHWHILE PLACES

Draft

Dear Mr. Wirth:

Your very interesting and thoughtful letter of September 30th has been read a number of times with great care.

Both with reference to what restored Williamsburg and the National Parks have to offer the public, I must confess my views are somewhat old-fashioned. My feeling is that these areas are of such outstanding interest in themselves that they tell their own story if only they are made reasonably accessible to the public.

You feel about the National Parks as I know certain people feel about Williamsburg-that an active effort should be made to tell their story. That may be the correct view of the matter. If it is and you can get the funds with which to put it into effect, the three-fold program - (1) Research and Analysis; (2) Training; and (3) Adaptation - which you outline is very likely the answer to the question.

For myself, I like to be free to see interesting places and beautiful scenery on my own and not have it "spoon fed" to me. The expression "spoon fed" is probably an exaggeration. By it I mean that to be obliged, while enjoying beautiful and interesting sites and scenes, to listen to the story of their origin or development or meaning or significance whether I want to or not is disturbing rather than helpful. On the other hand, I am always glad to have a competent guide or person available from whom I can get information that I may want and of whom I may ask such questions as come to mind.

While I presume there are still people who feel as I do about being peacefully allowed to enjoy beautiful things, I suppose that the great majority of the traveling public believe they are getting more for their money if someone is always nearby telling them what they are seeing and what it means, even if in the process of listening to such explanations the sightseer loses something of the enjoyment of the things which he has come to see.

Having made these few observations, may I quickly say that I doubt not that the average tourist thoroughly enjoys

316

the method of interpretation which the National Park Service is now employing and which you are feeling should be improved and extended. Furthermore, I doubt not that these average tourists would greatly deplore my having made the comments I have and earnestly hope that you would not let them deter you from developing the very interesting program which your letter outlines.

Regretting not to be able to answer more satisfactorily your questions and with deep appreciation of your great interest in the National Parks and how they can be most fully availed of and enjoyed by the public, I am,

Very sincerely,
JOHN D. ROCKEFELLER, JR.

September 21, 1954

Dear Mr. Rockefeller:

Acknowledging your note of September 18th, I read your letter to Mr. Wirth, liked everything about it and promptly sent it to him.

Thanks to action you took a year ago, there have been no personnel disturbances of the executive group of the National Park Service, although there was authority to remove or demote officials without giving any reasons because of the classification in Schedule C removing them from the protection of the Civil Service rules and regulations. In other words, the promise Secretary McKay made to you has been strictly kept.

Again because of your intercession, appropriations for maintenance and protection of the parks were considerably increased, and I understand there was much less littering of the parks and less damage to them this year. Weather conditions were such that there were almost no fires.

You know, of course, that funds are now available to complete the parkway to Jamestown and the Park Service expects to move forward rapidly to get new contracts under way.

A setback occurred in the limitation passed on the power of the Park Service to condemn lands, rights-of-way, etc. It seems that before condemnation proceedings can be instituted now, at least during this fiscal year, the consent of the person against whom the action is to be taken must be first obtained. Mrs. Potter Palmer is still recalcitrant, and since she will probably not give her consent, there can be no proceedings against her to acquire the tract of land needed to protect the motor road. I will have more to say on this when I see you.

There are some items in the August report of the superintendent of Colonial National Historical Park which may interest you. The report is attached; there is no need to return it to me.

So far as I can see now, I will be in New York at least during the first two weeks of October. I expect to make a trip to the Great Smoky Mountains National Park during the last two weeks of the month. I have to attend a meeting of the National Park Service Advisory Board which is going to meet at Gatlinburg, Tennessee. I am also anxious to see the Park and Parkway country with its trees and shrubs in autumn garb.

Despite the rainy summer, I hope your stay at Seal Harbor was pleasant and restful.

Faithfully yours,
HORACE M. ALBRIGHT

January 14, 1955

My dear Miss Warfield,

I have your note of January 12th to which you attached Mr. DeForest Grant's letter of January 7th to Mr. Rockefeller.

Just before Mr. Grant left for Arizona I had quite a long talk with him over the telephone and I know he is still very keenly interested in doing something about an organization that, outside of government service, will protect the National Park Service and do whatever is possible to influence the public in the direction of respecting and observing the policies under which the national parks are operated.

I made notes of Mr. Grant's letter and I am returning it to you herewith.

If Mr. Rockefeller should read the article in the January Reader's Digest relating to the national parks, I would like to have him know that I am not entirely satisfied with this article. It was written with good intentions to bring to the attention of the public the needs of the national parks, particularly in the direction of protecting them.

Mr. Stevenson, the author, covered too much territory and I think the article for most people is complicated and confusing.

Sincerely yours,
HORACE M. ALBRIGHT

Mr. DeForest Grant. Leading conservationist. Member of the council of the Save-the-Redwoods League.

January 18, 1955

Dear Mr. Albright:

Thank you for the information contained in your letter of January 14th to Miss Warfield.

I have read the Reader's Digest article on National Parks to which you refer. It paints a pretty drab and discouraging picture but, unfortunately, I fancy it states the facts.

I suppose Mr. DeForest Grant is the best and most likely person to undertake to organize a movement for the support of the National Parks. I hope he may be successful and shall be glad to cooperate financially at any point and in such amount as you might suggest. This I am saying to you in confidence and will appreciate some recommendation from you if and when the opportune moment for financial help seems to you to have arrived. I am enclosing a copy of my reply to Mr. Grant.

Very sincerely,
JOHN D. ROCKEFELLER, JR.

January 20, 1955

Dear Mr. Rockefeller,

I appreciate very much your thoughtfulness in writing me on January 18th and sending me a copy of your letter to Mr. DeForest Grant in regard to the Reader's Digest article on the problems facing the National Park Service, owing to overwhelming travel to the national parks and national monuments.

I am going to be in Washington for the next two weeks, and while I am down there I hope to talk with people both in the government service and in the various associations regarding ways and means of dealing with the problem that concerns us so deeply.

As to the Reader's Digest article, I think the author, Mr. Stevenson, "drew a long bow" in certain directions, because conditions are not as bad as he pictures them. I think he was trying to frighten Congress into action, but his article was in some ways confusing and I am afraid it did more harm than good, as far as the general public is concerned. Of course the upper end of Yosemite Valley and the geyser basins of Yellowstone Park are where the most serious problems have arisen due to overpopulation and something has got to be done about the situations in these parks. As far as I can see, a park like Glacier National Park has not been injured in any degree whatever.

Your continued interest is most inspiring and encouraging to all of us. I will have some kind of a report for you when you return from the West.

Faithfully yours,
HORACE M. ALBRIGHT

January 21, 1955

Dear Mr. Rockefeller:

I am leaving the city on a trip and I know you are going west very soon. Therefore, I am writing this note a little early to convey heartfelt felicitations on your 81st birthday. Mrs. Albright joins me in these greetings and in prayers that for a great many years to come Mrs. Rockefeller and you will be blessed with happiness and health.

I often reflect on the fine, useful life you have lived sustained by the endowment of perfect character, highest integrity and spiritual strength which, fortunately for our country — and the world, has been yours. I have marveled at your achievements in your 81st year in your many fields of interest, and the years ahead, I am sure, will find you strong and active.

I am ever grateful for the high privilege of your friendship and for the inspiration of your vision and great works.

I hope your visit to the Southwest will be restful and beneficial in every way.

Faithfully yours,
HORACE M. ALBRIGHT

February 11, 1955

Dear Mr. Albright:

Your letter of congratulations and good wishes from Mrs. Albright and yourself on my birthday, was one of the most beautiful I received and I thank you for it from my heart.

What a wonderful friend you have been to me over these many years, what interesting things we have done together and what happiness we have had in doing them.

I have been richly blessed throughout my life. To few men have come such opportunities as have come to me. With them have come responsibilities, great and varied. These I could not have carried with any degree of success had it not been for a small group of able, high-minded, public-spirited men like yourself with whom I have been fortunate in being able to surround myself.

When someone once asked my father to what he attributed his success, he said: "To my associates". In even larger measure has that been true in my life. No man ever had finer, wiser, or more loyal associates than I have had. Without them I could have accomplished little. To have worked with them has been one of the high privileges of my life.

Mrs. Rockefeller and I are greatly enjoying our stay here and are profiting by it in every way.

With renewed thanks for your beautiful letter and above all for your friendship, I am

Very sincerely,
JOHN D. ROCKEFELLER, JR.

March 25, 1955

Dear Mr. Rockefeller:

May I recall to you the luncheon meeting that Mr. DeForest Grant arranged last September here in New York to discuss ways and means of providing better protection for the national parks and other areas of great scenic, scientific and historic importance, and also the discussion you and I had on the subject at luncheon later in the autumn or early winter.

To both Mr. Grant and you I pointed out that we have a number of fine organizations interested in the conservation of natural resources, some having as their special interest or interests forest conservation, others the protection of wildlife and still others the conservation of national parks and historic sites, and so forth.

The personnel of these organizations consist of a few individuals, and in carrying out the objectives of their employers these people have to be extremely careful not to be charged with professional lobbying lest the tax status of their societies be placed in jeopardy. What we have been talking about is an organization, probably temporary, that would do more than just engage in spreading information about conservation of natural resources and conducting programs in the fields of interpretation and education regarding these resources and their problems. This different kind of an organization would be one that would frankly do what many business associations undertake, and that would be the deliberate presentation to Congressional committees, individual members of Congress and to officers of Government agencies the opinions of conservationists with a view to influencing legislation and executive action.

In other words, a situation has arisen, particularly so far as our national scenic and historic parks and monuments are concerned, that requires some very strong presentations in the direction where action can be obtained.

Several of us have been looking into the status of the various organizations, and while we have reached some conclusions, I do not think we see very clearly just what can or should be done. Accordingly, a number of us have decided to try to bring together in Washington, May 22-25, a group of people from all over the country to look into the present status of the areas in which we are most interested and what can be done to meet the problems arising out of the enormous increase in the number of visitors to these reservations and what steps can be taken to assure their future protection.

We are doing this under the auspices of the American Planning and Civic Association and we are in close cooperation with several other interested societies. We are raising a little fund to carry out this Conference. Our expenditures will be limited to hotel rooms for the Conference, a luncheon or two and correspondence. People going to the Conference will pay their own expenses. Should you feel that you would like to contribute to this fund, we would very much appreciate your doing so.

I might add that we are also going to look into the activities of several new organizations recently established, one or more of which may be able to do the things that Mr. Grant and you and I discussed several months ago. One of these is the Citizens Committee on Natural Resources which has been organized in Washington, D.C.; another is the Council of Conservationists which was established here in New York and has headquarters at 161 East 42nd St.; and a third one is Trustees for Conservation, organized in San Francisco. It looks as though each of these new organizations has been set up for one or more limited objectives and probably do not overlap each other's programs very much, but there could be extensive overlapping. They are all of the nature of coordinating organizations and probably established on a temporary basis. All are non-profit agencies and will, as I understand it, be registered under the lobbying law and therefore contributions to them will not be deductible for tax purposes.

There is still another movement that is new and that is the incorporation of the United Conservation Fund, Inc., headed by Louis Bromfield, the well-known author, which has been set up to solicit in all parts of the country funds to finance some of the organizations that are concentrating on the protection of natural resources and engaging in the dissemination of information regarding the problems of these resources and the Government agencies concerned with them. I have no details regarding this fund raising campaign.

All of the above adds up to very considerable activity developed in recent months and has a very important bearing on matters which Mr. Grand and you and I discussed. I have no recommendations to make at this time other than to commend the program we have envisioned for May in Washington to such consideration as you feel you can give it. Of course, any comments you have to offer will be very greatly appreciated.

I know you have seen the article on national parks in the READER'S DIGEST. There was a splendid editorial in the Saturday Evening Post in February.

The President and the Bureau of the Budget were generous in their consideration of the estimates of the National Park Service for appropriations for the fiscal year beginning June 1, 1955, and from all I can learn, the Appropriations Committee of the House of Representatives acted favorably on the estimates. In other words, we have reason to feel that there will be a considerable increase in funds for protection of the precious resources in which we are so much interested. Last year it was your intervention which brought a substantial increase in funds, and had it not been for that increase, we do not know what might have happened in some overcrowded parks.

I apologize to you for this long letter but felt that you expected me to give a report in due time on these matters of mutual interest.

Faithfully yours,
HORACE M. ALBRIGHT

February 6, 1956

Dear Mr. Albright:

How thoughtful and friendly of you and Mrs. Albright to remember my birthday and to send me so beautiful a birthday letter. The day was indeed a happy one for Mrs. Rockefeller and me. It was the second day after our arrival here and it found us both in the best of health.

These have been for me eighty-two years filled with interesting opportunities for service in many fields, and overflowing with heaven's richest blessings. I am deeply grateful for all they have brought to me - my fine sons and daughter and their wonderful families - and also for the many good friends by whom I have been surrounded and with whom I have been associated. Among the latter, you have long and will always hold a prominent place.

Again, to you and Mrs. Albright, I send truest thanks for your letter.

Very sincerely,
JOHN D. ROCKEFELLER, JR.

July 25, 1956

My dear Mr. Rockefeller,

This is a note which you must not take the trouble to answer.

I thought you would be interested in knowing that at the Grand Central Station the Eastman Kodak Company has another enormous colored enlargement of the Teton Mountains about as they are seen from the new Lodge, and it is being admired by thousands daily. This is a different picture from the one that was shown in April 1955 and it looks as though the Eastman Company has on its program a picture of the Tetons for its wonderful space in the Grand Central Terminal for several weeks each year.

I am getting news almost daily from the Jackson Hole, and the references to the new Lodge are most pleasing and gratifying. Freeman Tilden, the author, who has written considerably about the national parks, is just in from the West and I quote the following from a letter from him:

> "I had eight days - glorious and profitable days - in Grand Teton. Jackson Lake Lodge is providing fine service at what seems to me extremely modest prices for these days."

Mrs. Albright and I are going back to the Yellowstone and the Grand Teton Park, leaving here August 28th. We shall see Laurance out there early in September.

I have just received word that the Virign Islands National Park Bill is about ready to go to the White House for the President's signature. It passed the Senate unanimously a week ago and the conference between the two houses has adjusted the differences between the House and the Senate bills, so the bill is ready to become a law.

I noted the death of Mrs. Potter Palmer. I have written Mr. Wirth expressing the hope that before she died, the tract of land needed to complete the motor road was made available to the National Park Service.

I had hoped to get into Maine again this summer, but this now seems impossible. It has been three years since I enjoyed that wonderful weekend with Mrs. Rockefeller and you at the Eyrie after my tour of the northern woods with former Governor Baxter. I shall always remember the consideration shown me by Mrs. Rockefeller and you during those beautiful days spent with you.

Mrs. Albright joins me in best wishes to both of you, and in hopes that your summer will be restful and enjoyable.

Faithfully yours,
HORACE M. ALBRIGHT

The Virgin Islands National Park is located on the island of St. John, the smallest of the three major islands in the American Virgin Islands. Between 1939 and 1954, studies were made about the feasibility of creating a national park on the island. In 1954, Laurance S. Rockefeller became interested in the idea of a park. Earlier, he had purchased the Caneel Bay Estate, a resort on the island. In 1956, Congress authorized a park of not more than 9,485 acres on and around St. John and 15 acres on St. Thomas. Later that year, the Rockefeller organization, Jackson Hole Preserve, Inc., contributed over 5,000 acres to the nation for the park. The Park was dedicated in 1957.

July 28, 1956

Dear Mr. Albright:

Many thanks for your two letters of July 25th, one enclosing a bulletin containing much superlatively good news about the Colonial Parkway and also saying that the Virgin Islands Park bill awaits only the President's signature. How gratifying both these items are!

It is interesting that the Eastman Kodak Co. is giving Jackson Hole such splendid, free publicity. The photograph, I am sure, brings daily inspiration to the many people who pass through Grand Central. Mr. Tilden's comment about the new Lodge is also most gratifying. I am delighted that you and Mrs. Albright are going out there again.

I assume Mr. Wirth will let me know when anything new develops in the Potter Palmer property matter in view of Mrs. Palmer's death. I shall be greatly interested to hear of what progress, if any, can now be made.

Mrs. Rockefeller and I, too, remember with great pleasure your visit to us here and look forward to the time when you can repeat it. We unite in warm remembrance to you and Mrs. Albright and best wishes for a pleasant summer.

Very sincerely,
JOHN D. ROCKEFELLER, JR.

P. S. Since dictating the above, I have just learned through Mr. Smith, my lawyer in Bar Harbor, that sometime this past year before she died, Mrs. Palmer and her son gave a deed to the government of the property we have wanted so long and that contracts are being let for the construction of the connecting link. At long last, this is wonderful news.

(As I am just going out, I am sorry not to sign this myself)

December 28, 1956

My dear Mr. Rockefeller,

Mrs. Albright and I extend to Mrs. Rockefeller and you our New Year's Greetings and our high hopes that it will bring you both health and happiness in abundance.

We are not unmindful of the fact that in a month you will arrive at the eighty-third birthday anniversary in your long and exceedingly useful life. It is our heartfelt wish that you will be spared for many years ahead, as was your great father.

We have seen a copy of the new book recording in pictures and text many of your outstanding achievements in the conservation of natural resources and the restoration of historic sites and structures, assuring their preservation as vital parts of our American heritage. The design of the book is superb and it is beautifully illustrated.

We have also derived infinited pleasure from reading your biography by Dr. Fosdick. These books mean so very much to us because, among other things, we have been privileged to know you and your family for over thirty years.

I cannot mention the family without telling you that during 1956 I have had most interesting experiences in association with Laurance and Winthrop. I have been in the Teton country and the Virgin Islands with Laurance as well as serving on the Palisades Interstate Park Commission with him. He is brillant in his thinking and planning and modest and humble in recognizing appreciation expressed to him for his good deeds. He is a sound and practical executive.

His work in establishing our twenty-ninth national park on St. John Island gives him great prestige as a conservationist. I wish you could have seen him in action the day he turned over the lands to Secretary of the Interior Fred Seaton and the latter declared the park in being. The many natives standing near the official party spontaneously cried out, "God bless Mr. Rockefeller!" when Laurance rose to speak, thus eloquently and poignantly expressing the hope they felt that at last their island has a future.

WORTHWHILE PLACES

Winthrop had the Williamsburg Boards meet at Winrock Farm in November and we lived and worked together for three days amid beautiful surroundings - the farm with its fields and trees and lakes, the scenic splendor of the autumn colors and the landscape lying below and beyond the rim of Petit Jean Mountain.

Jeanette and Winthrop were perfect hosts and we were all delighted with their hospitality and generosity in filling in the hours when we were not at work on Williamsburg problems and projects.

Winthrop has done a phenomenal job in organizing his personnel and developing his farm. One is amazed that he has accomplished so much in three years. At the same time, he has made a profound impression throughout the State as an industrialist and planner, and civic-minded worker in the causes of better education, medical services and racial understanding. Of course, he is an exceptionally good speaker and is by nature and experience a talented and effective public relations man. He is on his way to greater fame in several fields of endeavor.

And David's advancement has been most gratifying to all his friends. I have just read his address "Are We Going Too Fast?"which he gave on October 12 before the American Life Convention. His stature is so great as to make him one of New York's most influential and effective citizens.

And the prestige of John and Nelson in business and foreign and other affairs is attaining new heights all the time. Of course I follow all your sons' activities as best I can. It seems as if I must be as proud of them as you are!

I know how busy you are; I only hope you can find time to read a letter as long as this one. Please do not expend any in reply.

Faithfully yours,
HORACE M. ALBRIGHT

The book in text and pictures was: A Contribution to the Heritage of Every American, The Conservation Activities of John D. Rockefeller, Jr. Text by Nancy Newhall. Prologue by Fairfield Osborn. Epilogue by Horace Marden Albright. Alfred A. Knopf. New York, 1957.

The biography was: John D. Rockefeller, Jr.: A Portrait. Raymond B. Fosdick. Harper & Brothers. New York, 1956.

Winrock Farm. Winthrop Rockefeller's farm located on Petit Jean Mountain in Arkansas.

Jeannette Rockefeller. Winthrop's wife.

May 16, 1957

Dear Mr. Albright:

Although you thoughtfully suggested that I should not reply to your gracious letter of December 28th, I cannot lay it aside without telling you how much it meant to me.

What you say about my sons naturally touches their father deeply and I appreciate more than I can tell you your writing me as you did.

You speak as well of Mr. Fosdick's biography and also of the conservation book which Laurance went to such pains to compile for me and to the development of which you yourself gave so much thought, time and energy. I find it difficult to express in any adequate matter my appreciation of the Epilogue which you wrote for this book. Written by you, my highly valued friend and associate of the long years, it has special meaning for me and I am most grateful to you. The book is, indeed, a most beautiful and handsome one and will always give me pleasure.

With many thanks for all these things and with warmest remembrances, I am,

Very sincerely,
JOHN D. ROCKEFELLER, JR.

WORTHWHILE PLACES

November 21, 1958

Dear Mr. Rockefeller:

This is just a little note to tell you that Mrs. Albright and I have thought of you often as Nelson's campaign progressed and after his great victory. We have been very happy that you have this further cause for rejoicing in the success of your sons and, of course, you are very proud of Laurance's selection to head the National Outdoor Recreation Resources Commission.

I well remember my first meeting with Nelson and Laurance, then sixteen and fourteen years of age respectively, and your gentle advice to the boys that they help the overburdened porter move the baggage from the train to the bus at Gardiner, Montana. That was in 1924.

A new publication on the Colonial Parkway has just been issued and I am sending you a copy herewith.

Please do not take the time to acknowledge this letter.

With every good wish for health and happiness to Mrs. Rockefeller and yourself, I am

Faithfully yours,
HORACE M. ALBRIGHT

Nelson A. Rockefeller was elected governor of New York in November, 1958. He resigned from the office in 1973.

National Outdoor Recreation Resources Review Commission. Laurance was named chairman of the Commission by President Eisenhower. The Commission, created by Congress, studied the recreation needs of the nation for the years 1958, 1976, and 2000. The final report was made to Congress and President Kennedy in January 1962. The study looked for the resources available to fill the needs and the policies and programs that should be adopted.

December 2, 1958

Dear Mr. Albright:

Your letter of November 21st, referring so graciously to Nelson and Laurance, is received with deep appreciation. Many thanks to you and Mrs. Albright for your friendly thought.

I, too, well remember our meeting in 1924 in the West. What a significant meeting that was from my point of view starting, as it did, our long association together in many fields, of which the completed Colonial Parkway is only one of the projects in which we have had a mutual interest. I am delighted to have the folder about the Parkway which you kindly enclosed.

With thanks for your good wishes for Mrs. Rockefeller and me which we cordially reciprocate for you and Mrs. Albright, I am,

Very sincerely,
JOHN D. ROCKEFELLER, JR

January 20, 1960

My dear Mr. Rockefeller:

I assume you will be going to Arizona again this winter and will leave soon; I am going to Washington, D. C. for a week.

Your 86th birthday anniversary is approaching, and Mrs. Albright and I want to extend our heartfelt felicitations to you on this occasion, and with them our high hopes and earnest prayers that you will have many years ahead of you and that they will bring you sound health and much happiness. Yours is a life so useful and valuable in the progress of our country and so inspiring to our people that surely it will be spared for many years to come.

Mrs. Albright and I also want to tell you that we are deeply grateful for the part you played in the testimonial dinner that was tendered me in Washington on December 4th under Kenneth Chorley's Chairmanship. Your wire that was read at the dinner by Mr. Chorley and your support of the Lectureship in Conservation at the University of California which is to bear my name gave us more pleasure than we can express in words.

You have been most considerate of us over a period of more than thirty-five years, and I never forget that neither the National Park Service as a great Government agency, nor I as an individual conservationist could have succeeded on the scale of achievement attained had it not been for the inspiration of your ideas and ideals, and the support you gave our projects and policies.

And now your sons are brilliantly carrying on in the fields in which you were so active, as well as developing new avenues of public service in the best traditions of your family. And let me say too that I see in Steven a third generation conservationist of clear vision, sound thinking and courage combined with an extraordinary personality for both public service and private business.

With another expression of our gratitude, and every good wish for a relaxing, enjoyable visit in the west, and kindest regards to Mrs. Rockefeller and you, I am

Ever faithfully,
HORACE M. ALBRIGHT

The Horace M. Albright Lectureship in Conservation at the University of California, College of Natural Resources, Department of Forestry and Resource Management. Albright gave the first lecture, entitled <u>Great American Conservationists</u>, in 1961. The 28th lecture, given in 1988 by Esther Gulick, Catherine Kerr, and Sylvia McLaughlin was titled, <u>Saving San Francisco Bay; Past, Present, and Future.</u>

Arizona Inn
Tucson, Arizona
January 27, 1960

Dear Mr. Albright:

Your letter of January 20th was forwarded to Mr.
Rockefeller in Arizona and he has asked me to thank you for
it on his behalf. He deeply appreciates all that you say in it:
about his birthday, with the good wishes from Mrs. Albright
and you which it brings him; about the dinner and the
lectureship; your association over the years which has meant
so much to him; and your friendly reference to his sons and
to Steven.

With his thanks Mr. Rockefeller sends you his warm
remembrances in which Mrs. Rockefeller joins.

Very sincerely,
Ruth Norris

*Ruth Norris was secretary to Mrs. Rockefeller and traveled
with Mr. and Mrs. Rockefeller to Arizona in the winter of
1960.*

May 26, 1960

My dear John: (3rd)

I saw you the day after you lost your beloved father and
tried to tell you then how deeply Grace and I sympathize with
Blanchette and you and your young folk.

Mr. Rockefeller was a continuing inspiration to me for
thirty five years because of his character, his way of life and
his good works. He was wonderfully considerate of me and
the opportunities he gave me such as membership on the

WORTHWHILE PLACES
=================

Williamsburg Board, as well as his magnificent help in worth
while conservation projects enriched my life and enabled me
to be more effective in all my conservation activities.

He was one of the greatest Americans of our entire history
and will ever be so regarded.

We are on a trip in Europe now and many times already
we have heard your father mentioned in terms of highest praise
and respect.

I find I am writing on Laurance's 50th birthday. He was
only 14 when I first met him in Gardner, Montana.

Grace joins me in another expression of heartfelt sympathy
and kindest regards to Blanchette and yourself.

Horace

*John D. Rockefeller, Jr., died in Tucson, Arizona, on May
11, 1960.*

EPILOGUE

Between 1960 and 1980, Horace Albright wrote about once a month to members of the Rockefeller family or their staff in New York. He wrote his last letter in 1987, shortly before he died.

His letters ranged from nostalgic reminiscences to incisive comments on the conservation movement in America. He reported on personnel changes in the Park Service, on shifts in its policies in the field, gave his views on national politics, and on the fortunes of the changing cast of characters in and out of government who tried to maintain a balance between preservation and the providing of space for the people's enjoyment and understanding of their natural environment.

In 1972, Albright was particularly critical of a change in Park Service policy from fighting fires set by lightning to letting such fires burn. The Park Service reasoning was that such fires cleared the forests of dead and aging trees and undergrowth letting the forests regenerate themselves. "I think somebody is 'nuts' in the Park Service," Albright wrote the Rockefeller office, "and I intend to see that the policy is changed."

He was not successful, but later fires in Yellowstone and Yosemite forced the Park Service to put the policy under review and it moved toward a compromise. Under the compromise, local conditions would determine when a fire would be fought and when it would be left to burn. There is no single, final solution.

WORTHWHILE PLACES

For Albright, the upsetting change in fire-fighting policies was echoed in changes in Washington, D. C. Again, in 1972, he deplored the appointment of a new Park Service Director, who, he said, had only seen the Statue of Liberty, spent one day in Jackson Hole and although educated at the University of Arizona, had never visited the Grand Canyon. Within eighteen months, the lobbying efforts of Albright and others, including four former directors of the Park Service, led to the appointment of a new Director selected from the ranks of the Park Service.

In spite of the pressures created by fires in the field and politics within the Capitol Beltway offices, the national park system continued to grow. The policies Rockefeller and Albright had followed in Acadia and Yellowstone are still being implemented and tested. Albright called those who want to keep the parks pristine and natural, "purists." Others, like Rockefeller and Albright, would strive to preserve the parks while making them accessible to the people. They would build and clear roads, build hotels and restaurants. They would fight fires, build lookouts, clear vistas, and create parking places.

These policies made the parks accessible. In 1928, there were 2.5 million visits to the 23 areas under Park Service jurisdiction. In 1988, 282.6 million visitors poured through the 375 areas under the care of the Park Service. Over 21 million went to the six national parks in which Rockefeller had made significant contributions: Great Smoky Mountains, 8.8 million; Acadia, 4.5 million; Yosemite, 3.3 million; Yellowstone, 2.1 million; Shenandoah, 1.9 million; and Grand Teton, 1.2 million.

The growth, use, and care of the national parks, monuments, preserves, historic sites, trails, parkways, and seashores under park service administration is recounted in books by two former Park Service Directors. Conrad Wirth, Director, 1951 to 1964, wrote *Parks, Politics and the People*, published in 1980. George B. Hartzog, Jr., Director, 1964 to 1973, wrote *Battling for the National Parks*, published in 1988.

Both Wirth and Hartzog continued their interest in parks and conservation after leaving the Park Service. Wirth became a conservation associate of Laurance S. Rockefeller.

Laurance S. Rockefeller, born in 1910, has described himself as an apprentice to his father in conservation. He learned

338

from his father, and others, such as Albright, to look upon the outdoors as a natural essential ingredient in the full development of the individual. Like his father, he has declared himself for conservation, preservation, and use. He considers outdoor resources important as the setting in which people develop and strengthen their own inner resources.

With his associates, Laurance S. Rockefeller has established and supported conservation organizations such as the American Conservation Association, Inc., a conservation agency servicing other agencies. Between 1960 and 1989, the ACA made contributions to over 170 conservation organizations. Total gifts to any one organization ranged from $750 to over $875,000. Among the major recipients were the National Parks and Conservation Association, the National Recreation and Park Association, the Natural Resources Defense Council, Scenic Hudson, and the Sierra Club Legal Defense Fund. Rockefeller also has had an active role in the New York Zoological Society, Resources for the Future, Inc., the National Park Foundation, and the Conservation Foundation.

One of his main vehicles for the support of the national parks and other conservation agencies has been Jackson Hole Preserve, Incorporated, (JHPI), founded by his father in 1940. He spearheaded the JHPI program to preserve areas of outstanding primitive grandeur and natural beauty and to provide appropriate facilities for their use and enjoyment by the public.

In addition to contributions of land made to Grand Teton National Park, the Preserve has contributed to California redwood parks and the Hudson Highlands State Park in New York; improved visitor facilities in two national parks; made large grants to the American Conservation Association, Sleepy Hollow Restorations, Inc., now Historic Hudson Valley, and other parks in New York State.

Acting through JHPI, Laurance S. Rockefeller took the lead in creating the Virgin Island National Park on St. John Island in the Caribbean. The park was dedicated in December 1956. In 1969, Rockefeller and the Nature Conservancy donated over 4,000 acres to Haleakala National Park on Hawaii's Maui Island.

Beyond his direct involvement in creating and expanding national parks, he followed in his father's tradition of service in other ways. He served as chairman of the Outdoor Recreation Resources Review Commission from 1958-1962; the White House Conference on Natural Beauty, 1965; the President's Advisory Committee on Recreation and Natural Beauty 1966-1968; and the Citizen's Advisory Committee on Environmental Quality, 1969-1976.

Laurance S. Rockefeller continued his family's interest in the Palisades Interstate Park, an interest that began with his grandfather, John D. Rockefeller. He became a commissioner of the park in 1939 and served until 1978. During that time, he was successively secretary, vice president, and president from 1970-1977.

The Rockefeller family's commitment to the natural beauty ideals of John D. Rockefeller, Jr., is also reflected in the works of Mr. and Mrs. David Rockefeller, Abby Rockefeller Mauzé and Laurance Rockefeller, son of Laurance S. Rockefeller.

David Rockefeller, the youngest son, and his wife have been active in garden and horticultural activities. They supported the publication of the multivolume *Wildflowers of America* series. They maintain the Eyrie gardens in Seal Harbor, Maine, and, in 1988, funded the Peggy Rockefeller Rose Garden in the New York Botanical Gardens. The two-acre garden is a reconstruction of a 1915 Beatrix Jones Farrand design. David Rockefeller has led in fostering urban open spaces at Rockefeller Center in New York, Embarcadero Center in San Francisco, and L'Enfant Plaza in Washington, D.C.

Mrs. Mauzé, John D. Rockefeller, Jr.'s only daughter, who died in 1976, developed Greenacre Park, a sparkling vestpocket park in New York City, through her Greenacre Foundation. The Foundation has continued Mrs. Mauzé's interests by fostering the preservation of open spaces in Manhattan.

Laurance Rockefeller has chosen to follow in the footsteps of his father and grandfather. He is president of the Palisades Interstate Park Commission, the Beaverkill Mountain Corporation, and the American Conservation Association. He is a trustee of Jackson Hole Preserve, Inc. and active in the Alaska Coalition and the Barrier Island Coalition.

EPILOGUE

For four generations, the family, with the advice and support of advisors such as Horace M. Albright, has sought to achieve the goal articulated in the organic law that created the National Park Service:

> To conserve the scenery and the natural and historic objects and wildlife therein, and to provide for the enjoyment of same in such a manner and by such means as will leave them unimpaired for the enjoyment of future generations.

SOURCES

The 211 letters in this collection were selected from over 1300 letters exchanged between Horace M. Albright and the Rockefeller office between 1924 and 1960. The letters are located in the Rockefeller Family Archives now in the Rockefeller Archive Center in Pocantico Hills, North Tarrytown, New York.

The letters are in Record Group 2 of the Rockefeller Family Archives. They are in several series within the group. The series name and box numbers for the letters are:

Cultural: Boxes 47, 78, 80, 81, 83, 86, 88, 92, 93, and 94.

Friends and Services: Box 42.

Homes: Boxes 78, 86, 88, 92, 93, 104, 118, 120, 122, 126, and 127.

Personal: JDR. Jr.: Boxes 17, 18, 42, and 43. Abby Aldrich Rockefeller: Box 17.

Welfare: Box 25.

FURTHER READING

Albright, Horace M. *The Birth of the National Park Service, The Founding Years, 1913-1933.* Salt Lake City. Howe Brothers. 1985.

Albright, Horace M., Dickenson, Russell E., and Mott, William Penn, Jr. *National Park Service. The Story Behind the Scenery.* KC Publications. 1987.

Bartlett, Richard A. *Yellowstone. A Wilderness Besieged.* Tucson, Arizona. The University of Arizona Press. 1985.

A Contribution to the Heritage of Every American, The Conservation Activities of John D. Rockefeller, Jr. New York. Alfred A. Knopf. 1957.

Fosdick, Raymond B. *John D. Rockefeller, Jr.: A Portrait.* New York. Harper & Brothers. 1956.

Hampton, H. Duane. *How the U.S. Cavalry Saved Our National Parks.* Bloomington. Indiana University Press. 1971.

Harr, John Ensor and Johnson, Peter J. *The Rockefeller Century.* New York. Charles Scribner's Sons. 1988.

WORTHWHILE PLACES

Hartzog, George B. Jr. *Battling for the National Parks.* Mt. Kisco, New York. Moyer Bell Limited. 1988.

Ise, John. *Our National Park Policy. A Critical History.* Baltimore. Johns Hopkins Press. 1961.

Righter, Robert W. *Crucible for Conservation; The Creation of Grand Teton National Park.* Boulder. Colorado Associated University Press. 1982.

Roberts, Ann R. *Mr. Rockefeller's Roads, The Untold Story of Acadia's Carriage Roads & Their Creator.* Camden, Maine. Down East Books. 1990.

Simon, David J. ed. *Our Common Lands. Defending the National Parks.* Washington, D. C. Island Press. 1988.

Wirth, Conrad L. *Parks, Politics and the People.* Norman. University of Oklahoma. 1980.

The Complete Guide to America's National Parks. New York. Prentice Hall. 1988.

INDEX

There are only selected entries for John D. Rockefeller, Jr. and Horace M. Albright.

A